AM I AN AFRICAN?

H M Basner
1944

AM I AN AFRICAN?
*The Political Memoirs of
H M Basner*

MIRIAM BASNER

WUP Witwatersrand University Press

Witwatersrand University Press
1 Jan Smuts Avenue
Johannesburg
2001 South Africa

©Miriam Basner 1993

ISBN 1 86814 210 8

All rights reserved. No part of this publication may be reproduced, stored in a retrieval system, or transmitted in any form or by any means, electronic, mechanical, photocopying, recording or otherwise, without the prior permission of the copyright owner.

First published 1993

Cover designed by Lee Stupart and Sue Sandrock
Typeset by GraphicSet, Johannesburg
Printed and bound by Galvin & Sales, Cape Town

In
remembrance
of
Kwane Nkrumah

Acknowledgements

My gratitude must first be expressed to Tom Lodge, not only for his meticulous annotations, but also for his sturdy general support over a long period of time. To Basil Davidson and to Charles van Onselen go thanks for what can only be termed their 'launching' of this book; and deep appreciation to Baruch Hirson who has, with typical generosity, shared his great storehouse of South African historical facts with me whenever called upon to do so.

Contents

Foreword ix
1 Prologue 1
2 On Not Finding a Country 6
3 On Finding a Country 14
4 People 22
5 Two More People 31
6 A Start in Law 38
7 Looking Beyond the Law 47
8 Into Politics 53
9 The Hertzog Bills 59
10 The Politics of the Nonpolitical 67
11 Candidates Without Electorates 75
12 Seeds in Neglected Soil 85
13 Bedevilled Times 92
14 Sparks Among the Stubble 99
15 Consensus in a Political Wilderness 109
16 Ending a Beginning 117
17 Another Place 125
18 Tremors Underground 137
19 Oh, What a Beautiful Harmony 146
20 Much Saying, Little Doing, Some Thinking 155
21 Better a Living Dog Than a Dead Lion 163
22 The Sleep of Reason Produces Monsters 172
23 A Small Glimmer of International Light 182
24 Epilogue 194
Notes 200
Who's Who 232
Index 244

FOREWORD

Opinions used to differ sharply about Hyman Basner, the 'native senator' for the four million African inhabitants of the Transvaal and the Orange Free State between 1943 and 1947. According to the members of the Moroka Vigilance Association, writing to Dr A B Xuma in 1947 he was 'indispensable and cannot be replaced'[1], a view endorsed by Eddie Roux who wrote admiringly in 1948 that it was 'Basner, more than any other Native Representative, who is known as an agitator among the people who sent him to Parliament'[2].

In contrast, the standard histories of African electoral politics accord short shrift to Hyman Basner. C M Tatz's *Shadow and Substance* avoids mentioning him by name but does refer to 'the presence of extremists' amongst the native senators who made the work of their colleagues — 'men of calibre' — much 'more difficult and embarrassing' than it ought to have been[3].

Those of Basner's Parliamentary colleagues who wrote about their own careers chose to omit any reference to him[4]. A recent doctoral dissertation on 'native representation' records disparagingly that 'blacks themselves did not attach much importance' to Basner's election as Senator[5]. At the peak of his influence, press cartoonists depicted Basner as a principal antagonist of General Smuts, yet his death in exile passed unnoticed in most South African newspapers, though *The Times* in London published a warm obituary of the man it called 'an outstanding defender of African rights'[6].

Today, he is all but forgotten except by chroniclers of black South African opposition movements who depend on his testimony in recording the stories of struggles which would otherwise remain hidden from history.

Basner's public life, though, may have a more lasting significance than merely his role as a witness to important events in the narrative of black South African resistance. For a time he was an actor in that narrative and within it, arguably, he played a formative role. Certainly the story of his life merits more than the occasional acknowledgement in academic footnotes or the odd nod of approval or dismissive comment in the public record. In any case, people do not have to be important to live interesting lives or to be interesting personalities.

As a man and a politician, Hyman Basner was brave but flawed, a tough and fearless advocate of popular causes but a political and social maverick who fought his battles in an increasingly lonely and erratic fashion leaving behind no comrades, colleagues or movement to mourn his passing or celebrate his memory. But memories which are celebrated often make for dull biography, and whatever the faults of which Hyman Basner could be accused, dullness was not one of them.

He was born in Dvinsk in Latvia in 1905 and emigrated with his mother to South Africa in 1912, joining his father who had opened a dairy in Johannesburg. His parents originally intended their stay in Africa to be temporary and in 1922 they despatched their son to Los Angeles to stay with his sister and train as a lawyer at the University of California.

As a consequence of Basner senior's financial misfortunes, Hyman was compelled to cut short his American legal career and return to Johannesburg in 1927. Here he served articles with a legal firm which was exceptional in acting largely for Indian businessmen and African petty offenders. It was in this capacity that he first encountered members of the Communist Party who began to use his skills in their efforts to protect African tenants against the provisions of the Urban Areas Act.

Basner opened his own practice in 1930, building a mainly black clientele from 'pirate taxi drivers and slum landlords, burglars and receivers in stolen goods, and liquor sellers and dagga dealers' as well as more respectable people — the chiefs, school headmasters and ministers — whose communities were beginning to experience the full weight of segregationist legislation passed in the 1920s. His practice became increasingly rural at a time when few Africans in the countryside other than chiefs could either afford or arrange legal defence.

From 1931, Basner became the principal lawyer engaged by the Communist Party's workers' defence organisation, *Inkaka laba Sebenzi*.

He joined the Party in 1933 at a time when it was fractured by doctrinal disagreements and rapidly losing its black following as a consequence of the strategic turnabouts engendered by Comintern policies. Conspicuous as a campaigner in the Party-sponsored Anti-Fascist League he was too intellectually unruly to be brought within the CPSA leadership.

He proposed himself as the Party's candidate in the 1937 elections for the new native senators and managed to convince key African communists that 'land was the key issue' and that they should direct their campaign at rural people. He lost the 1937 election but nevertheless constructed the support base which would win him the senatorship five years later. Though by the 1942 election he had left the party, resigning in 1939 after the Soviet invasion of Finland, he was still perceived to be the candidate of the left and he served his term in the Senate as a lively and vociferous exponent of the causes which were beginning to be contested by popular movements outside Parliament: trade unions, African nationalism, and the direct action of the poor in both the cities and the countryside.

In October 1946, incensed by the government's violent suppression of the African mineworkers' strike, Basner travelled to the United States to help Indian government representatives prepare their indictment of South African segregation at the opening session of the United Nations, the first skirmish in the long international offensive against apartheid. By this time, though, Basner's relations with the Communist Party and the African National Congress were mutually antagonistic; despairing of ANC willingness to commit itself to militant action he had helped to found a rival African Democratic Party while simultaneously establishing a short-lived Socialist Party.

By 1947 Basner had lost the support but not the friendship of his African helpers in the 1942 elections and he believed the potential force of black politics was about to be dissipated as a consequence of Congress's pending adoption of Gandhist passive resistance. He resigned his senatorship and revived his badly neglected attorney's practice.

Basner was politically inactive through the 1950s but this did not prevent him from being detained during the 1960 State of Emergency. After his release, government restrictions made legal work impossible and he left South Africa with his family, first going to Tanzania, then to Ghana, arriving in Accra in 1962. There for four years he wrote a newspaper column for the *Ghanaian Times* and became a confidant of Kwame Nkrumah. He was imprisoned once again in 1966 by the soldiers who deposed Nkrumah and was subsequently deported. Reluctantly admitted to Britain in 1968 after spending a year in Israel, Basner settled with his wife and children in Herefordshire where he remained in retirement until his death nine years later.

In retrospect, as a politician Hyman Basner's most enduring contribution was where he would have wanted it to have been, in the arena of extra-parliamentary politics. As this book makes clear, his election campaigns of 1937 and 1942 were vital episodes in the reconstruction of organised mass opposition amongst Africans from the stagnation into which it had fallen after the disintegration of the Industrial and Commercial Workers Union in 1929.

In most academic analyses of black political history, a sharp dichotomy is drawn between officially institutionalised politics and activity outside government sponsored representative bodies; it is a dichotomy which is depicted in terms which are essentially moral — collaboration as against resistance. In reality, the division between the two was never so simple nor so stark. Basner was unusual amongst left-wing activists in recognising the opportunities for mobilising a political following that existed in elections even for powerless representatives[7].

In the only detailed published account of the Senate contests, Eddie Roux attributes Basner's success to the personal connections he had formed 'as a lawyer with a Native practice and as such known to many chiefs and other Native leaders'[8]. There was more, though, to Basner's electoral victory than a network of supportive notables. Basner succeeded in re-igniting the 'elderly political cinders' left as a residue by the ICU 'in all the small dorp locations'. These men supplied him with lists of the names of office holders and organisers in the years when the ICU had built a following of thousands through the farms of the Orange Free State and the Southern Transvaal. The lists were important — they represented a much more tightly woven web of connections than the network of important clients referred to by Roux.

Basner was exceptional amongst his political contemporaries in the sociological imagination and historical perception with which he sought to arouse these veteran activists. In the early stages of industrial revolutions the wellsprings of revolt are often stronger in social groups threatened with extinction than among those in the process of being born[9]. Basner directed his exhortations at the people who were being crushed by the emerging capitalist social relations in the countryside, the 'flotsam and jetsam' left behind by the defeated African peasantry: 'teachers, self employed artisans, clergy, general labourers, hawkers' as well as those communities who had yet to be completely dispossessed of their rights over land. The support he received in both the 1937 and the 1942 elections was an early expression of a massive and protracted rural revolt which ended only three decades later. It helped to awaken the Transvaal ANC leadership to the possibilities of systematic local organisation amongst the poor and rightless in the cities as well as the countryside. Basner's friend and principal collaborator in the 1937 election, John Marks, was a key figure in developing a more populist predisposition amongst ANC leaders.

Basner's special acumen was in recognising the symptoms of profound social changes for what they were and in perceiving the political opportunities they represented. Though he called himself a Marxist[10], he at first intuitively and later more self-consciously recognised that local realities often failed to conform with the schematic order proposed by the more dogmatic applications of Marxist social theory favoured by South African Communists during the 1930s and 1940s. In the countryside he was willing to enlist the support of supposedly reactionary landowning millenarian church leaders. As an urban politician he was the first to attempt to harness the energy represented in the 'direct action' of the poor — action undertaken usually at the behest not of virtuous proletarian tribunes but of the disreputable prophets, charlatans, and visionaries of an only partly urbanised society, one dominated by the politics of patronage and by ties of personal loyalty.

He was unsuccessful in his efforts to promote more radical and popular political alternatives to the ANC and the Communist Party but his own involvement in the bus boycotts and Mpanza's squatter community magnified the inspirational impact of such movements and rendered them visible to African political elites in ways they might not otherwise have been. Of course, he was not alone in this — young African nationalists were also beginning to consider ways in which the ANC could tap the power invested in the armies of the urban poor and connoisseurs of historical coincidence will appreciate the presence in Basner's attorney's office of two founding members of the Congress Youth League, Macdonald Maseko and Nelson Mandela.

Basner surely deserves a place in any pantheon of South African radicalism. Ironically, the most serious academic evaluation of his career to date recruits him instead into a canonical tradition of democratic liberalism, a view Basner himself would have found most uncongenial[11]. He claimed he disliked liberals and liberalism. In fact, though, his relationship with South African liberalism was more complex than he allowed for in such protestations.

Certainly, Basner believed that capital was malign and moreover, in South Africa, retrogressive. It is also true that his understanding of local liberal institutions and leading liberal personalities was conspiratorial; they were the agencies and agents of big business, unwitting perhaps, but essentially malevolent. As a public critic of the paternal and protective liberalism which helped to supply some of the intellectual underpinning of segregationist policies, Basner had few equals. Paul Rich has argued that he made a major contribution in detaching African politics from the becalmed ideological moorings established by such bodies as the Joint Council Movement and the Institute of Race Relations. But in helping to undermine the political standing of a socially conservative and politically elitist generation of liberals, Basner may only have cleared the way for the gestation of a more democratically inclined South African liberalism.

Basner was intellectually attracted by the analytical and methodological dimensions of Marxism, but his political career was motivated by outrage at social injustice and engagement with people whom he perceived as individuals with strengths and failings rather than as idealised representatives of vast impersonal social forces. He found political fellowship amongst a variety of souls: with African Communists, especially those less compelled by dialectical acrobatics, amongst non-Marxist social democrats, and towards the end of his Parliamentary career, within the growing group of democratic liberals fostered by the wartime climate of social reform. Whatever his private inclinations may have been, Basner's political allies were increasingly located among the less revolutionary sections of the left and the more democratically inclined liberals.

Neither of the political parties he helped to establish had a radical programme. In 1945 he was being mocked by the Trotskyist Workers International League for his association with Michael Scott's Campaign for Rights and Justice, a coalition of labourites and clerics, the WIL said, dedicated to winning 'support of a very strong sector of capitalist opinion in the Union'[12]. Two years later Basner was reported to be calling 'for a non-socialist party of young churchmen, Indian merchants, African chiefs and European trade unionists'. One of its objectives would be the summoning of a national convention to rewrite the constitution[13].

Influenced perhaps by his association with white trade unionists in the Socialist Party, Basner was prepared in 1945 to advocate increased white immigration in order that white working class fears evoked by black 'numerical superiority' would be assuaged[14]. The text of this book concedes that many of Basner's utterances at this time 'seem downright liberal' (though encouraging white immigration was not a policy typically favoured or emphasised by white liberals) expressing a 'moral wrath that seems to accept the South African power structure as something capable of amendment'. Such mistaken perceptions, the text suggests, were attributable to South Africa's participation in a war against fascism and the 'significant change of attitudes' of many of the 'ordinary whites' who helped to fight it.

That may have been the case, but it is possible that in a more profound way, Basner's participation in Parliamentary politics itself may have prompted visions of political change which though democratic were distinctly non-revolutionary. 'Native representatives', he told a meeting of the Cape Town Joint Council, should 'correlate the activities of all those who are exploited and unenfranchised in their efforts to achieve the general franchise and to abolish general exploitation'. They should also undertake 'to educate the native people to realise the necessity of industrial organisation, peasant leagues and political parties to become pressure groups on the Government for change of the present laws and policies. Otherwise native representation is completely useless, and by confining itself to parliamentary advocacy can be very harmful'[15].

Leaving aside the paternalism of the language which reflected the conventions of the time, this was by no means a completely unrealistic scheme, not if Basner's own example is taken seriously. He was a ubiquitous presence in even minor protests; Basil Davidson records him in 1946 standing on the Johannesburg City Hall steps in front of a line of coffee carts, denouncing the municipality's efforts to clear African food vendors off the streets. After an hour of the Senator's hectoring the mayor conceded that there would be no further prosecutions[16].

Paul Rich has argued that Basner's confrontation of the moral and political authority of traditional liberal elders helped to alter the course of black politics:

> This challenge to the traditional institute hegemony in the co-optive structures created in 1936 had a significant impact on the movement of African political consciousness in the coming years. It contributed to a growing democratic liberalism amongst younger Africans and white liberals influenced by the wartime alliance against the Axis.[17]

This may be overstating the case, but even so Basner's senatorship was a very different kind of 'representation' from those forms which were customarily offered to Africans, encouraging as it did active assertion of rights rather than passive dependence on mediators to secure concessions. As such it may well have helped to strengthen constitutionalist predispositions in African political thought.

Quite apart from the ways in which he as an individual may have altered people's perceptions, Basner's life is interesting as an expression of wider social changes. He belonged to a generation which grew up in a community of Jewish immigrants, 45 000 of whom arrived in South Africa from Russia's Baltic provinces between 1890 and 1913. It was a community of small traders, artisans, and clerical workers. Its exodus was prompted by racial and political persecution as well as economic hardship. Continuing poverty in South Africa, local anti-Semitism, and in some cases experience of European revolutionary politics were all factors which may have motivated a tiny but conspicuous minority within this community to join the fledgeling South African Communist Party (though much larger numbers were active in a vigorous Zionist movement).

In the 1920s and 1930s a disproportionate number of the Party's leading members were born in Lithuania or Latvia. This book joins a number of other biographical and autobiographical writings which document the social roots of white left-wing Johannesburg politics in a world of young men and women growing up in intimate but austere inner city neighbourhoods of comfortless homes, precarious business ventures, economic worries, and increasingly irksome religious etiquette[18]. This marginality of existence was an essential ingredient of Basner's upbringing; he remained all his life an outsider in many senses, never quite accepted and never quite 'respectable'.

Being an outsider may have helped to cultivate his capacity for social observation. For professional historians, Basner's story constitutes authoritative testimony on rural African politics during the late 1930s and early 1940s; the book includes the most detailed portrait existing of the heroic Alphaeus Maliba with whom Basner worked closely for a while. He was unique among white political activists in the degree of his involvement 'in the terrible problems of those two-thirds of the African population who lived on the land'. His analysis of the impact of 1936 laws on the Transvaal reserves is only beginning to be rivalled by academic researchers and his speeches on the topic still constitute a vital primary source for them.

This book is not quite biography. To begin with it contains two voices — Basner's own and that of his second wife, Miriam, whom he married in 1950. The text is adapted from an incomplete autobiographical narrative supplemented by information drawn from interviews Basner gave to researchers in the 1970s as well as by Miriam's own memories. She worked as Basner's secretary during his senatorship. In this book she appears briefly and anonymously on the steps of the Johannesburg Magistrates' Court just after Basner's acquittal on a charge of incitement. Portions of Basner's original text have been excised; in Miriam's judgement they represented indiscretions about Basner's private life which could hurt people without adding any useful understanding of his character, motives, or actions. This has not been done in such a way as to hide Basner's imperfections as a man. Even so, the main narrator is Basner himself; the text is largely his story as he would have liked it to have been told and representing his perceptions and opinions.

This is especially evident in his depiction of his opponent in the 1936 and 1943 election, John David Rheinallt Jones, for whom Basner felt intense dislike as well as political antipathy. The narrative does not altogether explain the depth of Basner's feelings. Jones was a widely admired figure, a 'superb social worker'[19] according to Edgar Brookes (another figure for whom Basner had little time) and in the opinion of his academic colleague, Julius Lewin, a 'straightforward and honest man', dignified, well mannered, and modest[20]. He was certainly a more complex and substantial figure than the mean spirited and duplicitous character Basner took him to be. He was an inept politician, though; his willingness to associate with government officials — 'the splendid lot of men in the Native Affairs Department' as he termed them[21] — and his conviction that lobbying and persuasion were more useful tactics than confrontation and mobilisation made him increasingly insensitive to the perceptions of his African constituents.

His defence of the South African Native Trust's management of the land acquired after the 1936 legislation was an example of his naïvely benign view of government intentions[22]. By 1947 his critics could be found even within the Institute of Race Relations for which he ceased working that year to take up a post as adviser to the Anglo American Corporation. Basner's harshness towards Jones in the text may reflect the bitterness of the 1943 election in which the incumbent injected an element of personal nastiness which had hitherto been absent, accusing his opponent of doing nothing for the voters other than 'taking cases in the courts for which he has been paid in money taken from African pockets'[23].

Autobiography tends to be more selective than biography though both types of writing are often teleological; they attempt to make sense of a life by turning it into narrative, granting it point, purpose and achievement by endowing it with plot, progression, consistency, and development. In biography, the overall design is usually less symmetrical and there is more room for critical interpretation. This text is closer to autobiography and in reading it we should be aware that memory and retrospective perceptions have been the main elements in its composition. In narrating their own stories people often 'read history backwards', for example in attributing to themselves beliefs or opinions or motives at an earlier stage than they actually held them.

In his account of the events leading up to the 1946 mineworker's strike, Basner is heavily ironical about the Party's anxiety that no labour disruption should hamper the war effort. In fact, however much he may have disapproved of such concerns afterwards, they were ones which Basner himself shared at the time. At the April 1945 conference of the Council for Non-European Trade Unions Basner delivered the keynote address, helping to sway delegates against a Trotskyite attempt to win control of the Council's leadership. In his speech, he praised the 'loyalty' of African workers in the previous five years 'in not striking and in not upsetting the economy of the country'[24].

One year earlier, Basner, according to the evidence he gave at a 1947 sedition inquiry into the strike, actually dissuaded miners from striking while he and other native representatives attempted to extract concessions from the government[25].

Basner's depiction of the Alexandra Bus Boycott is equally forgetful. His story ends with the triumphant conclusion of the 1943 boycott, the first 'marching' boycott which owed much to Basner's own leadership. It is a victory of little people representative of 'the unity that can underlie diversity'. But at the end of 1944 there was another boycott of which there is little mention in the text. On the eve of this boycott, Basner made what a Communist Party newspaper called a 'thoroughly defeatist speech' telling his audience there was no point in walking to town unless the residents of Orlando and the Johannesburg Western Areas also boycotted trams and buses[26]. The boycott lasted seven weeks and did secure a partial reduction in fares (through a weekly coupon system) but it progressed as it began with constant acrimony between the different organisers over tactical options and led to the collapse of the African Democratic Party in its Alexandra stronghold with the departure of its more active participants to the ANC, the Communist Party and the Workers International League.

A biographer might have been more critical of the moral and political lapses which are recorded in the text. Basner's deal with the slumyard owner to collect her rents in exchange for her financial backing of his new attorney's office makes for unattractive reading particularly because of the way in which it is presented as almost endearingly raffish behaviour and especially when read in conjunction with his often caustic comments about the personal failings of African notables. In fairness to Basner, he was genuinely tolerant of other peoples weaknesses and for this reason probably saw no reason to be unduly censorious about his own.

A more defensible but nevertheless wrong-headed decision by Basner was to restrain himself in 1944 from publicising the murders by foremen of labourers on farms around Bethal owned by Jews. Basner was anxious not to add fuel to any local anti-Semitism. Instead he left it to the Jewish Board of Deputies to secure vain assurances from the farmers that the abuses would cease; the brutality continued to become the subject of press exposures by Michael Scott and Ruth First. The Board of Deputies, motivated by similar fears of anti-Semitic reactions was to assist Basner three years later, when it helped to arrange a loan to pay back funds embezzled from a trust fund by a partner. In this, Basner was guilty of neglect rather than dishonesty — but the disarray of his legal practice and the misbehaviour of his colleague earned him the antipathy of the profession.

In 1952 the Transvaal Law Society sought to have Basner struck off the Roll of Attorneys for failing to render a properly detailed account for work undertaken on behalf of the paramount chieftainess of Basutoland. The judge ended the case by merely telling Basner to bring his accounts up to date, recognising the case for what it was, an unfair instance of professional harassment[27]. To this day he is still remembered with disapproval by Johannesburg lawyers, though his legal papers, now in the University of Witwatersrand Library indicate that through the 1950s he maintained a high reputation amongst a rural African clientele, people for whom he acted conscientiously without receiving very generous material rewards. Basner lived and died a poor man.

Though one should keep in mind that this text has had some of Basner's original material removed, it records a very public life. We learn a few anecdotal details about Basner's parents but very little about his feelings for them and how they altered or developed over time. Similarly neither his wife nor his child are presences in the text; we know that his first marriage was an unhappy one but this is mentioned in passing. We are informed that Basner had a frustrated ambition to be a writer but we are told very little else about those interests he had outside politics[28].

Few of his friendships seem to have endured or been regularly renewed: Eddie Roux, once a close associate if not a friend, in both his history and his autobiography refers to Basner only in impersonal terms. Occasionally, the text explores doubts and uncertainties in Basner's mind, for instance, in the case of his confused feelings during his first day in Parliament, but on the whole the narrative leaves little room for introspection. This reflects its essentially autobiographical character: Basner chooses to perceive and describe his public career as something apart from and unrelated to his private or his inner life. In reality, though, the distinction is much less easy to make, particularly in determining the motives which inform people's actions and decisions. For example, in the text Basner ascribes the evolution of his social attitudes to a series of political revelations: witnessing the 1922 Rand Rebellion, reading Plekhanov, visiting the jailed participants in the Californian oil workers' strike. Doubtless these experiences were important, but attitudes usually have more complicated origins; we know too little about Basner's childhood and upbringing to understand his moral passion for justice, his dislike of authority — any authority — and his inclination to be alone.

In a final and more obvious sense the text is incomplete because its chronology stops in 1947, thirty years before Basner's death. Basner wrote two drafts of another substantial fragment of his autobiography which concern the four years he lived in Ghana, but the years which passed between 1947 and his departure from South Africa in 1961, he dismissed as inconsequential, 'a political sleep for twelve years'.

Basner explains his withdrawal from political activity as prompted partly by the threat of bankruptcy in his legal firm but he also felt that the ANC's adoption of civil disobedience in 1949 was leading the organisation up a blind alley. Without being specific, he wrote in his Ghanaian memoir that Gandhism threatened to 'neutralise all the political efforts of the Africans to resist openly the fascist measures of apartheid'[29]. In addition, he was demoralised by the collapse of the two political parties he helped to form.

There may have been other considerations as well. After his resignation from the Senate, Basner, his wife and his daughter, Marcella, spent a year, mainly in Switzerland, returning, Marcella believes, only after South African currency regulations prevented Basner from drawing on his Johannesburg bank account. She remembers him being dismayed after the 1948 election, and saying 'Now that the Nationalists are in there is nothing for me here'. At that stage, Marcella thinks, the Basners planned to settle permanently in Britain.

Basner was not the only left-wing white politician who was reluctant to make the transition from socialist to African nationalist politics. When the South African Communist Party regrouped underground in 1953 after its banning, many former Communists were left on the sidelines, some because they were unwilling to undertake the risks of illegal politics but others because they had principled objections to the alliance with the ANC becoming the main focus of the Party's efforts. Those who shared Basner's view (which he held at least as late as 1947) that white workers could yet be won over to class politics would have found the 1950s orientation of the SACP particularly difficult to accept.

Basner left South Africa resolved 'to find an African newspaper in an independent African country in which (he) could campaign for a reconstruction of the United Nations and continue to fight against apartheid'. Once in Accra, though he did his best to persuade Kwame Nkrumah to sanction a more sympathetic official disposition towards the ANC within the Bureau of African Affairs, Basner became increasingly involved in the Ghanaian President's pan-African projects as well as in local politics as a member of Nkrumah's staff and as a journalist. He was deeply impressed by Nkrumah, believing him to be a visionary moderniser constructing 'the infrastructure of a modern industrial state' and enabling 'the clouds of ignorance and scientific backwardness (to) lift from Ghana'. For Basner, Nkrumah's project of imposing 'socialism from above' was both noble and plausible; to him it justified the attacks on the judiciary — 'the judges and lawyers in Ghana were not the kind of men for whom I would risk wrecking my friendship with Nkrumah' — and the debasement of constitutional procedures — 'any form of government which resembles the multi-party rule of Western democracy will not function in any developing countries'. It needs to be said that these were views which were widely shared by academic specialists on Ghanaian politics at the time who like Basner were enchanted with Nkrumah's idealism and his charm[30].

Not that Basner was an uncritical admirer of Nkrumah's leadership. In his manuscript he makes illuminating observations about Nkrumah's accelerating abandonment of political reality, about the degeneration of political institutions, and the 'weakness and danger of Nkrumah's practice of by-passing the ministries to assume personal control'. Ironically, it was this particular habit of Nkrumah's which enhanced the influence of people such as Basner who had no official status but had direct access to Flagstaff House.

Such access represented considerable privilege but it carried risks as well: in 1965 Basner began to assume an active role in Nkrumah's efforts to check official corruption and in the process acquired powerful enemies. Basner believed that public venality and misappropriation of resources were at least partly the outcome of political conspiracies by an 'establishment' hostile to socialism; he also insisted that Nkrumah was innocent of any personal self enrichment[31].

For a while Basner was closely implicated in Nkrumah's efforts to develop pan-African unity. He began to help draft Nkrumah's OAU speeches and memorandums in 1963 and attended the summit conferences in Addis Ababa, Cairo, and Accra. Given the failure of Nkrumah's foreign policy initiatives in this direction and especially his isolation at the Cairo summit when he delivered a speech co-written with Basner[32], it would be foolish to ascribe too much significance to this. To be fair to Basner, though, his main concerns seem to have been to restrain Nkrumah's more utopian impulses and to encourage him to be sensitive to African national sovereignties. And in his Ghanaian newspaper column he was an early and far-sighted critic of the shortcomings of the OAU's pretensions concerning continental solidarity[33].

Basner's detention and expulsion from Ghana were dryly noted in a brief report in *West Africa* magazine:

> Mr Hyman Basner, a South African refugee who was a leading political columnist in CPP newspapers, was released from protective custody, and flew to Rome[34].

His fellow prisoner in Accra, Nkrumah's former attorney-general, Geoffrey Bing, attached much more significance to the South African's enforced departure. Later he wrote of Basner:

> He was a brilliant journalist and man of high personal courage ... Accra had seemed to him then the best centre from which he could continue the political objective he had set himself in South Africa, the destruction of apartheid and the creation of a planned economy throughout the African continent.
>
> His complete acceptance by Ghanaians as an African like themselves, despite his colour and his faith, had symbolized Nkrumah's dream of a united Africa free of prejudice on grounds of race and religion. His imprisonment signified more clearly than anything else, that the old values were gone'[35].

Bing's tribute is generous but not overstated. In Ghana Hyman Basner came closest to becoming an African and nearest to finding contentment.

TOM LODGE
September 1992

1

PROLOGUE

Before he died in Britain in 1977, HM Basner was able to write a substantial part of his recollections of a life spent mostly, and occasionally prominently, in Africa. This was never completed as a fully consecutive autobiography, though it covered the period from his childhood and youth in Latvia, South Africa and the United States to late middle age in Tanzania and Nkrumah's Ghana. Some of his text was extremely lengthy, some of it sketchy, and a great deal missing altogether.[1]

One period he tackled, however, clearly constituted a whole in itself, despite some sizeable gaps in the narrative. This was the period between 1927 and 1947, which coincided with his active participation in South African politics. Furthermore, it coincided with a palpable acceleration in the drift of historical processes set in motion by the discovery of gold on the Witwatersrand, the Anglo-Boer War and the establishment of the Union of South Africa. For these reasons, and because of the considerable amount of material he provided, I decided to confine the contents of this book to little more than those twenty years.

It is usual to begin a formal biography with a full account of the antecedents and early experience of its subject. This work, because of its limited time-scale, traces the thread of Basner's younger days in little more than a single chapter, and mainly in terms of his subsequent political development. I have not only put that chapter and all those following into the third person, but have abbreviated or expanded them.

In view of the treatment to which I have subjected so much of Basner's writing, it seems to me that he and the reader are entitled to have at least a few preliminary pages set down in his own words. These will, I hope, not only provide some elementary information about his background, but do a little justice to his style and intent. His original narrative soon ceased to refer in any detail to personal matters (such as the deaths of his parents, his first marriage, and the birth of his eldest daughter). This was quite simply because the more he wrote, the more he became absorbed in recollection of his political world, and the less it occurred to him to discuss his private one.

'Am I an African?' he began.

'No matter which flag flew, or whether they called it by the Russian name of Dvinsk or its Latvian name Daugavpils, or by the ancient Scandinavian one of Danneborg[2], the town in which I was born had for centuries been a Jewish one. Every invasion and pogrom somehow left, in this important centre on the banks of the River Dvina and the railway line between St Petersburg and Warsaw, a remnant of Jews to carry on the timber trade for the Baltic barons, establish markets for the peasants, keep the brothels and shebeens for the railwaymen and soldiers, and provision the rafts that made long journeys from the Volga provinces to the Gulf of Riga.

'In this community, more prosperous than most among the ghetto towns of the Tsar's Jewish "pale of settlement", I was born in 1905, a week before the high festival of New Year, summarily placed in the Julian calendar as the thirty-first of August when the time came to include my name on my mother's passport to travel to South Africa.

'My father's name was Abraham. He had already been to South Africa and had returned at the end of the Anglo-Boer War on the first train to pull out from Pretoria to Cape Town when hostilities ended (a convinced pro-Boer by that time). He returned there shortly after my birth, and did not really become a personality for me until years later in our South African setting. My mother's name was Hannah, and her maiden name Elitsofin. I know nothing of her family except that it was comfortably off and belonged to the Chassidic sect. The Chassids were mystics, with their own synagogues, forms of worship and Talmudic lore, who seldom mixed socially with other Jews and were considered eccentric and disreputable by the orthodox majority in spite of the piety and learning of their rabbis and the considerable prosperity of their leading families[3].

'My paternal grandfather, Baruch, known among Latvians by the literal translation of his Hebrew name as Benedictus, and by his family as Bendik, was an outstanding citizen, though not sufficiently pious or well-to-do to be considered a notable in the community. He was taller and broader than most Jews, and gentle and soft-spoken despite his size and strength. He was a fisherman, with his own boat on the river in summer, who acted as night-watchman for the town's only substantial department store in winter when the Dvina was frozen. The store was owned by a syndicate of businessmen in Riga, headed by a Latvian baron with whom Benedictus was a great favourite. This was useful to the community as well as to my grandfather, since the baron was very influential with the police and other uniformed proconsuls.

'Bendik had three married sons and one ageing spinster daughter, and owned three wooden houses which he did not let, since they were occupied by himself and his sons and their families. In one lived his eldest, Israel, who was a rabbi; in another, his second son, David, who was a cabinet-maker; and he himself lived in the third together with his daughter and my mother, my elder sister Marusya and me (and my father, when he was not away).

'Israel was not a proper rabbi, despite his title[4]. He was a petty state official whose duty it was to record Jewish weddings, births and deaths. For this he got a small salary from the government but no payment from the congregation, so had to farm a small plot of land in order to make ends meet. It was his own fault that he received no help from the congregation, because he did not even go to the synagogue regularly and was rumoured to smoke on the Sabbath.

'My uncle David the cabinet-maker was a drunkard and whoremonger, but, like most black sheep, the favourite of the family, though with the exception of myself. I never liked sitting on Uncle David's knee, even when he was sober. I preferred riding with stiff, silent Uncle Israel in his trap to his field in summer and to the river in winter, where he would make a hole in the ice and dip himself in. That was his flagellation for violating the Sabbath, it was said, but I thought he was the bravest man in the world.

'My father was the maverick of the family, and, I suppose, of the whole community. He joined the Tsar's army at an early age, not waiting to be called up and, when discharged, took up employment in the non-kosher food department of the store, where no Jew had ever worked before. Tiring of that after a few years, he ran away to South Africa, somewhere around 1895.

'It is not quite correct to say he ran away, for one cannot say that men emigrated from Dvinsk as did large numbers of respectable Jews who were driven by economic pressure from the 'pales' to heathen lands like the United States, the Argentine and South Africa[5]. In Dvinsk, anyone who wanted to work could earn a living, and those who went away did so mainly because of creditors, the police, or to avoid military service. My father, as everybody knew, left only because he was being pressed by his own restless nature, and not by the natural enemies of a pious Jew. (My mother also told me, much later, that he was beginning to associate with some of the revolutionary workers in a local factory, and that she encouraged him to go because she did not want to spend the rest of her life with him in Siberia.[6])

A little more needs to be added about Basner's personal names and date of birth.

His original given names were Hebrew ones — Chaim Meir. When he was three, his mother took him with her on a long visit to the Prussian city of Koenigsburg (now Kaliningrad) where she went for medical treatment for her eyes, and lodged there with a married sister who had completely adopted German culture and had come to consider that Dvinsk's Russo-Yiddish ways were downright uncivilised.

Under her influence, Chaim and Meir were translated into Hermann and Meyer — and Hermann he was to remain until six years later, in Johannesburg at the outbreak of the First World War. In those days of ferocious jingoism, his school's headmaster felt it wise to recommend that his parents make another change, thinking that 'Hermann-the-German' could become a nasty cry in the playground.

So, at a family conference, Vivian, the literal version of Chaim, was considered and rejected as too fancy. The alternative, 'Hyman', which inevitably takes on the diminutive 'Hymie' was chosen, but came to be disliked by his parents nearly as much as by him. As a result, they, and all who knew him well, eventually called him by shortened forms of his surname, which is the reason why only his surname is used in this book.

As for his age, early official documents confirm that he was born in 1905, but passports issued between 1937 and the end of his life make the date two years earlier. He had changed the date himself on discovering, when he was about to stand for the Senate in 1937, that the electoral laws demanded that he be a little older than he actually was.

Basner finished his first chapter like this:

'Were the next few years — that is from my third to my seventh, when I reached South Africa — the important ones which formed my character and conscious mind? They certainly left nostalgias and memories deeper and stronger than any other time. But what happened in my mother's womb? What happened at the huge breasts of my Latvian foster-mother and in puling, incontinent months in the cot? I know as much about it as the reader.

'What sounds like a pointless digression has special point for South Africa, where the geography of birth is used more often than patriotism as the last refuge of the political fanatic, opportunist and scoundrel. The right skin is not enough: it has to be the right skin born in the right place. In that country, among whites, when discussing apartheid, the causes of the Anglo-Boer War, wildlife conservation, the smell of the Transvaal lowveld at dawn, you are liable to be asked, "What can you know? You weren't born here". It used to infuriate me as nothing else did, when, as a member of the South African Senate, speaking of some of the cruel grievances, pains or problems of my African constituents, I was countered by a bearded Boer patriarch (whether a rabid Nationalist of Dr Malan's party or from the more "liberal" ranks of Jan Smuts's United Party) with "You weren't born here. How can you understand?" '

'I would ask, "Could it have helped if I'd come when I was two instead of seven? If I arrived when I was six months old?" There would be blank, not necessarily hostile, faces all around me. Could I not understand that it was the first breath you drew which counted . . .? The first drop of mother's milk decided whether you understood why there could be no equality in church or state between white man (Nordic, Jew, Syrian, and later, by honourable adoption, Japanese) and the black man, who was born to serve.

'As a fair-minded man, I had to remember that Sir Walter Scott had put it in nobler words, but with essentially the same meaning:

> Breathes there a man with soul so dead
> Who never to himself hath said
> This is my own, my native land!

'And did not Thomas Jefferson and the Founding Fathers, intimately involved with great revolutions, trust geography more than humanity with their provision in the United States constitution that no one born outside the United States could become President?'

2
ON NOT FINDING A COUNTRY
(1912-1926)

Basner thought it probable that Balmoral Chambers was the only furnished apartment house in Johannesburg in 1912. That was the year when, aged seven, he came from Latvia with his mother to join his father in South Africa, and the three of them spent several months in rooms there.

A few of the tenants were in families, but most of them were better-off bachelors and single women who had someone to pay the rent. The building occupied nearly half a block on Commissioner Street, in the middle of town, and had shops on the ground floor. Behind was an ample courtyard, entered through gates by lumbering carts delivering goods to the tradespeople. The horses would drop enough manure there to give the whole place a distinct farmyard smell.

Two of the shops belonged to butchers who slaughtered their own sheep and calves in the yard. This would happen nearly every morning except Sunday, and there would be frantic bleating and pools of blood and children would stop on their way to school to watch the performance.

Some black and coloured children also made up the audience, but had to stand at the back.

Another attraction was the Gaiety Cafe, an all-night establishment which sold penny cold drinks and hot lemon tea in the daytime and was a centre of life for cabbies, prostitutes and revellers who wanted food and shelter when other places closed. Outside its doors were two distorting mirrors — one in which you became as small as a dwarf and the other in which you were marvellously attenuated — and during the day there was never a moment without a crowd in front of them. White miners (not yet Afrikaners, but mostly Cornish 'Cousin Jacks' and Australians[1]) had good sport there, coming out of neighbouring bars to chase gaping blacks off the pavement.[2] They were not enforcing apartheid. They were only 'bloods' expressing the high spirits of their masterful birthright.

Because he did not know enough English yet to go to school, Basner had plenty of free time and spent hours outside Balmoral Chambers with other small children, watching the many passers-by moving down from the Indian Market in Diagonal Street towards Rissik Street and the commercial centre.

The Indian hawkers came first, some in rickshas or carts, but the majority trudging along to make their way out into the suburbs, laden with panniers of fruit and vegetables or silks and beads and silvery trinkets. There were more white miners, off the night shift, in gumboots and tin hats. Later, perhaps, an ox-wagon would fill half the street, causing all the traffic to swerve and manoeuvre to get past. The black teamster in front would pull frantically at the leading span; his mate with the whip would crack it like thunder and shout, Witbooi! Bosman! or whatever the dilatory ox was called. It would take several minutes for the great wheels to roll by the gateway of Balmoral Chambers. A man in a black suit and bowler hat might hurry on his way from the Stock Exchange to the Rand Club for his first drink, or to the headquarters of Rand Mines at Corner House in Commissioner Street, for a board meeting, taking care to keep his boots and trouser bottoms clear of puddles and horse dung.

Best of all was when the whistles blew madly and a newly recruited contingent of half-naked Shangaans or Swazis or blanketed Basotho marched down from the municipal single male quarters in the Wemmer Compound towards Crown Mines or City Deep. More often than not they would be chanting and their walk would be a rhythmic prance. One of them would be leaping ahead, waving his sticks, and uniformed *indunas*[3] strode alongside to keep the ranks. All traffic would stop until they were gone and every passer-by would pause to look at them. It was a common sight, but not to be taken for granted, since the flow of tribal manhood into the deep shafts of the gold mines was the lifeblood of Johannesburg itself.

For the next ten years, until he matriculated and left South Africa for the United States and the University of California, Basner's home was a house behind the dairy his parents ran in Doornfontein, a once-prosperous suburb of Johannesburg which, by the late 1920s had become a multiracial slum. After primary school, he was awarded a place at Jeppe, a government high school of considerable standing[4], run on English public school lines. Its aim was to turn English-speaking sons of farmers and shopkeepers into administrators, officers, sportsmen, gentlemen and scholars, and so provide an indigenous establishment for the country.

The emphasis was on cadet drill, cricket and football, but there was also an insistence upon high standards in Latin and English which could lead to admission to good universities 'at Home' (in Britain). The education at Jeppe suited Basner. It helped him to escape from the ritualist traditional life which corresponded with his mother's ambition to make him a conforming Jew, if not a rabbi, and to find his way into the pagan world of the classics and the renaissance life of the Elizabethans.

It was possible at that time for whites to grow up in South Africa's largest town without realising that brown-skinned people were the same kind of human beings with the same needs, feelings and rights to respect, dignity and justice as they had. Basner and his contemporaries could spend all their youth in Johannesburg without knowing enough about the African — or the Afrikaner, for that matter — to have the slightest understanding of their own country.

It was possible, if you were English-speaking and brought up in the suburbs, to think of Afrikaners not as fellow white South Africans, but as conquered people who had to be kept by force under British rule. It was true that Prime Ministers General Botha and General Smuts were Boers, but they had sensibly decided to serve the King, the Governor-General and the British Empire. It was true that Dutch, as well as English, was an official language, but most of the Boers did not speak it, but a jargon called Afrikaans which people in Holland were said to have difficulty in understanding.

These attitudes were not found in the same degree or form throughout the country — neither in the Cape Province, where the two white races had lived together for generations, nor in the Orange Free State, where the white population was entirely Afrikaans-speaking, nor again in Natal, where English was completely dominant. They were typical, however, in Johannesburg as it grew and grew at speed, ever luring and drawing into itself all races, all tribes, all the variations in religion, culture and skin which go to make up the South African nation.

Johannesburg was a British town. Afrikaners there were poor-white ex-farmers and their families who had drifted in from burnt-out homesteads and lands ruined in the campaign which ended the Anglo-Boer War in 1902, or workers beginning to replace the earlier wave of English-speaking immigrants employed on the trams, railways and mines and in the building trades. The poor-whites lived in Vrededorp and adjoining slums, the workers in mean suburbs developed round each important shaft of the largest mines — Crown Mines, City Deep, Robinson Deep. For them there were no parks and few trees, and civic amenities were of the most grudging kind.

The municipal councillors were British — heavy burgesses allied to a handful of very venal Labour Party members. Primary schools for Afrikaans-speaking children were scarce, and until 1921 the nearest secondary schools for them were in Pretoria, thirty-five miles away, and Potchefstroom, seventy miles away.[5] The African and coloured population, on the other hand, was everywhere[6], in sheds in the back yards of houses in every street, rich or poor. Each white house needed domestic servants, each shop or trade, cleaners and messengers. But these were not working people — not servants in the European sense: they were part of the environment which made life easier than in Europe, like sunshine and mild winters. Their children did not go to school at all.

There must have been some missionary education for Africans and coloureds in Johannesburg in those days, Basner later realised. But he could not remember ever seeing a black child carry a satchel or hold a book.[7] His parents employed about ten 'boys' — grown men who lived in a yard behind the house with their families — and he later came to feel that had he seen their children go to school as he did, the sight could have awakened his imagination to include them among his fellow-humans.

His first sight of a place of education for Africans was to come when he was twenty-four, at Evaton, a black township twenty miles from Johannesburg.

Before Basner reached his final high school year it had been decided that he was cut out to be a successful barrister. For that, he would go to Oxford or Cambridge. His headmaster thought he had literary ability and should aim at journalism, but only Basner took this notion seriously. For his parents, the idea was so unfitting as to be nonsense. The ideal for Jewish Doornfontein boys was the medical profession, and failing that, law. Commerce was less worthy, and anyway needed capital. (His mother's hope that he would become a rabbi had, to her regret alone, inevitably proved forlorn.)

He would certainly have gone to England and Oxford had not his sister Marusya intervened. Her husband, Gregor Cherniavsky, a distinguished Russian violinist, had been so successful in the United States that he had decided to settle in Los Angeles, of which a suburb, Hollywood, had become the centre of the film industry and a magnet for actors, writers and musicians from all over the world. The phenomenal growth of the place had persuaded the University of California to open a branch in the south, and this had prompted Marusya to invite her young brother to stay with them and study law there.

Basner had thought himself committed to literature, but dreaming spires and the noble music of Milton and chiselled prose of Walter Pater had occupied his mind for so long that their charm had worn a little thin. From Hollywood came not only the vulgarities of the Keystone Cops[8], but the curves of Mack Sennett bathing beauties[9]; not only the stereotyped excitements of the Wild West, but the exotic and languorous movements of Gloria Swanson[10] and Pola Negri[11] in bedroom scenes. There was the Fatty Arbuckle scandal[12] and the death of Wally Reid from an overdose of drugs, mourned by the whole film colony.[13] The writings of Oscar Wilde, Arthur Symons and Edgar Allan Poe and English translations of Gautier, Verlaine, Rimbaud and Baudelaire were full of scarlet sins and dark mysteries that could be relished far better in the United States than in Britain.

An American law degree would not qualify Basner to practise in South Africa, but it was likely that his parents might emigrate one day and they could all be together in the States.

His departure was due to take place in March 1922, but shortly before that, the Rand Revolt of white miners took place. He had to wait for the Prime Minister, General Smuts, to fusillade, deport and hang a number of miners and other trade unionists before he could go. The issue which supplied the catalyst for the strike was the 1918 status quo agreement in which the industry was committed to providing jobs for skilled and unskilled whites — jobs which were either superfluous or were already being undertaken by black workers.[14]

Because Ellis Park, one of the big open spaces in the city, had become one of the battlegrounds, a great deal of sniping went on in nearby Beit Street where he lived. A neighbour was accidently killed by a bullet and several bullets came through the dairy windows. Basner did not see white miners marching but the Transvaal Scottish Regiment, the Durban Light Infantry and Smuts's Boer Commandos on their shaggy horses often paraded through Beit Street on their way to the hostilities.

The battle of Ellis Park occurred when, during the afternoon of 11 March, a group of armed strikers attacked an Imperial Light Horse encampment. Forty soldiers were killed or wounded by the attackers and in the subsequent skirmishing in outlying streets, forty-seven strikers lost their lives[15]. The Transvaal Scottish contingent was led by Major Ford, a solicitor from a firm acting for the Chamber of Mines; the officers of the Durban Light Infantry were sons of sugar planters from Natal and the Boers were from the veld — farmers who hated revolutionaries, even if many of them were by now their own Afrikaner kin.

The rebellious workers had formed commandos, too, heralded by banners proclaiming *White Workers of the World, Unite!* and *Fight for a White South Africa*. They had struck mainly to have the colour bar on the goldmines and railways reinforced, and had shot a number of African migrant workers in the mine compounds for no better reason than that they happened to be around.[16]

At that time, Basner was only beginning to understand the crude outlines of South African politics, in the same way as did the combatants in the Rand Revolt. Like the white miners, he thought it unnatural that black men should do skilled work and receive high wages, although he did consider it criminal to shoot innocent blacks who had come to the Rand to do the heavy labour which was appropriate to them. It seemed a sign of progress that English-speaking regiments should join Boer burghers to put down a rebellion against the government, but he also had vague feelings that General Smuts was excessively rough and unsympathetic in not negotiating a settlement with the strikers.

By now the influence of Jeppe High had made him sufficiently pro-British to disagree with his pro-Boer father, and he had read a few articles about the Russian revolution and some books by Bernard Shaw and other socialists which made him wonder if the poor-whites and white workers should not get better treatment. Brutality and injustice — of which he had seen little — made him distressed and uneasy, but when he thought of any social or political matters, it was only in terms of whites.

The sprawled, sunbaked city of Los Angeles had no patina of age to disguise its warts. Downtown was dirty and crude, despite many tall new buildings. Here the horse age had almost gone, and motor traffic was already heavy. There were lots of bars and sleazy little hotels, the streets were full of down-at-heel men and girls smarter than those in South Africa, though the number of plain ones was the same as anywhere.

Hollywood was even more disappointing to look at. The part where Basner had come to live was attractive enough, with clean streets lined with palms; the houses handsome timbered bungalows with open lawns and large, well-kept gardens. But the film studios were invisible behind enormous fences guarded by uniformed men, the whole district was chequered with development plots marked off with string tied to wooden pegs, and little huts for the real-estate agents were almost as numerous as the buildings.

The coming years in Basner's Russian-speaking sister's house were to be animated by the visits of exiles who had fled from the Bolsheviks through Harbin in Manchuria to California after the collapse of Denikin and Kolchak's counter-revolutionary armies. The great bass singer, Chaliapin, had to stay with the Cherniavsky family because he could not risk being prosecuted under the law which made it a crime to travel from one state to another with one's mistress and cohabit with her in an hotel. The great (and rather trying) Pavlova, was also a friend. There were music critics and journalists from the demolished press of St Petersburg and Moscow. There were real aristocrats and some self-made ones. They all opened the mind, as no others could have done, to what had happened in Russia.

Coming to California had raised the standards of material life for Basner, but had failed him academically. He had looked for a university, only to find himself in a glorified version of secondary school. Sport was the test of success for the college as well as for the students, and though there was respect for scholastic attainment, there was none for learning. He knew nothing about baseball or American football, and no one else had heard of cricket or soccer. His enthusiasm for modern European literature was an irritation rather than a delight to his tutor in English. His second major subject was logic, but he had enough sense not to refer in class to Kant, Hegel, Swedenborg and Nietzsche. His other courses were French, astronomy (because it promised field work at night with girl students) and civics (because he was going to become an American citizen).

Life here was as different socially and intellectually from that of the Oxford he had imagined as if he had blundered into an amusement arcade meaning to visit a museum. The disillusionment was all the greater because his sister's household was such a remarkable centre of musical and artistic talent.

He put up with it in a state of suppressed rebellion for a year, after which he would have dropped out had he not by then made sufficient friends on the campus who had similar sentiments. There were Chinese from Singapore, sons and daughters of British film actors, black students and a small number of Americans from the eastern states. By the end of his second year, however, his attendance record had become so bad that he did not qualify to write exams. He found a job in the office of a prominent Hollywood attorney and transferred himself to evening classes at the Los Angeles Law School.

He now began to take some interest in law, and through an almost accidental experience, learnt to be interested in justice.

A strike of Mexican workers on the Julian oilfields near the city spread to San Pedro, the harbour of Los Angeles, where the majority of dockers were Mexican[17]. The mayor and police chief responded as Smuts had on the Rand four years before, only here the conflict was entirely racial and there was no need for troops or guns. Police with batons and the oil company's security force with pickhandles were enough for the dark-skinned, undersized migrants from over the border, with no work permits and therefore no legal rights.

Daily arrests and beatings went on until, after about a week, the writer Upton Sinclair[18] and his wife — then living in southern California — called a meeting at which the strikers' leaders could explain their case to the public. When this meeting was broken up by the police, he announced another at which he intended to read the American Constitution aloud to an audience which included a number of students.

The second meeting, too, was brutally broken up and Sinclair and many of those present were arrested and thrown into prison. Claiming, as clerk to an attorney, that he had clients to see, Basner found his way to the prison, partly to find out whether any of the student acquaintances had been taken in, and partly out of curiosity. He had never seen prison cells before.

No visitors were allowed except lawyers. There were dozens upon dozens of people squeezed into a circular cage in the basement of the city hall, some with bloodstained bandages and some with open scalp wounds still bleeding. They had difficulty in breathing because there was not enough air, and no one could lie down, as there was no space for that. Everyone, however, was determinedly singing[19], which infuriated the guards in charge of the cage, who were moving around rattling the bars and swinging their clubs. The prisoners could have bought relief with submissive silence but would not, and the hatefulness of the scene was ameliorated by their obstinacy.

The next day, everyone got bail. In the end, they paid small fines to avoid the useless tedium of a trial before a police judge. The strike petered out and the Mexicans returned to work, no better off.

A side-swipe from a baton on the solar plexus, which was Basner's parting gift from the guards, did no more than emphasise painfully thoughts that had been going on in his mind for some time. His eyes were clearer now than in the days of the Rand Revolt.

The October Revolution in Russia had taken on a meaning which had not yet been poisoned by the Moscow Trials, Stalin's labour camps or Harry Pollitt's shifty polemics in Britain. His knowledge of Marx was confined to a book by Plekhanov[20], but that was something of an introduction. He had Negro and Chinese friends, and there could no longer be any question of his regarding white as the normal and natural colour for humans. He had outgrown the aesthetics of Oscar Wilde and was reading Henry Mencken religiously,[21] sharing his hilarity and exasperation over the 'boobus Americanus' and the morality and social aims of Main Street, USA.

When the news came that his parents could not come to the United States because his father had lost all his savings in an unlucky investment, he was almost glad to return home. At least he did not want to be an American any more.

3

ON FINDING A COUNTRY
(1927)

There was no one to meet him in Cape Town when he landed because his parents could not afford the fare for even one of them to make the journey. He arrived wearing an American suit and had a light American accent and a careful air of combined boredom and swagger as cover for a less than victorious return.

The situation at home was far worse than he had been led to believe. His father, who had been a diabetic for years was now very ill, in part because of worry over his business affairs, and his mother was struggling to run a smaller dairy in the district of Belgravia, which was rapidly running to seed with big houses downgraded to lodgings or second-rate boarding houses and the white population merging with that of the mining suburbs of Denver and George Goch. The trade was mostly in milk and bread for the whites and sour milk for the blacks in the backyards. The sour milk came in massive steel drums and was almost a staple food, together with mealie porridge, for black children. The cream, butter and eggs which had been consumed in great quantities by the customers in Doornfontein were rare luxuries in the new shop. His mother, greyer and frailer, was, however, insistent that this was a passing phase in their fortunes, and felt she could manage to support him if he went to the new University of the Witwatersrand. Meanwhile, she would find another shop with which they would fare better.

Between his mother's gallantry and his father's illness, any remaining thoughts of leaving South Africa disappeared and Basner had, even though faintly, the beginnings of a feeling that the situation held a challenge.

He had been receiving copies of South African newspapers during his years in the United States, but had begun to read them with interest only towards the end of 1926 when the time for his departure neared. He had a fair idea of political changes in the government, and also of attempts by a section of the blacks to resist the effects of the legislation which that government had brought about.

He knew that General Smuts had been beaten in 1924 by a coalition of Afrikaner Nationalists under General Hertzog and Labourites[1] under Colonel Cresswell. He admired Hertzog and approved of him as a champion of the poor-whites. He knew almost nothing about Cresswell and the Labour Party, although Tom Paine, Jack London, Shaw and Plekhanov's book on Marxism had made him think himself a socialist.

He felt that in South Africa he might satisfy both the romantic and the cerebral strains in the temperament he had developed when he turned his back on America. He was nearly twenty-two — the age at which his father had turned his back on Dvinsk in Latvia to become a recruit in the Tsar's army. But the father's education had been limited to the Hebrew *cheder*[2] and his horizons narrowed by lack of knowledge of the world outside the Russian Jewish 'Pale'. The son, on the other hand, could not have had much better schooling or seen more of the world had he been descended from British gentry. Mavericks they both were, but Basner was not built to be an aimless rebel and did not want to be one. For that, he would have done better to stay in California.

He made enquiries and was very indignant when the new university offered him only one year's credit for all the work he had done at UCLA and the Los Angeles Law School. The authorities were right, of course, but he thought it impertinent of a university whose buildings were not even completed. He began to consider the alternative of serving three years' articles with a solicitor and practising as an attorney only in the lower courts.

In South Africa's English-style two-tier legal profession, four years as a student dependent on his mother would only turn him into a barrister who would be obliged to spend more years waiting for briefs. Financial considerations, therefore, not social or intellectual ones, determined his choice.

Among his interests in Hollywood had been the Theosophical Society which sought to promote a synthesis of religion, philosophy and natural science, drawing on Western and Oriental intellectual systems. A number of fellow students, under the influence of Indian friends, found nothing incompatible with their socialist leanings in attending lectures delivered by the followers of Krishnamurti. Despite his material outlook on the world, Buddhist myths and religious actuality as combined in the lively western intelligence of Annie Besant and the brooding Slavic mysticism of Madame Blavatsky fascinated Basner. They presented fanciful forms of existence with which his mind liked playing, but as toys rather than valid aids towards a transformation of society.

Loneliness as much as interest often took him to the Johannesburg Theosophical Lodge and its library where he became friendly with a lawyer, Frederick Lowenberg.

Fred Lowenberg was a handsome man in his early forties, a tall, very thin Jew who had first arrived from London trained as an accountant, and then become a moderately successful solicitor with a commercial practice. Latterly he had joined in partnership with another Jew, Herman Wasserzug, a South African of German extraction who had made his mark as the best fly-half of his time at Pretoria High School and in provincial junior rugby, and was very popular with Afrikaner police and civil servants, who by that time were already rugby fanatics.

Wasserzug was not very bright as a lawyer, but was the only person Basner knew of whom he could say that he had a heart of gold. He and Lowenberg (who had a cool heart and a sharp brain) made an ideal combination. Civil servants referred plenty of domestic, accident and workman's compensation cases to Wasserzug, and Lowenberg dealt with them very capably.

It was not surprising that Lowenberg should agree to article Basner as a clerk to train as an attorney, yet it was probably Wasserzug who persuaded his partner to forgo the high premium which was customary, but would have been hard to raise. Basner was at least three years older than the average articled clerk and had had nearly two years' experience in a busy American legal office. Although the routine and formalities were different from those in Los Angeles, it was not hard for him to adjust, and he was soon able to finish all his work in the morning and have the afternoons free. Life was not very interesting, but he was paid ten pounds a month, and in three years' time could put up his own brass plate.

It became obvious that it was a waste to keep him at the office-boy tasks which a first-year clerk is required to perform. Lowenberg found that he could take a satisfactory statement from a witness, or notes in court, and could handle debt-collections better than the older man who was employed for the purpose. But here again, it was probably the guileless Wasserzug who first appreciated the best use to which the newcomer could be put.

A Chief Magistrate had recently been appointed in Johannesburg who tackled in earnest a scandal which concerned many people, though nobody did anything about it. Although justice was not a commodity generously distributed to the African community, the conditions in the Magistrates' Courts were intolerable even by the meanest standards. Most lawyers in those days would not bother to appear for an African client unless pressed to do so as a favour by his employer, a clergyman or some philanthropic body. The fees were not the problem as much as the loss of prestige, the unpleasantness of having blacks in the waiting room, and the possibility of having to contradict (or even impugn the veracity of) a white policeman or white witness giving evidence against a black.

This situation led to the evolution of a group of solicitors who for a variety of reasons were unable to earn an ordinary living in their profession, and therefore specialised in appearing for African clients, using touts to obtain them. The touts were usually educated blacks, often discharged teachers or mine clerks who had themselves taken to drink or petty crime.

They would hang about the courts and police stations on the lookout for anyone who seemed to be distressed and searching for a missing relative or friend who might have been arrested. If the seeker had money, he or she would be rushed to the tout's employer and something might be done to help, but more often, after the lawyer had received his fee and the tout his commission, the client would sit waiting for hours until he or she was told to go home because all efforts had been in vain.

The police would not prosecute the touts, saying it was too difficult to get reliable evidence. The Law Society made feeble gestures but never seemed to succeed in getting the lawyers who employed the touts struck off the rolls. The magistrates complained about attorneys who came to court without having interviewed their clients or knowing what their cases were about. The appeal judges fulminated, but their lightning never seemed to strike. Hundreds of hard-working black women drudging in kitchens and fathers in the countryside who sold their cattle to find fees were robbed by these pests each year, sometimes without their imprisoned relatives even meeting an attorney, let alone getting legal help.

The Chief Magistrate decided to set up a bureau in a small hut in the crowded prisoners' yard, where an official could interview any arrested person or relative wanting — and having the means — to consult a solicitor. This officer could then get in touch with a reputable man who would come to be instructed. The idea was to bypass the touts who swarmed round the courts and could no more be dislodged than flies from a dunghill.

To be effective, the 'Prisoner's Friend' had to be a responsible, educated African who belonged neither to the clergy nor to a political movement. There were functionaries high in the Department of Justice hostile to the new move who predicted that it would have undesirable social consequences. On the other hand nobody should be given an opportunity to label the new office an evangelising enterprise. African trust in lawyers was already strong and distrust of missionaries was a heritage from colonial times.

What happened was remarkable. The person chosen for the job could not have been bettered. She was Mrs Charlotte Maxeke, who, under her maiden name, Manye, had graduated in social science at the black university of Wilberforce in the United States, and had already spent some years as a welfare and probation officer. She was of Sotho-Hlubi stock, both chieftainly and mission-bred (not an unusual combination), and the widow of a Xhosa clergyman. Originally a Wesleyan, she had played a considerable part in the early campaigns of the African National Congress, but above all had been active in the 1890s in the Ethiopian Church movement, which was in essence a reaction of black clergy against the paternalistic white missions. At present, Charlotte Maxeke had no political affiliations. She was a devoted member of the African Methodist Episcopal Church (AME),[3] which, largely through her agency, had developed from an amalgamation between the solidly established American black church of the same name and the Ethiopians in South Africa. She had, too, been largely responsible for founding the notable AME educational centre (also called Wilberforce)[4], at Evaton, an African township in the Vaal Triangle, south of Johannesburg.

When the time came for the Senior Public Prosecutor and the police to draw up a list of respectable and reliable attorneys to whom black clients with enough money could be referred, the name of Herman Wasserzug led all the rest. From the point of view of the office it was a good arrangement: they already had separate waiting rooms for Indians and whites. Wasserzug seldom went to court (as the clients usually insisted on Lowenberg acting in that role), and was so genial and popular that he could be trusted not to lose face or to get into unseemly clashes with the police if he happened to appear for African *dagga* (marijuana) and illicit liquor sellers — the people with the money to pay really worthwhile fees.

Wasserzug and his partner agreed that in Basner they had a competent clerk who would be valuable in handling what was soon to prove a very lucrative part of their practice. He was competent because he liked reading law cases for precedents and was good at sifting and judging the weight of evidence. Interest, however, not competence, was what really made him useful to his employers. He was no more built to be an articled clerk than to be a freshman at UCLA. He had fought boredom and idleness in his first months in the office as hard as he could, but it had been a losing battle, leading to the habit of eating huge Chianti-soaked lunches at an Italian restaurant and then spending his afternoons in a torpor. For the small stakes he could afford, he had begun playing poker with people with whom he had nothing else in common.

The new kind of client, however, brought work which kept him busy all day and did not bore him. The hours spent in the criminal courts — so different from the civil ones where he had occasionally been with Lowenberg — began his true education and understanding of the society and the country in which he lived and brought his first realisation of what he wanted to do with his life.

Basner and his clients often had to wait for hours for their particular case to begin. If the prosecutor was friendly, he would give an indication that they could return to the office for a while. If rushed or harassed or not well-disposed, he would make them stay. As they waited, Basner could see a South African court at work. It did not differ much from such places all over the world, with drunks, prostitutes, petty thieves and common ruffians receiving summary justice, short sentences or small fines. But in South Africa there was the added dimension of colour-obsessed officials, special offences, specifically racial victims and switches to loud bullying or quiet, cruel indifference when the accused was black and obviously in a state of confusion and pathetic fear. Basner's skull would prickle with horror and there would be a painful feeling in his chest. The skull and chest reactions lessened with time, but his capacity for rage and disgust did not.

Among the accused on any one day would be deserters from the mining compounds. They would be cut short as they were telling how they had been assaulted and robbed in a shebeen: 'Ten shillings — or seven days imprisonment'.

There would be the passless ones: 'I lost my pass and was on my way to the Pass Office to . . .'. 'Ten shillings or seven days.'

A man living with his wife in the backyard of a private house . . . 'Ten shillings or seven days.'

Urinating in the street . . . 'I tried to find a latrine, but . . .' 'Ten shillings or seven days.'

Living in a municipal native location without a permit: 'Ten shillings or seven days.'

The batch of prisoners came and went in procession. They would spend no more than a few moments in the dock. The magistrate wrote nothing but the verdict on a prepared, typed charge sheet. Bullying was not for him or the prosecutor, but for the interpreter, who argued and shouted at the witnesses until he could say 'The accused pleads guilty, your worship.' The monstrous injustice and wickedness of what happened was not the fault of the interpreter, however. He had his job to do, and would lose it if the string of petty cases took longer to pass than usual. The fault lay entirely with the magistrate, who should have asked what the accused was saying, but did not because it was just a 'kaffir' in the box.

The weight of impersonal cruelty crushing a multitude of bewildered, simple and guiltless people sickened Basner. Not many could pay the ten shilling fine; a labourer's wages then were about two pounds a month. Many would lose their jobs when they went to prison, and with that the right to live legally anywhere near the city. Many were not just imprisoned, but sent to work in potato or mealie fields on the Transvaal Highveld farms, whilst frantic children, wives or parents spent agonised days looking for them. A few tragedies, and who knows how much suffering and hardship, followed the casual, brutal and pointless racial violence of 'Ten shillings or seven days.'

With Basner back, his father's mood and health improved and, as a result so did the family's fortunes. His parents had owned three small plots in the suburb of Mayfair which, when they had found themselves in serious need, turned out to be so valueless that nothing had been done to dispose of them. Now public transport in Johannesburg was extending and had reached two of these stands, and his father was able to raise a loan to build two houses and two shops. They could move into a relatively prosperous mixed Afrikaans and Jewish area and become comfortably off once more.

It was as well that this happened and that they could return to an environment in which they were able to find some of the ease and communal dignity they had enjoyed in Doornfontein, since it would have spelt misery for them and their son had the problems of poverty combined much longer with the problems of two generations. Basner had completely lost sympathy with religion and Jewish affairs and his present concerns, his few new friends, and even the food he liked, had no place in his parents' home. Their improved situation made it possible for him to continue staying with them, to be on happy terms with them, yet lead his own life.

He had fallen in love with a girl who lived far from his home. On evenings when he visited her, he would catch the last tram back to the middle of town and so miss the connection to get to Mayfair. Sometimes he felt rich enough to take a cab, but more often he would visit the Gaiety Café in Commissioner Street, which stayed open all night and did a busy trade because all other places closed at twelve.

Balmoral Chambers was by then a ruin, with all the shop fronts and upstairs rooms boarded up. The financial centre of Johannesburg was developing in that part of the city, and many of its older buildings were awaiting demolition. The distorting mirrors were still at the entrance, and occasionally a passerby would stop to look. There were no Africans at night, however. Curfew began at nine, and after that no black could be in the street without a 'special' — a special pass, written by a white on any scrap of paper, giving details of when and where he must return to his job. Police vans toured the town on the lookout for curfew-breakers.[5]

A common sight was a sudden chase — a man running, the van hooting and a mob joining in — white South Africa hunting and rounding up its unpenned slaves.

Inside the Gaiety Café, the air was heavy with smoke and bad ventilation, yet Basner could sit there for hours over dry beef sandwiches and a cup of coffee.

At one table would be young Afrikaans girls, tall, emaciated, badly dressed, tired from walking their beats on notorious Troye Street, waiting for the dawn so they could go home and wash before going to their daytime work. Most of them were employed in clothing factories in Langlaagte, where the pay was twelve shillings and sixpence for a six-day week. Two Communists who were trying to organise them into a trade union were facing charges under the Riotous Assemblies Act, designed by a Minister of Justice elected to maintain white supremacy.[6]

Other tables would be occupied by members of the 'sherry gang'. These were tramps — mainly old British working men who had lost their jobs and could not find a place in the labour teams on the railways and roadworks set up by the Nationalist government for poor-white Afrikaners.[7] They would keep enough money for a single cup of coffee which would allow them to sleep all night with their heads on their hands at a table.

There were cabbies whose dilapidated vehicles and starved horses plied all night because they could not compete during the day with the new motor taxis, and a tableful of noisy men and women in evening dress finishing a bottle of whisky they had brought with them. There were fat white waiters and a thin little Coloured girl wiping the floor where someone had vomited.

He would walk home in the clean, cool air under the Southern Cross. Who could see more, out on the town, in Paris or London?

4

PEOPLE
(1927-1929)

Charlotte Maxeke, the 'Prisoner's Friend', and Basner became friends the moment they met. Wasserzug introduced them to each other in the round hut-office that had been used to store old records and discarded correspondence. Now whitewashed and furnished with a desk, a telephone, a vast armchair for her ample bottom and some benches, it was a cool and restful room for legal business and exchanging reminiscences about America.

She had visited the University of California at Berkeley and had also been to Los Angeles to see black acquaintances, and when she heard about his musical family in the US, offered to take him to the Wilberforce Institute at Evaton, where her friend the Rev Dr Francis Gow, an African American AME pastor who was the Principal, had trained a wonderful pupils' choir to sing spirituals. 'Go down, Moses', Basner told her, was his favourite. 'He must have been a black Jew', she said, 'Jews in South Africa don't seem a bit like Moses', and they both laughed. His parents did not laugh when he told them the story that night.

She was an enormous woman in her middle fifties, always dressed in sober black; groaning with difficulty when she had to rise from her chair to fetch a file from her cupboard or walk to the car which kindly white philanthropists connected with an accountant, Howard Pim, who handled the charitable side of the gold-mining industry, had provided for her.

For all her surplus fat and age she still had the keen mind of the first black South African woman graduate, together with all the charm of an African maiden. Her strong frame, upright carriage, shining skin and brilliant brown eyes all showed what a beauty she must have been as a young matron.

Second only to the God of her late husband and her present church, she revered Dr W E Burghardt du Bois, the founder of the National Association for the Advancement of Coloured People (NAACP) in the United States, who had been one of her teachers. If she could have known of the hours Basner was to spend nearly forty years later in Ghana at the bedside of the dying Du Bois, discussing the past and future of South Africa, she would, he came to suspect, have started to revere him too.

He must have been rather novel to her — a young white, not brought up in Cape Liberal or missionary and negrophile circles in the Transvaal, who nevertheless thought about race in terms of straightforward egalitarianism. To him, Charlotte Maxeke was not the human novelty she might have been had he not made friends on the campus at UCLA and among the actors and musicians in the film studios of Hollywood, but she was a virtual treasure-house of knowledge about the history of African political movements, and a unique chaperon to acquaint him with old and contemporary personalities and political leaders.

Before the beginning of the 1914-18 War, she had been deeply concerned in the foundation of the South African Native National Congress, renamed the African National Congress in 1923. She had been a leader in the protest movement against the extension of the pass laws to women in the Orange Free State in 1913, when hundreds of followers of the Bantu Women's League, which she had helped establish, were imprisoned. In 1918, as President of the League, she had led a women's deputation to General Botha, which contributed to his decision to leave the issue alone.

She was ruefully resigned as she described her own acceptance, and that of Congress leaders in the northern provinces, of a compromise over the pass laws as they affected men, and humorously resigned herself to the Congress constitution of 1919, which only accepted women as an associate body in the form of her Bantu Women's League, certainly not as full individual members. 'They needed us to help by making the tea', she said, anticipating a plaint still heard (though more loudly) in political parties all over the world.

The excitement and difficulties of enlisting chiefs, clergy and teachers to build the African National Congress in order to oppose the Natives Land Bill in 1912 were particularly interesting. The Treaty of Vereeniging after the Anglo-Boer War and its logical successor, the Act of Union of 1910, had harnessed the white tribes of the Cape and Natal colonies and the Transvaal and Orange Free State Boer republics into nationhood for strictly practical reasons, which had been accepted by them as such (either with enthusiasm or on sufferance). The black tribes had not been asked whether they accepted the new state and they had definitely not been required to participate in it *en masse* or in any manner at all. Indeed, 'divide and rule' as a cry concerning the management of blacks was as good a one as any to rally the divergent whites into a single body politic.

The blacks were a fragmented majority in their own country, conquered, custom-bound and ignorant of all the ways of an industrialised society — what more was needed to ensure their subservience? Much more, since mere subservience was not enough, displacement from the land itself was the only way to impel the blacks to satiate the huge hunger of the white Union for cheap labour.

So, the Natives Land Act was designed and passed in June 1913. It restricted African land ownership to 'scheduled areas' and prohibited African land sales within these areas. The Act also made sharecropping illegal in the Orange Free State where all Africans settled on white farmland had to work for a white landowner for at least ninety days a year.

Buttressed by illiteracy and the colour-bar, the Land Act would cause thousands, rendered homeless, to seek out helotry for themselves on farms, in towns and, above all, on mines.

In the eyes of the small western-educated section of the African population, the implications of the looming act were plain and to some of them the necessity of uniting at least the leaders of the people in protest was both obvious and urgent. That they should fail against the Act was inevitable, but they did succeed in something else — in creating a national framework for the development of a political movement, the Congress, which has endured and grown ever since, despite long periods of grave internal weakness and brutal external repression.

In long hours in Charlotte Maxeke's little office and in drives at weekends to concerts at the Wilberforce Institute, Basner learnt a great deal, and heard amusing comments about events and people in the days before 1913. She was gently critical of the Jabavu family, the black intellectual aristocrats of the Cape Province. She had known their distinguished forbear, Tengo Jabavu, now dead, who preferred diplomatic pressure through favourable whites and electoral pressure through the still substantial coloured and African vote in the Cape to involvement in popular organisation.

It was illuminating to be told about Jan Smuts's friendly relationship with the Jabavus and to grasp its political meaning through Mrs Maxeke's sharp mind, to have read the noble speeches of Merriman Sauer and other white liberal legislators in the Cape[1] and then realise their shortcomings in action when she told their tale. On the whole it was her anecdotes and introductions, not her political observations, which held Basner spellbound.

She would call him to her office to meet old friends like the Rev John Dube, the first President General of Congress. He already seemed an old man, though he was not yet sixty. Short, heavy of figure, with the dignity of a Zulu chieftain even in his clerical garb, he had a magnificent voice — like an organ even when he spoke most quietly. It was a voice Basner was to hear again one day in the speaking tones of Paul Robeson.

Dube was a 'moderate', already a has-been. Yet, Mrs Maxeke pointed out, when Basner was born, his newspaper, *Ilanga lase Natal* (the Sun of Natal)[2], had been shining — into the eyes of the British Governor and all his Commissioners. It was because of his fighting spirit, she felt, that the hated poll-tax was not introduced into Natal[3] until years after it had been imposed on the rest of South Africa.

It was enchanting to hear their recollection of the days when the Congress was being planned ('In vain . . . in vain . . .' said Dube in his organ tones), to fight the Land Act. He had not expected to be chosen President General. Indeed, when the call came, he had been at home at the Ohlange Institute, an educational establishment which he headed and ran devoutly according to the principles of Booker T Washington.

A remarkable educator and orator with a fine mind, his integrity so manifest that he could coax the fiercest tribalist out of his tribalism, he was, in 1929, nearing the end of his political day. Yet such a man was he that despite all criticism — most of it reasonable — he was still the provincial president of Congress in Natal, and would remain so until not long before his death in 1946.

Many African chiefs visiting their tribesmen in the compounds of the Rand were taken by Mr Pim or someone from the mines' labour recruiting corporations to see the innovation at the magistrates' courts for helping black people in trouble. Among them was Sobhuza II, King of Swaziland, who had been a student at the famous Lovedale Mission Station in the Cape and who maintained a house in Sophiatown where he stayed during annual visits to Johannesburg to attend the Rand Show and to hold audiences with Swazi mineworkers. Seven years older than Basner, though still slim as a boy, he never journeyed without a small army of retainers, but did not as yet have the imperious air which was to become a feature of his personality.

He had been befriended by Charlotte Maxeke's late husband, and she must have spoken kindly of Basner, because Sobhuza did much to persuade him to come and open an office in Swaziland as soon as he was free to venture on his own. This Basner later did, but only for a very short while, since that beautiful little country was still too simple, placid and remote to provide a way of life for an energetic and politically-minded young lawyer. Although, as time went by, Basner found Sobhuza increasingly domineering as well as increasingly amenable to the requirements of the South African government and the British Commonwealth Office, he nonetheless remained one of his legal advisers for many years and, in the earliest of those years they were sometimes close companions.

They both loved driving at night, and would go in the King's heavy car — Sobhuza kirtled in leopard-skin to the knee; riding over the rutted red laterite Swazi roads, talking, till dawn. In the cool morning mist, Basner would get out at his office in the diminutive hill settlement of Mbabane, the British administrative centre, and Sobhuza would drive on down to the plains, to retire in the thatched village of one of his growing number of wives.

On the occasion of Basner's first meeting with Sobhuza, a message from Charlotte Maxeke brought him to her office to find the King accompanied by Dr Pixley ka Seme. The two were in Johannesburg on some official business, and had called on her as a mark of respect.

The magnificently built Dr Seme, a graduate of Columbia and Oxford, and a London-qualified barrister, was related by birth and marriage to both the Zulu and the Swazi royal houses. He had all the opportunities nature could provide to unite the chiefs and the main South African tribes into one mighty political union. The kinship he could claim with the African ruling clans gave him an unrivalled position in tribal society which, in the early part of the twentieth century, was still conscious of recent freedoms and powers. His academic qualifications were well beyond those of all but two or three of the clergy and teachers who made up the bulk of educated African society.

After returning to South Africa in 1911, it was Seme who, first with an article in Tengo Jabavu's *Imvo Sabantsundu* (Native Opinion), and then by his passionate eloquence on many platforms, had gathered together important chiefs, joined them with educated commoners and inspired both to form the Congress — against the will of the hitherto magisterial Jabavu. It was Seme who had founded and edited the Congress newspaper, *Abantu-Batho* (The People)[4], financed by the Queen Mother Regent of Swaziland while Sobhuza was still a child. The first meeting of Congress in 1912, which elected Dube President General, elected Seme as Treasurer.

Dube and Seme did not get along well. There was at least one obvious reason for this: Seme was a drunk. Liquor had begun to destroy him even before he came back from England. By 1929, he was a burnt-out wreck, run to fat, with a hoarse, asthmatic voice and speech so rambling that it was difficult to follow him at all.

Utterly unlike Dube as he was, they shared a common inheritance: public respect for their past attainments so great as to transcend their present potential. Dube, unable to renounce the values in which he had been reared, or to share the feelings of newer, more uncompromising generations, could still, year after year, be re-elected to leadership in Natal by Zulus who revered him for the deeds of his younger days. The same respect, but taken far beyond reasonable bounds, made it impossible for Seme's family to shift him from the public scene, despite their efforts to pension and keep him in a royal kraal near Eshowe or Manzini (the Zulu and Swazi tribal capitals). In 1930, Congress, making a virtually suicidal decision, was to bring him back to office, as President General, this time for seven disastrous years, during which only the provincial branches kept it alive.

When the Congress came into being to meet the national disaster of the Land Act of 1913, the African people flocked to it, bringing their cattle (their most precious possession), money and a readiness for greater sacrifices. Their leaders, themselves inexperienced in modern politics, advised by white negrophiles, and full of trust in the mighty justice of Parliament at Westminster, spent the money on large deputations to London, and misspent the energies of the aroused people on huge mass meetings which passed terrific resolutions which led to nothing.

When the deputations returned empty-handed and the negrophiles wavered and the tribal chiefs left Congress because of government threats to depose them, and the leading intellectuals split into provincial and ideological factions, the rank and file returned to a lethargic, if resentful, acceptance of the facts of white supremacy. Since the early 1920s, Congress as a national institution had lacked militancy, membership and cash. Its central organisation had been become a shell, housing a few hundred educated chiefs and clergy together with a handful of professional people, to most of whom mass action appeared impracticable or distasteful, or both. Indeed, it may be said that 1919 was the last year in which it gave real backing to popular protest — when major demonstrations against the pass laws and other injustices took place in and near the Witwatersrand.[5]

A new personality had, however, roused the population from its lethargy. Clements Kadalie[6] — a man with the physique, voice, personality and courage of a young black lion, who yet lacked the roots, the contacts and the intellectual development essential to help him understand the problems of capitalist and colonial exploitation. He was the forerunner of Nkrumah, Nyerere and Sekou Touré without their education and experience, but his senses knew the burdens of oppression and his lungs expanded to the air of freedom like those of any Chartist, Blanquist or early Communist in Europe at the beginning of industrialisation.

As he strolled past Johannesburg down the continent from his birthplace in Nyasaland (today Malawi) — a journey undertaken by hundreds of thousands of blacks from central Africa who exchange the tedium and poverty of tribal life for the tedium and poverty of the mining compounds — he grasped the concept of organising men, not on tribal or national lines, but on the basis of bargaining for their labour.

Kadalie reached Cape Town and founded his ICU among African dock-workers encouraged by a white trade-unionist, AH Batty. There it spread as if by spontaneous combustion into the cities, small towns and farmlands of South Africa, though it could not get a hold on the gold mines because their compounds had fences of iron and overseers and espionage systems. Even so, a strike of more than 40 000 black miners on the Witwatersrand in 1920 lasted a week and had to be put down by police methods of violence and terror.[7] Dock workers' strikes and some other actions succeeded in winning higher rates of pay in urban centres and the ICU's enthusiasm did much to sustain the militancy of the thousands of nameless women who in country districts as well as in the towns — between 1913 and 1923 — compelled the government to drop all further attempts to make them carry passes in the Orange Free State and the Transvaal.[8] The mood of the African population had become so dangerous in relation to the pass issue that the police chiefs advised its abandonment, which was probably why Mrs Maxeke and the Bantu Women's League were given cause to feel that their earlier approaches had been effective.

The ICU was too amorphous and too unprogrammatic to last long. By 1930, its huge membership and budget had destroyed the aims and balance of its leaders.[9] The strong personalities of Kadalie and his Natal lieutenant George Champion had clashed. There was too much oratory and not enough discipline, too many colonels and privates and not enough NCOs, too many staff cars and not enough footslogging, too many monster parades and not enough staff meetings. But the greatest lack was trade union experience and a clear objective.

By the time Basner met Kadalie in about 1929, the African people were already coming to know that his movement, too, had failed them.[10] It was the second occasion on which, having flocked to an organisation which was to redress their wrongs (and prepared again to sacrifice their pennies and their lives), they saw quarrelling leaders with unformed aims dissipating all their energies and hopes.

Charlotte Maxeke's office was once more the meeting place. Even in decline, the man from the mountains of Nyasaland was still a lion, though often, like Seme, a befuddled one. In later days, he would come just to sit and pass time away, complaining about the white do-gooders who had ruined his ICU.

Mrs Maxeke was a temperance and church woman by conviction as well as the conditioning and requirements of her upbringing, marriage and present job, yet Basner had never heard her moralising or being censorious about the army of liquor-sellers, prostitutes and thieves who passed daily through her hands. She took it as a matter of course (as he agreed too) that no African could live within the law, or live at peace within himself in the conditions created in South Africa. Where they differed when discussing the problems which brought and kept them together was in her belief in religion as salvation while he was becoming convinced that dedication, the way the Communists embraced it, was the only solution.

'Political dedication!' Mrs Maxeke would snort through her short, shapely Sotho nose. Would he deny that drink took its toll of the best sons of Africa whether they were sent to a university or became leaders through their natural abilities? 'Kadalie, the best activist you could want, is drinking away his dedication and his ICU. You have met Seme. He was once our Moses. Now we pick him up from the gutter every day. One day you will meet our best journalists. The white men can get them to write anything they want for half-a-crown.'

Basner could have answered that he was not talking about the politics of desperation but of intellectual conviction; not of wanting to dominate the world, but of wanting to change it. But the daughter of the mission, the wife of a clergyman, the fast friend of Dr Gow of Wilberforce, would not have understood him. The philosophy of Karl Marx was proscribed by her past and her job.

The political disabilities and physical hardships of the non-white population were so great that the ICU and Congress could have led it into battle against all opponents except for one enemy, which came, not in battalions, but in bottles. For that, the South African liquor laws were mainly responsible. By declaring 'European' intoxicants illicit, they created a thirst which came from bravado and defiance as well as taste. By prohibiting 'Native' brews (made from millet or maize) in the urban areas, the laws deprived the black community of a natural drink used for generations with meals and on festive occasions. The aim had probably not been deliberate and its effects were not as devastating as those of supplying the American Indians with unlimited supplies of firewater. The laws were offshoots, rather, of the Calvinist and missionary roots of certain aspects of 'Native' policy.[11]

But the result was to create a class of criminals not unfamiliar to Basner, who had lived in the United States during Prohibition, and one especially dangerous in the conditions prevailing in South Africa. The gangsters in America who became professional bootleggers were not themselves created by Prohibition and returned to their other lawless activities once it was abolished. There was no need, however, for a white man to become a gangster to obtain liquor for illegal sale in South Africa. Any white could buy it, and the whole trade — from large distilleries to suburban shops — was naturally interested in selling as much as possible.

All a white person had to do was go to a number of retailers, using different names, so that his big purchases would not become noticeable to the police, and find a black 'runner'. Most of the slum landlords and plenty of whites fallen on evil days became sellers. The danger and violence began at the black end, because from there everything — purchase, possession, drinking — became unlawful. A black runner would be murdered because he took money and failed to deliver, a drinking-place would become a shebeen, with prostitution as a sideline, and robbery of the drunken customer an easy source of income for the lovers or associates of the shebeen-queen. The police would use informers, raid constantly, and be met with violence. The civil war was with batons, not with revolvers and machine-guns as in Chicago, but it was racial and widespread wherever black people lived in towns.

These who suffered most were respectable African women who were expected to brew 'kaffir beer' for their husbands and families. A process which was carried out with pleasure and dignity in the tribal home had to be finished quickly, in secret, with all sorts of unpleasant additions, such as rotting pineapples, to speed fermentation. Tins of beer would be buried in holes outdoors, and the police would find them easily. If no one admitted ownership, all the women in the house and yard were arrested and imprisoned, leaving the stench of poured-out liquor to pervade the street.

Communism was a subject Mrs Maxeke would rarely discuss, and Basner could guess that it was not only the difficulty of atheism, but strict warnings from the authorities which kept her back. He was sure of it because the most reliable lawyer for African cases, Sidney Percival Bunting, a Communist, was not on her panel. When his name was mentioned because Lowenberg and Wasserzug were too busy and looking for someone else to take a case, she would turn it down. The omission was so obvious and absolute that Basner did not have to be told what it meant.

5

TWO MORE PEOPLE

Sidney Bunting was not short of African clients in spite of the proscription imposed by the Chief Magistrate and Charlotte Maxeke's sponsors. As a Communist lawyer, he was kept busy defending his party's members against numerous charges, and since he was the only reliable lawyer before the 'Prisoner's Friend' office opened, many Africans who were not subject to clerical or official pressure found their way to his office.

It was inevitable that he and Basner should soon make contact, though about professional and not political matters; and Basner did not at first mention (and Bunting did not remember) that they had been, in a manner of speaking, acquaintances fifteen years before, in Doornfontein.

In the Beit Street of Basner's childhood, opposite his parents' dairy, three little houses stood together as if part of an interrupted ribbon-development project, all alike, with green tin roofs, wooden verandahs and garden-fronts each with the same kind of flowers and patches of grass invaded by cosmos, a beautiful and ineradicable weed. In one of them lived Mr Radin, an accountant and excellent customer for cream and butter until he absconded to Brazil with a great deal of money belonging to wholesale merchants in Johannesburg's Market Street. In the middle one lived a woman doctor — Dr Bessie Sieff — small, thin, quiet and shy as a mouse, with large brown eyes, and the terror of all the children in the district with her castor oil, epsom salts and cascara.

In the third house lived Bunting and his wife Rebecca, easily the most interesting people in the neighbourhood; mysterious and sinister characters to the young, and a source of endless gossip for their elders. For one thing, he was said to be the son of an English Lord and she was a Jewish woman, the only mixed marriage known to Doornfontein apart from that of Langley Levy, the editor of the *Sunday Times*, and for another, they were dangerous revolutionaries who had been in prison, and their house was constantly watched by the police.

Bunting never came to the dairy, and his wife only came on Sunday mornings for the fresh bread which arrived from the Jewish bakery or for items she might have forgotten in her shopping in town. She never stopped for a chat like all the other customers. Hence discussion about them was more frequent in the shop than about any other subject except the elections for the committee of the Doornfontein Synagogue.

His physical appearance was as unusual as his reputation. Then a middle-aged man, he was heavily built, with rounded shoulders and a very large head and when he walked across the street, he kept his eyes on the ground. Waiting for a tram, he was an awesome character, but it was an exciting game trying to catch a glimpse of his face. Children would bump or push one another into him to make him look up.

The Buntings moved away from the district whilst Basner was at Jeppe High School, and he forgot about them until he returned from America when the papers were full of their name, because Sidney Bunting was *the* leading Communist and the cases in which he appeared for people on political charges were always reported.

Most of the information Basner received about him was from Fred Lowenberg, who knew him well. They had both come to South Africa as soldiers and had studied law and been admitted as attorneys at about the same time. Basner's employer, who was not in the habit of speaking with particular tolerance of people or of espousing unpopular causes, surprised him by an unusual lack of distaste for Bunting and his political career.

He was not the son of a Lord, and neither he nor Rebecca had guilty secrets or criminal convictions. He was as good a viola player as he was a lawyer ('better' — the acid-tongued Lowenberg could not help adding), and music had brought the pair of them together. His father was only a knight, Sir Percy Bunting, who had received the royal tap for his support of good causes as founder and editor of the English *Contemporary Review*[1]. The family were Wesleyan Liberals who had sent Sidney to South Africa to help Cecil Rhodes and his mining philanthropists, the Chamberlains and their fellow idealists, Lord Milner and his team of dedicated administrators, to end the cruel regime of the black-hating Boers. (Lowenberg could be as scathingly ironical about politics as about legal decisions not in his favour).

Basner was bold enough to ask Lowenberg why and how Bunting had become a Communist. 'Sidney, like a lot of us,' was the answer, 'decided to stay on after the war, but his conscience couldn't adjust itself to what was happening either to the Boers or the natives. He gave up music to study law, not to earn a better living but because he confused law with justice, just like his dad at home. He's been somewhat confused ever since, and has had some hard knocks. He's fulfilling his Karma, I suppose.'

'Why didn't he join the Labourites, or start a Liberal party here?'

'What would you do, with his background?' asked the astute Mr Lowenberg, who would no more dream of joining a political movement than of dipping into the freezing waters of the Dvina River through a hole in the ice, as Basner's uncle the Rabbi used to do. 'The only thing for a liberal who thinks Russian peasants and native tribesmen are ready for socialism is communism.'

For all his critical resumé of Bunting's biography and political directions, Lowenburg could not hide a sneaking envy for the passionate courage and faith in humanity with which Sidney Percival Bunting made so many mistakes.

There was another and closer source of information about Bunting. Among the boys at Jeppe High School in Basner's time was Edward Roux, two years older than he and therefore not more than an acquaintance. After matriculating, Roux had studied botany and zoology and then taken a postgraduate science degree at Cambridge, whence he had recently returned. They had not met again until now, in the late months of 1929, when Roux had occasion to come to the office in connection with some African clients. He had relinquished his career to be a full-time member of the Communist Party, and joined Bunting in attempting the formation of a mass 'front' organisation called the League of African Rights.[2]

Though a Huguenot Afrikaner by paternal descent, Roux was English speaking. His mother had come from England to South Africa as a military nurse at the time of the Anglo-Boer War and his father (a chemist in a small way of business) had fought for the British, to the dismay of his family in the Cape, and was a radical and an atheist who became a pacifist in 1914.

Roux started bringing Communist comrades to Lowenberg and Wasserzug's office when Bunting was busy elsewhere, because Basner's name was beginning to be mentioned favourably among members of the 'Native Advisory Boards' that had been officially constituted in the municipal black locations.[3] This came about more by chance than through Basner's own doing. Herman Wasserzug was very popular with the Syrian community, some of whom were slum landlords whose yards were being cleared of tenants by inspectors proceeding under the Urban Areas Act of 1923. It had become an offence to rent, and an offence to reside in, certain areas if the tenant was an African. The prosecutions which followed neglected eviction orders were, of course, always against the tenant, who was black, and not against the landlord, who was white but it was naturally upsetting to the latter when he found himself threatened with loss of income.

With Wasserzug knowing little law and Lowenberg being busy with more important matters, these Urban Areas prosecutions were left to Basner. Not yet qualified, he could not appear in court, but could prepare the legal defence and in the first case they had, he noticed a loophole, based on a simple principle recognised in American justice. If the municipality could not offer a black tenant and his family alternative accommodation in a location, it had no right to eject him from his residence. In other words, *lex non cogit ad impossibilia* — the law does not expect the impossible.

One would think such a simple axiom would be too obvious for debate, but it burst upon the legal world of the Transvaal as an extremely novel postulate of justice.[4] The startling discovery that the law may not demand the impossible was the foundation of Basner's professional reputation. A young lawyer, it was felt, who would think of such a thing could think of anything to get an African out of trouble.

Although Wasserzug was the victor in the courts when the tenants were acquitted, all the black people sitting around their fire-tins that night discussing the great event knew that it was the clerk in the office who had thought of that remarkable line of defence. The elected members of the location advisory boards, one or two of whom were Communists[5], and all of them adherents of the African National Congress, knew it particularly well, because it had been necessary for Basner to explain the nature of their evidence to them with care.

They had to swear and produce proof with official documents that the locations were chock-a-block, with no houses or rooms remotely available. If the Minister of Native Affairs, proclaiming any part of Johannesburg as prohibited to native occupation, could not satisfy himself that the municipality had space to spare, then his proclamation was as invalid as snow in summer. The simile (somewhat faulty but picturesque), pleased Wasserzug and impressed the magistrate.

At the time he started to come to Basner's office, Roux, who was twenty-seven years old, did not seem much older than he had at Jeppe, when he was about eighteen. He was fairly tall, slender, with a fresh, light complexion and what Basner could only describe as a winning smile. He was as mild as the milk which was his only drink during the time they knew each other, and he never seemed to get angry. He was to prove, however, always ready for a set-to with the Nazi Greyshirts who tried to break up Communist meetings on the Town Hall steps of a Sunday in the late 1930s.[6] He was a food-faddist, mostly vegetarian, and his life was as devoted and poverty-stricken as that of an early Franciscan. But what he missed in other pleasures he seemed to find in amorous adventures. Communist Party members quipped that if Eddie could manage that well on milk, heaven help the girl comrades if ever he took to beer.

There was a simple — even simplistic — side to Edward Roux which went together with an extraordinarily energetic and meticulous mind in pursuit of knowledge which did not require theoretical confirmation. This made him outstanding, if not originative as a botanist. He was also the author of *Time Longer than Rope*, which has remained since its publication in 1948 an extraordinarily reliable general account of African experience and struggles in South Africa (as well as a mainspring for contemporary research). It does not expunge or try to belittle the role of non-Communists as the Communist writers do nor does it misinterpret or misreport the role of the Communist Party as the non-Communists do. It has its own bias but never fiddles with the truth or indulges in malice, and is crammed with solid facts.

Basner's long association with him was punctuated with many political disagreements which, though often personally painful, could never be truly profound, because Roux's integrity was far more to be valued than the political shrewdness of his party opponents; and because he could not be taken seriously as a Marxist, only as an honest and fearless radical.

Their first disagreement was about Bunting, to whom Basner made a personal visit at Roux's urging.

Though he was becoming very interested in Communism, Basner was as yet cautious because his articles were coming to an end and he hoped for a partnership in the firm of Lowenberg and Wasserzug. Also, in spite of his long friendship with Charlotte Maxeke, it would have been impossible for her to give him the free run and help of her office had the slightest taint of 'redness' impinged on their relationship.

He was being respectable and hypocritical only to a limited extent. He still had intellectual reservations about Marxist politics, though not about Marxism as a political philosophy. His chief interests were still music and literature, and he found labels like 'bolshevik' and 'proletarian' repellent. The Stalin regime was unsavoury and the Trotsky expulsion dismaying. The copies of *Moscow News* which he bought occasionally at Trades Hall meetings were dull and depressing. Kadalie's section of the ICU was at war with the Party as well as with a breakaway group led by William Ballinger[7] and most of the leaders of the African National Congress whom he encountered in Mrs Maxeke's office complained of being slandered and harassed by the Communists[8].

It was this last aspect which led him to seek more than his usual superficial contact with Bunting, but Bunting simply said there was nothing to be done about local difficulties. The Comintern wanted a small elite Bolshevik party controlling all indigenous political movements.[9]

Basner found Bunting no more heroic or attractive than the figure he remembered from Doornfontein. He was older and heavier, with a rasping voice and a big head. He was still given to looking away from rather than at people. Was this the leader every missionary saw as the devil incarnate and every Boer on his farm as a white Dingaan, plotting new massacres and other outrages against the Afrikaner nation?

It was true that Bunting was very tired. He had recently been through a turbulent election campaign in Tembuland in the Cape, constantly tormented by hoodlums, police, mindless prosecutions and (unknown to Basner) the disloyalty of those he thought his comrades.[10] But there was a leaden quality about him which seemed intrinsic to his nature and not just attributable to temporary exhaustion.

When they met professionally, they might perhaps chat a little, but usually about topics such as the slackness of the Law Society in dealing with touts, or the misdeeds of interpreters, and would sometimes reminisce about Doornfontein. But Basner could never go much further afield with Bunting. He seemed to have no intellectual curiosity or enthusiasm, and once remarked that he had not read a book in years. When asked if he meant that literally, his reply was, 'Where would I get the time?'

This answer seemed shocking to Basner, who hotly told Roux so and, perhaps pompously, added that when politics meant you had no time to read, those politics could not benefit human beings. This was a view he continued to hold for over forty years of political life, and one from which he was not shaken when he learnt of that split-minded genius, Smuts, leading a commando raid into the Cape during the Anglo-Boer War with Kant's *Critique of Pure Reason* in his saddle-bags. It was more than confirmed for him in the abilities of Kwame Nkrumah who never stopped reading whilst living under far greater pressures than Bunting.

Roux was upset and as near to anger as his nature allowed. Sidney was his hero, which was not remarkable. What was remarkable was Basner's reaction to the pains to which Bunting subjected himself; the poverty that stemmed from his often sentimental reluctance to charge proper fees; the number of times he had been beaten up at elections and public meetings. The more Eddie told him, the more his blood ran cold, not so much with pity as revulsion. This was the sort of career which he himself contemplated, but not in Bunting's way, which called up the image of a bull rushing into the ring to be wounded again and again by the darts and lances of the picadors.

Basner refused to be a bull. Yet he had so many heroes of his own whose lives had been wrecked: Tom Paine, Parnell, Trotsky and, in South Africa, the eighteenth century missionaries Johan van der Kemp and John Philip, and even those misguided Labour leaders in the Rand

Revolt whom Smuts had deported or hanged. If they were romantics, Bunting's life was romantic enough. Was he envious? He did not envy Bunting's passion as did the cold Fred Lowenberg. He felt he had enough passion himself, and decided it was Bunting's vulnerability and lack of understanding of how society functioned that repelled him. To be at the head of the Communist Party and preach to the Africans to make a revolution but establish no power-bases — not even defence committees when appearing in hostile territory — was an unpardonable contradiction.

There was no charm in Bunting, though he had a very kindly manner. In short, Basner did not like him much, and did not think Bunting took to him, either.

Despite his desire for political commitment, Basner's role in 1930 was still that of an onlooker. His primary concern was to become a really good lawyer.

6

A START IN LAW

Although Basner's days and weekends had been full enough, his evenings at home in his parents' latest house in the dreary suburb of Mayfair had been lonely, and he had had plenty of time to ponder on the conditions he saw in South Africa. He began to read as much history as could then be found because he was interested, and the legislative enactments because he had qualifying examinations to face.

He came to know something about 'Onze Jan' Hofmeyr, the leader of the Afrikaner Bond party in the Cape and his struggle with Cecil Rhodes to save the Kruger Republic, and about 'Cape Liberals' such as Merriman and Sauer, and their efforts to save the franchise for the educated African and Coloured people there.

He learnt the surprising provenance of the laws and policies that had driven the blacks into helotry — they came from Lord Milner's administration together with its new allies, the Boer generals Botha and Smuts.[1] The philosophies of the two sides were epitomised by Rhodes's ambiguous cry 'Civilised rights for every civilised man' and the fight of the Boers to maintain a constitution which demanded 'No equality between white and black in Church or State'.

He found everything — the history as well as the legislation — written literally in black and white, in racial terms which referred to 'Europeans' and 'Natives'. But the more he read, the more it seemed that this history was as much about property and labour as colour and race.

The numerous 'Kaffir Wars' were not over cattle raids for the juiciest steaks, but about land on which to graze cattle. The great Boer treks away from the Cape into the hinterland were not about the right to own slaves, as was usually asserted. The Boers did not want to make slaves of the blacks in their new republics, but drove them off the land to lay out vast farms, and then called them back to be farm labourers. The Anglo-Boer War was not a fight to do away with 'no equality', but to secure imperial ownership of the goldfields of the Witwatersrand (the Treaty of Vereeniging which ended the war made that very clear).

Reading law made things clearer still. The Mines and Works Act of 1911 could seem an innocent measure for safety on the mine workings but for a provision which was suddenly included that the Minister might make regulations as to which 'class of persons' could work with machinery. In this way, the colour bar was effectively born.[2] The Masters and Servants Act regulated the relationship between all masters and all servants, but, in practice, only the black servant could be sent to prison for breaking the contract, and be returned to his or her master if he or she absconded. As regards public order, the Governor-General was transmogrified through the Natives Administration Act of 1927 into a supreme chief in the Transvaal, Free State and Natal with the power to issue proclamations affecting all Africans which had the force of law.

Basner decided that once he was qualified he would be able to find plenty of loopholes in such legislation, just as he had found them in the Urban Areas Act. But loopholes can be closed. Legislation can be made ever tighter. Legal triumphs would inevitably become nothing but cruel preliminaries to further legal battles. Real success could only be achieved through political action, and that, Basner felt, should be undertaken by the Communist Party, since the African National Congress and the ICU both seemed in an equal state of disintegration.[3]

The fate of Trotsky, who had been expelled from the Soviet Union, and his account of what was happening in Russia made Basner doubtful about drawing closer to a local movement controlled from there, especially after its reorganisation in the course of 1931.

He immediately took to some of the African Communists he had recently met, but they seemed none too happy with their party's arrogant attitude, especially towards Kadalie's ICU.[4] On the whole, he decided, he felt far more at home with the characters he encountered through Charlotte Maxeke.

It was not difficult for Basner to pass his examinations and become an attorney, and he had already begun to negotiate with his principals about remaining with them. The difficulty was that he wanted to be a junior partner and they preferred him to be an employee, which he considered unreasonable since it was obvious that most of their African clients and some of the Indian ones would follow him if he left the firm. In this he ignored a factor which influenced white traders, businessmen and professional people like — fear of a prosperity which depended in large part upon black goodwill.

Mrs Maxeke was all for his establishing an office of his own. She had been having arguments with Wasserzug because he would not take his fair share of *pro deo* work — that is, unpaid and done for God and not His bounty — and she wanted her young nephew, Samuel Radebe (whom, in tribal fashion, she regarded as a son), to leave the firm.

Independence presented daunting hazards, of which lack of money was the greatest. For Basner to open his own door he would naturally require furniture, rent and stationery. Besides other incidentals he would need a car, because the work promised by members of advisory boards in other towns on the Witwatersrand and chiefs in remoter districts would require one. Even if he earned enough in the first month to pay the salaries of Samuel Radebe and a typist, he would need about five hundred pounds. His parents were able to help him with two hundred, but other relatives and friends could not be approached for the rest, since they knew he had the option of a well-paid job should he want it.

As with many dilemmas, the horns proved more fearsome in appearance than in substance. A frowsy, elderly woman, in a skirt too short for her spindly legs, walked into the office accompanied by a very attractive young one, whose clothes were obviously made in Europe. The old woman wanted to see Basner and nobody else — he had been recommended to her by a pianist friend. Her married name was an Afrikaans one, as common as Smith or Jones. Her accent was Irish-South African. The young woman was her daughter (here to be called Nadine), who had just arrived from Vienna where she had been studying music.

Nadine's mother's troubles were the same as those of Mr Zock, the Syrian landlord whose tenants Basner had rescued from the Urban Areas Act. She was the owner of a particularly large and notorious slum yard[5] which lay not a quarter of a mile from Marshall Square, the Johannesburg police headquarters, and was renowned for its shebeens and prostitutes. It was a favourite resort for black miners on a spree or deserting from their compounds, and the numerous intertribal affrays and murders which occurred there were often mentioned in court reports in the newspapers. The police constantly raided it, but because they could not see what was going on from the outside, all the liquor would be gone and the violence over by the time they managed to gain entry.

The yard had a high corrugated iron barrier all round, topped with barbed wire, and the gates to it were reinforced from within by iron bars. The surface of the yard and all the rooms in it was made of solid cement. For this reason it was nicknamed the 'Cement Fort' a reference too, to the

Johannesburg prison called The Fort (having originally been built as one in Republican days).

Basner had been to the yard with Mr Wasserzug *in loco* during preparatory examinations and he heard magistrates comment and police explain that they could do nothing about the place without a court order to destroy it with dynamite. The police also added that it was full of unmarried women with small children for whom there was no accommodation in the municipal locations. Unmarried men could be sent to hostels — crude barracks, in fact — but not women and children or married men with families.

Now the police, under pressure from the Chief Magistrate and the municipal councillors, had become desperate and had started issuing eviction notices to some of the tenants. 'It's such a shame,' said Nadine's mother. 'What's going to happen to all those poor little children?' Neither her daughter nor Basner smiled or moved a muscle. He knew that the rentals from those rooms must be enormous, and had heard how the yard's caretaker, Jacob, collected the rent. Jacob was a grotesquely muscular Xhosa and had assistants with huge knobkerries. If a woman would not or could not pay the rent, Jacob never resorted to solicitors. He borrowed a knobkerrie from one of his men and wrecked everything in the room. He would then say he would come back the next day and use the knobkerrie on the tenant but he never had to, the money would be waiting.

Nadine's mother's proposition was simple. She wanted Basner to take charge of the Cement Fort. She had been advised to leave South Africa for a while in case the police decided to prosecute her. Now that Nadine was back, she and Basner could handle all legal and financial matters together and send a regular remittance to mother in Dublin.

Basner was startled, indeed shaken, by the proposal. It had unsavoury features which rendered him squeamish. Would he not be privy to rack-renting and also to making a secret deal with someone who had to be considered a client of his firm, even though he had been consulted privately? Nadine, however, was undeniably appealing as a partner.

He put it to her mother that he could not be a party to collecting rent the way Jacob did.

'I don't know how he does it,' she lied, 'and you can get it any way you like so long as I'm not the loser.'

He started to explain his ethical difficulties about being an employee of Lowenberg and Wasserzug and mentioned his hope of starting a practice of his own.

'All the better,' she interrupted. 'I'll walk out right now and won't bother you until you've opened your office.'

It was then necessary to point out that his pecuniary plight made this unlikely.

'I'll finance you. How much do you want? . . . What's three hundred pounds? You can pay me back when you're rich and famous,' said the woman, who had answers for everything.

Basner had a terrible time with the Cement Fort in the beginning. Were it not that his relationship with Nadine had become romantic and intimate almost immediately, he would have given up within a few weeks.

When he took over, he gave Jacob a month's notice, which was a mistake. He should have paid double his wage and ordered him off the premises at once. In that month Jacob discovered his affair with Nadine and employed a letter-writer to inform her mother that the pair of them were getting rid of him in order to defraud her. The result was frantic cables from Dublin, threatening to cancel their powers of attorney — and worse, a return to Johannesburg — should her henchman be forced to go.

Jacob was cunning and ruthless but here he met his match. Basner was already an instinctive criminal lawyer, despite his lack of experience. He called in a competent bookkeeper who soon found out that Jacob had been taking a rake-off from the rents for years. When Nadine threatened to bring in the police, Jacob disappeared and, on her mother's receiving proof of his peculations, peace was restored.

It became possible to remove the barbed wire and iron bars from the Cement Fort, and it was agreed that the police might drill holes in the metal fence so that they could keep an eye on the place. Gradually the liquor-sellers and prostitutes moved to safer quarters, and the yard could be filled with more respectable tenants, who were never hard to find in the overcrowded suburbs.

There was no question of reducing the rents, however. Africans argued no more about rent than strayed travellers about the cost of Sahara water.

Nadine's mother died about a year later, only a short while after Basner had repaid her three hundred pounds and Nadine's grief was able to tolerate his joke that she had seemed to be waiting for that event before her final departure. By then property near the centre of the city had become so valuable that the yard could be sold for a very good price.

Basner and Nadine were still very fond of each other, but Basner was far from ready for marriage and she missed Vienna and did not like South Africa much, so decided to go back to Europe. The only person who might have missed the Cement Fort was a woman in her grave in Dublin.

Basner opened a legal office in Asher's Buildings with a small sherry party at which he broke the law by supplying liquor to non-whites. The building was right opposite the Magistrates Courts so the touts had only a short distance in which to waylay clients coming from Mrs Maxeke.

Samuel Radebe had accompanied Basner. Not well-educated, but literate enough for his job, he was neither ambitious nor very clever. He could never be persuaded to try to matriculate by correspondence in order to become articled, and would have nothing to do with politics (Basner never knew whether Samuel approved or disapproved of his own, in all the thirty years they were together). But when Basner left his office for weeks and sometimes months at a time, it was this barely-lettered clerk upon whom he depended to run it properly, to report intelligently and to handle thousands of pounds of fees and trust money honestly. On several occasions when he broke this rule and left his affairs to better-qualified clerks and partners he ran into trouble, and, once or twice, into near disaster.

Basner, at twenty-five, had started his career with the world depression that began in 1929 well on its way, but was to weather the next few years comfortably, and much better than most young lawyers in easier times. He grew expert at — and eventually bored with — defending 'pirate' taxi drivers and slum landlords, burglars and dealers in stolen goods and liquor sellers and *dagga* (marijuana) smugglers from the neighbouring Protectorates of Basutoland and Swaziland. These were clients who had the money to pay good fees, and were also constantly in trouble. Their offences were racial in origin and the justice meted out to them was racial in quality, but they ran their businesses on more logical and less chancy lines than bankers and wholesale merchants are inclined to do.

Offenders of their kind in South Africa (and in most other countries) supply needs which never slacken and for which cash is always obtainable. They lie and cheat without hypocrisy, so no one really hates them. If they are caught, they go to prison, but that does not mean social ruin or economic extinction. When the gates of the prison open, they are greeted by their families and friends with parties and jubilation — and then they start again, with profitable experience.

Basner's success as a criminal lawyer was swift, and due as much to South African conditions as to personal merit. The laws were full of loopholes, the prosecutors were lazy and not too bright, the police overconfident and given to careless perjury because they were not used to anyone challenging their testimony. As for him, he was on the side of his clients, which was a great help, particularly because he was not sentimental enough to believe them, pity them, or abet them. (A defendant who regards his lawyer as his accomplice acquires a false sense of security which can end in ruin.) He was sympathetic, but aggressive and impatient, logical but imaginative, with some histrionic ability: just the right combination for criminal law and the jury system which existed in South African courts until 1969, but ill-suited to a commercial lawyer, who must be shrewd and have a very cool nature.

His presence in court became embarrassing to the police to the extent that they would often throw in their hand if he appeared for the defence. Their problem was always 'possession'. Did they see the accused handle the liquor, *dagga* or stolen articles found in a place where several others might have put it? Was the housewife bending over or running away from the hole in which the tin of brew was buried? Did the packet of *dagga* found in the room of the cleaners of the block of flats belong to

John or Jim or Isaac? (All flat caretakers smoked the stuff in their leisure hours, as they had in their tribal homes for years without apparent ill-effects.) Was the stolen coat hanging on the wall brought in by the head of the house, one of the lodgers, or any of the grown-up sons?

The police could never establish a connection unless they were lucky, or good at perjury. They were seldom lucky, because the Africans were as wary and quick as any springbok in the Kalahari, so they just lied and lied, but not competently, because they were mostly raw recruits working under pressure with no time for careful preparation. The magistrates would do their best to believe them as a matter of racial solidarity and state security. But the accused, as long as they got a fine and not imprisonment, and had their day in court with their lawyer challenging and denouncing the police in a loud and angry voice, were highly satisfied.

More serious crimes were unprofitable for solicitors. These went to the Supreme Court, and Africans could rarely raise the large sums required by the barristers, whose society refused to fix smaller minimum fees for them. If a black could just manage to pay counsel there was nothing left for the solicitor. The result of this stupid ruling, based entirely on a blinkered class attitude on the part of the higher tier of the legal profession, meant that dozens of young advocates remained idle and inexperienced whilst Africans and other poor people were deprived of proper defence in serious cases (except for those carrying the death penalty, like murder and rape, where the State had to provide legal aid.)

In spite of the petty nature of his practice — and thanks to Charlotte Maxeke and the Advisory Board members — many important chiefs, school headmasters and ministers of the independent black churches gradually started coming to his office. They had considerable problems with property and finance, and most of their activities were hampered by racist regulations.

The richest and most substantial clients were the *ngakas* ('witchdoctors'). In a large city like Johannesburg these were really unlicensed herbalists, and were prosecuted at the behest of the white pharmacists and the Health Department, who considered most of their medicines to be injurious. A few of them accumulated really fantastic fortunes by selling powdered rhinoceros horn to make men potent, and noxious mixtures to women to interfere with pregnancy (and they were patronised by people of every race). Occasionally a customer would die, and the *ngaka* would have to part with real money for a senior advocate — who sniffed at his client, but not at the cheque he received from the solicitor.

Once in a while, something would come along which was of no great interest as a legal issue, but so dramatically unfair that correcting it seemed really worthwhile.

A not untypical case, ludicrous, but sensational and widely reported, whereby Basner became more generally known, was the Hospital police raid. Arriving at the office late one Saturday morning, he found an uproar. Charlotte Maxeke was there in person, so excited as to be almost incoherent. Nearly a hundred Zulu cleaners, porters and labourers — the whole African staff of the Johannesburg General Hospital in fact — had been arrested, charged and convicted of theft in 'F' Court. The two big dormitories in which they slept had, on a tip-off, been raided by the police before dawn. In the storage box under each occupant's bed they had found bundles of dirty hospital sheets, pillowcases and blankets. No questions were asked and the men were all rushed to court. It took hours to charge them and for the indictments to be framed and recorded. By the time they were lined up like a battalion before the magistrate it was well past ten o'clock.

They claimed that they had not pleaded guilty, as the interpreter said they had, and were refusing to pay the five pound fines imposed, even in instalments. They also refused to listen to the hospital superintendent, who had come to beg them to pay, and so be able to return to work. They insisted on changing their pleas to 'not guilty' and being defended.

Basner went to investigate and the first man he interviewed told a story he knew all too well. When the accused had come into the dock, the interpreter had asked if the pillowcases and sheets found in his locker were put there by him. 'Yes.' Did he know they were the property of the hospital? 'Yes.' Did anyone give him permission to take them? 'No.' 'The accused pleads guilty, your worship,' the satisfied interpreter had said. The magistrate then managed to write, 'Guilty. Five pounds or thirty days' nearly a hundred times in little more than an hour.

With Mrs Maxeke standing by, Basner asked — through the same interpreter, and in the presence of the hospital superintendent — 'Why did you take those things?' 'They were in the incinerator.' 'What do you mean?' 'They're from the isolation wards, *baas*. They can't go to the laundry, so they're sent to be burnt, but we take them out and wash them ourselves and send them home to Natal.' The superintendent was shamefacedly obliged to admit that because this practice was known to go on, he had asked the police to warn the men to stop it, but that instead, they had arrested everyone that night, and when he found this out it was too late to stop the prosecution.

In the Magistrate's office, Basner found a very worried man with a set of golf clubs by his side. By noon on Saturdays, the magistrates and court staff expected to be free, and he had an appointment at the Country Club. It would be necessary, he said crossly, to wait until Monday for a new trial if the plea was to be changed.

'Why should the accused spend today and Sunday in jail? What's going to happen to the General Hospital without native workers at the weekend?' Both parties were getting angry and voices were being raised, when in came the superintendent, together with the Chief Magistrate and the Senior Public Prosecutor. The Magistrate thereupon forgot about his appointment and endorsed every charge sheet to the effect that each of the prisoners was released on his own recognisances. It was long past two when he grabbed his golf clubs.

The labourers, who had docilely been paying fines for years for drinking and pass offences, had vindicated their thirst for justice by digging in their heels over a too manifestly unfair sentence. When the case came up, Basner was given an excellent opportunity to vent his own feelings as well as those of his clients, who were all acquitted. They formed an *impi* and danced all the way up the hill from the centre of the city to the hospital, chanting about the 'Lion of the Courts' who had roared for them that morning. In time, his fame reached Tugela Ferry in Zululand and all the huts above it (where most amenities were lacking, but not bed linen).

The press, having got hold of the story thanks to Mrs Maxeke, considered the case front-page material which illustrated both the hospital's shocking laxness and the human side of justice. There was considerable mention of Basner's erudite description of an infected sheet as a *res hullius* — a non-thing — which could not be stolen by anyone, let alone simple, honest Zulus.

7
LOOKING BEYOND THE LAW
(1931-1933)

If anyone doubted that Basner's role as a solicitor was only a disguise for a political animal, a few days in his office in Asher's Buildings would have been convincing.

Much of his legal work was only indirectly political — for instance, the defence of a beer-brewer or the prevention of the expulsion of a widow from a location because she had been married by *bohali* (payment of dowry cattle) and not in church or by a Native Commissioner. But there were many consultations and conferences which only had to do with legal business in a secondary sense.

In September, 1931, Sidney Bunting, together with a number of white trade unionists, was expelled from the Communist Party (for 'right wing deviationism'), and Basner became the only lawyer in Johannesburg to whom the Communists could turn for help. They had money and they did not want legal representation unless it was coupled with a Marxist denunciation of capitalist laws. It was the latter condition which appealed to him.

An organisation called *Ikaka laba Sebenzi* (Workers' Defence) had been set up at the beginning of that year (as a branch of International Red Aid) and was intended to replace — and be much more revolutionary than — Bunting's very broad-based League of African Rights, which had been summarily dissolved on Comintern orders the year before. It aimed in general at forming a disciplined as well as military organisation to defy racial oppression, and in particular, to give legal assistance to Communists and their allies charged with political offences. The first of its purposes was never achieved but the second was, in a manner, fulfilled for some years, although *Ikaka* came to consist almost entirely of one lawyer — Basner — and one source of funds — his petty cash box (much to the disgust of his clerk, Samuel Radebe).

Though he was disturbed at the Communists' drive towards isolation by cutting themselves off from the white trade union movement, and repelled by their Moscow-style attacks describing Bunting as a 'right-wing imperialist bloodsucker', he could not resist the temptation to have people to defend as a political spokesman rather than as a jurist. It was one thing trying to save a pathetic widow whose sole concern was a roof over the heads of her children and quite another to appear for a party activist who did not mind going to prison as long as Karl Marx had his day in court. In the widow's case, Basner used his histrionic and legal talents to soothe the magistrate with a plea *ad misericordiam* and to equity and in the other he could let rip with moral indignation and savage irony about a system of law designed to entrench privilege and exploitation.

In one sense black South Africans did not live under the rule of law as they had no say in the law-making process, very little hope of safeguarding those rights they possessed and very few activities which required the advice of attorneys or barristers in civil practice. In another sense, they lived completely circumscribed by draconian ordinances — rules over where they should live, when they should go to bed, what they should drink, what work they should do and where they should lodge their families.

Aftricans needed lawyers, not as citizens, but as outlaws. When Basner first met Charlotte Maxeke in 1927, Sidney Bunting and he — an articled clerk with nothing but American experience — were among the few legal men prepared to offer the services required. By 1936, when he had become too involved in politics to spend much time in the courts, there were already numbers of people, including some Africans trained in the Cape, ready to act willingly and conscientiously for black clients. Some spread of liberal thought played its part, but the main impetus was a growth in the economic importance and educational attainment of the African population which neither the Depression of the 1930s nor the colour-bar could halt.

With the Urban Areas Act of 1923 and its compulsion upon blacks to leave the towns proper and live in the municipal housing developments called locations, had to come a certain amount of trade and some token of popular representation. The shops and location advisory boards (mock town councils, mainly nominated by the authorities, partly elected by the inhabitants), attracted enterprising and educated Africans, many of them disillusioned or retired activists once prominent in the Congress or ICU.

Inevitably the white location superintendents tried to fill the shops and advisory boards with their own protégés and inevitably legal struggles occurred over the regulations and by-laws framed by the Native Affairs Department and white municipal councillors under the enabling powers of the Act.

At first, most of these court battles started with the help of Basner's office, but gradually, as their numbers increased, several other firms also became involved and it became apparent that not only did it pay them, but that some board members were finding it a profitable exercise to collect considerable sums from location residents to fight 'test cases'.

Basner became all the more convinced that political soldiering rather than legal sparring was the means of redress for most of the grievances which pressed so hard on his clients. The channels through which so many of the hopes and energies of the African protest movements had now begun to flow were leading nowhere except to frustration and damaging despair. For every instance of racial discrimination and injustice, the remedy had become a 'test case', and a test case, even when victorious, was as much use as a mustard plaster to a raging bout of sciatica. As he had earlier become aware, if a regulation, ordinance or by-law was upset as unreasonable or *ultra vires*, all the lawmakers had to do was change the wording or add a phrase or two, and there it was — the same construction with neatly mended masonry, and another loophole stopped up.

It was a painful irony to remember how, a few years before, Charlotte Maxeke and he had started out to defeat the touts and the drunken, dishonest crew of broken-down lawyers who employed them to rob Africans and deny them real legal aid. Now, there was no lack of a new breed of young, intelligent, and in some instances, idealistic, solicitors, aided by young barristers, who were able, conscientious and ambitious. Yet things were scarcely better.

The African's hunger for justice, numerous disabilities and the cash reserves of a growing urban population all provided more than ample work and rich rewards for a non-white practice. With it came what can only be described as a new kind of tout, the semi-educated, semi-political, semi-honest leaders in the advisory boards, tenant associations, lodgers' committees, small independent church congregations and associations of workers not allowed by law to form or join proper trade unions.

The money side was handled by collectors who worked on commission; legal work was handled by responsible attorneys who charged legitimate fees and ultra-respectable advocates who had no personal contact with their clients and would not accept emoluments except through an attorney. In return, however, the African did not even get his 'day in court' (which Basner could at least give the liquor-seller, the thief and the Marxist).

The Magistrate's Court hearing would be attended by the 'tout', the Supreme Court hearing by the attorney. All the client would hear was that the appeal had been dismissed or won, but that the Minister of Justice was already framing and promulgating new regulations.

Johannesburg is the metropolis of a sprawl of towns lying west and east of her, each an outcrop of the great gold-bearing Reef of the Witwatersrand that runs thousands of feet below them. Randfontein, Roodepoort, Boksburg, Benoni and Brakpan, to name a few, belong to a mining and industrial continuum that in the thirties was already unique in South Africa for size and the number and variety of its people.

This was the area, some sixty miles by fifteen, in which Basner had begun to learn about South Africa and because it had taken into itself every element of the nation, not to mention places far beyond its borders, it was a good school, though an elementary one.

Contacts with some chiefs, which started with his acquaintance with men who had been leading personalities in the African National Congress, led to his becoming legal adviser to many. It became necessary to see them and their people in their own surroundings — the Transvaal, Orange Free State and Natal 'native reserves' (predecessors of apartheid's so-called homelands) and the neighbouring British Protectorates of Basutoland and Swaziland. Contacts with advisory board members on the Reef brought further contacts in the locations attached to white villages and small towns (*dorps*), within the ever-widening periphery of Johannesburg, and cases like that of the General Hospital workers led to calls from as far away as the Natal coast.

In purely African areas there were no lawyers at all, and around them, in the white farming districts — in *dorps* sometimes fifty miles apart from one another — solitary attorneys would depend entirely on other whites for fellowship as well as for status and a living. For such men it would have been ruinous, even if they had had the inclination, to act for a black against a local farmer, trader or official.

The black field-workers and servants in and around the dusty *dorps* had special need of energetic defence. Basner was only asked to travel so far by these poorest of his clients if they were passionately convinced of the justice of their cases. It was a psychic as well as a practical matter. The pleasure a 'pirate' taxi-driver in Johannesburg could get from hearing magistrates and police treated with the reverse of obsequiousness was nothing to that of a gathering of scattered (and tattered) country folk with a chance to attend a trial when the accused had employed Basner to defend him.

These visits were worth while. He not only had every chance of winning the case, a fiercely-contested action provided for its audience the catharsis of classical drama. Remembered experience of tribal courts in which all adult males participate endowed illiterate labourers with subtle critical faculties, and reverberations of their own past protests hinted at a future restoration of self-respect.

Basner came inevitably to meet people who years before had formed local branches of Congress and the ICU, now seemingly resigned to inaction. This was the beginning of an understanding of regional matters and the friendships he started to make formed the foundation of an extensive political reputation never quite understood and hardly ever acknowledged by his white political associates.

The expulsion of Bunting and others from the Communist Party was occasioned by a doctrine originally imposed upon it by the Comintern in 1928 and worthy of mention as an example of the contentions which had always bedevilled that party and were an important constituent of the atmosphere in which Basner was to live for the next six years.

The edict was to the effect that Communists were to stand for a 'black republic of workers and peasants'. In this process, they should dissociate themselves from the 'black bourgeoisie'. This term presumably included not only the then existing handful of African business and professional people, but many thousands of near-poverty-stricken people such as primary school teachers, who were ready and able to press for properly organised resistance against unjust laws. Most of them may not have been prepared for dreams of socialism and those who were so prepared thought such dreams to be distant ones. They all, however, wished for a widespread movement that, just for once, would simply be well run.

Having founded the League of African Rights after the 1928 doctrine had been promulgated, Bunting presumably thought himself to be at one with Comintern policy since his intention was to create a mass organisation led by the Party (which itself was expected to be confined to trained Bolsheviks). He was temperamentally incapable of being doctrinaire, however, and his nature was above all humanitarian and hence, perhaps, inclined to be paternalistic. The politicisation of poor and illiterate blacks was close to his heart, but his League did not assume the form required of it in far distant, and often ill-briefed, Moscow.

Its initial aim, to present a great petition of rights to government, was manifestly appealing to a society only newly conscious of itself as a whole and unprepared both in mood and in theory for revolution. In the circumstances, neither Bunting nor his comrades in the Party were prepared for the telegram that arbitrarily bade them abandon the petition. They acquiesced. But more than acquiescence was demanded of them.

By 1931, a bigoted internal group, endorsing a further Comintern ukase demanding strict implementation of the 1928 instructions, took charge and began a process of Party purification. Bunting was to cease from 'opportunist conformism', or else. Communist trade union organisers should cease trying to create solidarity between blacks and whites in industry, since that inevitably meant compromise over the colour bar. (Some of those who were expelled had managed, against very great odds, to achieve a small measure of interracial collaboration in their unions. E S Sachs's Garment Workers, for instance, became notable for their Afrikaner women leaders amongst whom, if not amongst the rank and file, racism had no place).

The validity of this policy is still arguable. One can only say that at the time its positive effects were minimal. The slogan of the Black Republic might perhaps be imagined to have possessed a similar appeal to that of Garveyism or of later, overtly race-based black movements, but it did not . . . and for good reason. Away from the largest towns, scarcely anyone was aware of the Communist Party[10]. In such towns its members who thought like Roux, Bunting and the trade unionists were accepted as the valuable human beings they were and, if heard of at all, the refinements of political thinking which had suddenly turned people like them into pernicious agents of imperialism were not worth attention.

Inside the Party which was dominated by its white theorists, there were very few Africans really interested in conducting Soviet-style polemics. Many deplored their virulence but would do nothing and others drifted away in cynicism and despair. Eddie Roux's own willing submission to discipline came to cause him great remorse. The Communist ideals for which he and all his comrades, including the bigots, were so prepared to sacrifice themselves, prevailed over his love and respect for Bunting. He was to remain in the Party until the late thirties, when he too felt obliged to drift away.[6]

By 1933, when Basner finally decided to join it, the Party was in a poor state with a membership of no more than a hundred and fifty, and its past influence in the ICU, Congress and other organisations much diminished. From then until 1939 he played a considerable role in shaping its practical character. Where it erred whether theoretically or practically, he afterwards claimed no innocence and where it shed light to make the African nationalist movement less racial and more rational than some of those in other parts of the world, he had no need to deny his contribution.

8

INTO POLITICS
(1933-1935)

Basner had no doubts or reservations about Marxism but many about the Communist Party. Despite daily involvement in its affairs, until 1933 he rejected efforts to recruit him. Now, however, he became convinced that the monopolistic nature of the gold-mining industry was responsible for the legally built-in racialism of South Africa[1] and that it was an integral part of the international structure of capitalism. The expulsions and denunciations of old comrades-in-arms in South Africa were to his mind no more than the normal process of the revolution 'eating up its children' and were not to be compared to the insane cruelty and brutish irrationality of the capitalist world.

The shadow of Hitler's madness had reached South Africa quickly because the virus of his creed was already within her. The shadow of Stalin's madness, which was corrupting and decimating the only brotherhood of activists who could have united blacks and whites against their common enemy, the gold-mining industry, was not so apparent. The ferocious polemics and fiery debates of some dozens of people in drab meeting places in Johannesburg over the definition of a 'Black Republic' or the elimination of the 'Black Bourgeoisie' were irrelevancies. What mattered was the safety of the first Socialist Fatherland, its very borders menaced by Hitler.

With the spread of fascism in Europe and the appearance of local stormtroopers, the 'Greyshirts', in the streets, Basner's compulsion to take to active politics had become too strong to allow him to remain a bystander. There was only one movement, despite its defects, which had the courage and the will to meet Nazis wherever they appeared.

He was already the legal task-force of the Communist Party and was busy as a speaker in the evenings and at weekends in a society called the Friends of the Soviet Union (FSU).

This society (part of an international one of the same name) had been started some time before, not as a 'front' organisation but to combat the dearth of information and the plethora of hostile propaganda about the USSR in the capitalist press. Its aim was not to enlist members, though its activities had to include helping to spread Marxist thought. Meetings were held every Sunday evening in the Trades Hall, and non-Communist trade union members, preferably Afrikaners, were favoured. Occasionally there were large gatherings, to which blacks began to come. They and the whites sat together amicably enough, participating in discussions and asking questions without apparent discomfort or embarrassment.

Unhappily, Sidney and Rebecca Bunting decided to use the platform of the FSU to protest against their exclusion from the Communist Party and to expose the leadership as opportunist betrayers of the African people. It became Basner's unsavoury task to stop them, which he did by ordering the stewards to bar their attendance — an action which gave much pain to Eddie Roux and caused a coolness between him and Basner which was to last a considerable time.

In the beginning Basner's party membership brought little change in his way of life. The leadership considered him too intellectually rarefied to help formulate policy and tactics and too bourgeois to assist in the important work of writing for and distributing the party paper, training cadres and organising branches in locations and factories.

He felt somewhat isolated and dissatisfied. He had not become a Communist in order to intensify his activities as a lawyer or to exercise his eloquence as a mouthpiece of the FSU on the achievements of electrification plus socialism by Stakhanovites in the USSR. Gradually, however, his legal work began to lead to real fellowship with African comrades, both men and women, who were of a character he had not met before. They satisfied both his political and his social needs and did not cease to be his friends even after he left the Party (in 1939).

One of them was Edwin Mofutsanyana, an ex-teacher who, with his wife, Josie Mpama, had become a staunch Communist some three years before, and would remain one almost all his life.

Born in Witzieshoek near the Lesotho border and educated in Catholic mission schools in Lesotho itself, he had spent enough time on further education in Moscow to become a sound Marxist and to acquire healthy reservations about both the Roman Church and the Soviet Union. Basner was to become closely associated with Edwin who was a retiring and temperate person, not particularly clever, seldom a questioner of party dogma, and quite incapable of demagogy but always ready to face white police brutality. As if to contradict his own modest nature, Edwin loved to be well dressed, but in a different and more dandified style from that of his colleague, J B Marks.

John Marks and his wife were also teachers, though he had been dismissed from his post because of his politics. He was a dignified, large, coloured man, with a reddish tinge to his skin, like an American Indian, but was dark enough to pass as an African if it suited him. No one knew much about his parentage or background; but he was forceful, intelligent and well-educated and highly respected.

After two years of schooling in the USSR, he could debate as a Marxist with the necessary familiarity and vehemence, but also with the grace of humour. It was typical of him, in the midst of a police raid and the ransacking of his room, to have sat ostentatiously adjusting his trouser turn-ups as a preliminary to putting a shine on his boots with a feather duster. It was also typical that he was perpetually broke and in perpetual need of somewhere, anywhere, to sleep, since so much of his time was spent travelling to meetings and subsequently avoiding arrest. 'It's agony! The way money comes and goes,' he would say. 'And you're horrified when you wake up to find who's lying next to you in the bed.' He was to remain on affectionate terms with Basner until his death in Moscow in 1972 after years of exile.

Contact with Charlotte Maxeke was now virtually over. Although she never expressed her disapproval of his doings, Basner could not, as a known Communist, visit her office without endangering her job. However, since her nephew was his clerk, she contrived to bypass difficulties and prejudices, by using Samuel as a go-between over some serious cases.

A considerable number of his clients dropped away because of his involvement in the Communist Party and others came to him only on specific occasions when they thought his services preferable to those of new legal advisers.

His income fell substantially but only because he had lost all desire to act for townspeople on petty criminal charges. The liquor-sellers and thieves did not mind whether he was a Communist or a papal nuncio. What they did mind was his refusing to conduct their defence in person, and he would have to fight hard not to give in. They would imply 'You hate me' and he had to remember that they were not talking to him but to a whole race which was ill-treating them — not out of greed or for some other understandable reason, but out of irrational physical antagonism. (To make such people see differently, Basner felt he had to try turning them into Communists, and thereby risked losing yet more clients.)

Perhaps in view of his adherence to the Party line at a time when the Buntings' expulsion still caused tacit dissension and open falling away, Basner was in due course promoted to speaking at open-air meetings on the Johannesburg City Hall steps. He had a powerful voice which could compete against the Post Office clock when it boomed each quarter hour. Since he was a Jew as well as a democrat and Marxist, recent events in Germany gave an added power to his theme.

It was necessary now to recruit Jews to help combat the Greyshirts. Although anti-Semitism was the nub of their propaganda, most instances of their thuggery were against Africans and Indian hawkers and shopkeepers, especially in the isolated backveld *dorps* where Jews were hard to find.

A group of young refugees from Poland and Lithuania, organised as the Jewish Workers' Club[2], became a contingent of stalwarts, and they and the Communists had powerful auxiliaries among Afrikaner men and women from the trade unions, and a number of Afrikaner intellectuals. Early in 1934, together with these and many other English-speakers, Basner joined a new broad alliance, the Anti-Fascist League (AFL), launched largely through the efforts of a left-wing member of the Labour Party from Natal, Alec Wanless.

A band of them would rush off in force in a hired lorry to counter a Greyshirt meeting in a neighbouring town or village if they got to know about it in time. They would sing all the way there, and some would nurse bloody noses and broken heads on the way back. Most memorable of all to Basner were the trade unionists Johanna Cornelius and her sister Hester, and a sculptress, Hetta Crouse, all statuesque and powerful women, and J Larkin, a school headmaster and fiery speaker.

Among them, Johanna was outstanding. She came of a family of poor farmers which, like so many, had been driven off the land in the Transvaal by drought and the Depression. With her great abilities, she became a skilled trade union leader and, chestnut hair flying, was a right bonny fighter. From the time when, aged fifteen, in gym tunic and blazer, she was arrested for picketing a factory because of its wage of 7/6d a week for white women, she was a champion of justice for the rest of her life, and a democrat to whom racism of any kind was disgusting.

In 1935, still in her early twenties, she and four other Afrikaans girls were defended by Basner when prosecuted after an enthusiastic brawl with strike-breakers at a textile mill.[3] They refused to pay fines of a pound each, and opted for ten days in the Johannesburg Fort — the first white women to do such a thing. One of them, Bettie du Toit (then aged seventeen), recollects Basner's admiration for their decision, and his loud bellows of praise for them in the courtroom[4]. They were tough, but she also remembers how innocent they were. Each one had known real poverty, but the prison food, just boiled mealie-meal pap and rancid dripping to be eaten from dirty wooden spoons, reduced them to tears. They were puzzled by the other women who were inside. 'For what?' they asked as they sat on the latrines. 'For soliciting', was the answer. 'And what's that?' they wanted to know and needed a lot of elucidation.

The necessity to avoid racial encounters lent local credibility to a policy which was, as it happens, only another mutation of the Soviet strategies which were to destroy the Spanish Republic and thwart the growth of the British and other Communist parties.

There seemed to be sense at first in the sudden orders — no one knew for certain from whom or where they came — to divide the Friends of the Soviet Union into two separate organisations, one for whites and one for blacks. The white workers in South Africa had the franchise and the industrial power, and therefore their prejudices had to be considered in seeking friends for the USSR, and so bringing together more allies in a 'united front' against fascism. They would come to meetings more willingly and in greater numbers if they did not have to sit next to Africans and listen to non-white speakers. It sounded like sense until it could be recognised as blatant and self-defeating appeasement, in no way the same as simply preventing riotous confrontations[5].

Sidney Bunting's indignation at the behaviour of those who had expelled him in 1931 was more than understandable. Among the crimes of which he had been accused was the placation of well-disposed whites, such as liberal academics and social workers. Now, the blacks for whom he had fought so hard for twenty years were being degraded to placate the ill-disposed; and by the very people who had claimed to stand more squarely for them than he had. Had he been a different sort of man, he might have been grimly amused. Blacks lost interest in attending FSU meetings. Why should they come to hear about the equality of all races in the USSR if they were not fit to do so sitting next to white workers? Hardly any white workers came either, because by this time the Greyshirts had much more exciting news to tell — about the achievements of Hitler's Third Reich.

Among the expelled trade unionists, ES ('Solly') Sachs may have merely felt vindicated. He had failed to persuade the rank and file of his Garment Workers to admit Africans, and had accepted that failure as inevitable. But he had not only done great things to improve working conditions and wages for poor-whites and coloured women, but had trained up a whole generation of totally unprejudiced and highly able leaders like Johanna Cornelius and Bettie du Toit.

Personally, he had been born with awesome disabilities: the child of an unhappy family of Jewish immigrants; seemingly retarded; brought up in squalor; poor-sighted, pallid and stooped. He had somehow managed to become both expert and a success in a career which exposed him to ceaseless vilification and harassment. His rather rabbinical mind had something in common with the functionaries who had rejected him but he was a very practical man, and when his opinions became orthodoxy overnight, saw no reason to return to the fold.

The new doctrine of racial segregation in the FSU disturbed but did not horrify Basner. It would take international events to do that, and meanwhile, more horrifying and more immediately threatening things were happening in South Africa.

At the end of 1935, two proposed enactments generally known as the 'Hertzog Bills' had come before Parliament and there was no time for brooding over Communist faults, whether in Johannesburg or elsewhere. Basner, together with Africans whom he held in great respect, was now busy making plans to oppose the bills. The men with whom he was working were senior comrades like Edwin Mofutsanyana, John Marks and Moses Kotane who were not greatly interested in world events and only rarely voiced dissent about what was going on either in the Kremlin or in the Party at home.

What impressed him greatly was the complete lack of race bias with which they discussed black nationalism and white supremacy in Marxist terms. But even that was not half as important as the way they could all argue and shout. If a white and a black in South Africa can shout at each other and remain friends, then true equality has been established. If they have to be polite and circumspect in their dealings, that is 'race relations' — soothing ointment to film over nasty sores and hide the deep corruption within.

9
THE HERTZOG BILLS
(1935-1936)

In June 1934, General Hertzog, as head of the wholly Afrikaner National Party, and General Smuts, leader of the opposition South African Party (SAP), formed a coalition which came to be known as 'Fusion'.

Fusion had nothing to offer the country; it merely welded one political barterer whose chickens would not hatch to another who had acquired a store of bitter fruit. Such a government could produce nothing of any significance for the white electorate except more legislation to manipulate the blacks.

The chickens which would not hatch for Jan Smuts and the interests he represented — the goldmining industry and Westminster — were the appeasement of the majority of the Afrikaners, the confinement of the main African tribes within reserves and the creation of an establishment friendly to such ends.

Smuts's appeasement would not work in favour of Britain and the English-speaking South Africans for the simple reason that appeasement never works. The betrayal of the African population which commenced with the Treaty of Vereeniging at the end of the Anglo-Boer War had only sharpened the appetite of many of the Boers to fight another round once the situation became more favourable.

For every Afrikaner follower of Botha and Smuts and their policy of reconciliation, two could be counted upon to agree with Hertzog that the destiny of the country should not lie within the British orbit. Ever stricter colour bars and pass laws were mere palliatives that only intensified a longing for another Voortrekker Republic with Paul Kruger's motto 'No equality for white and black in Church or State'.

The bitter fruit Hertzog was harvesting can be understood through the character of his son Albert who considered him too moderate over Native policy, too constitutional in his struggle against the English-speaking whites and out of touch with reality in not supporting Germany in its war preparations against the British Empire. The wing of the Nationalists to which he belonged split from his father's party. Claiming to speak for the majority of Afrikaners, it certainly did voice the opinion of most of their intellectuals.

In April 1936 Fusion produced the so-called Hertzog Bills, the Native Representation Act and the Native Land and Trust Act, two measures which destroyed that last vestige of African political rights — the very limited Cape franchise, and laid new and even heavier burdens on the rural population. Taken together, they drove Basner into parliamentary politics and eventually sent him to the South African Senate in 1942 as the 'Native Representative' of the then three-and-a-half-million Africans of the Transvaal and Orange Free State.

Confinement of the Africans within reserves had not worked. It had been conceived, not by the pastoral Boers as a racist measure, but by the highly sophisticated goldmining industry as the only means of supplying a huge and constant flow of cheap and migrant labour to heave the gold-bearing rock from the deep shafts beneath the Witwatersrand to the mills for crushing. Cecil Rhodes and his magnates would doubtless have preferred to mechanise their mines to an extent that would allow them to employ a smaller, settled labour force. But the technological problems involved were (and still are) too great for that. They had had to employ the best brains of Balliol and the English Bar for the inhuman policy which culminated in the Land Act of 1913.

Nothing worked, however, because the land would not stretch, and the Africans did not stop procreating. And the white farmers wanted field-labour, the white housewives wanted domestic labour, the white shopkeepers wanted sweepers and messengers, the white municipalities wanted drivers for their mule-carts and sewage-buckets. For them, transient male muscle-power would not do.

For the blacks, it would not do either. As their population grew, the native reserves became over-stocked and over-ploughed. Thousands of families could no longer live on a mixture of subsistence agriculture and meagre remittances from their young men on the mines.¹ As the towns grew, the exodus from the reserves became a flood. Soil erosion and the human spate swept away the dreams of Rhodes, Milner, the Chamber of Mines and Jan Smuts.

To gauge the craft and cunning of the Hertzog Bills, it must be borne in mind that Smuts had won the highest prize in Cambridge for his law studies, was President Kruger's Attorney General and had drawn up the draft constitution of the League of Nations. Hertzog had been a judge. The Chamber of Mines employed outstanding barristers.

In the Cape Province, the voting rights of a limited number of Africans, with property and educational qualifications not required of whites, enabled balance to be maintained in a sufficient number of constituencies to return white members of Parliament who held mildly liberal beliefs.² These, although few, were enough to prevent any government from gaining the two-thirds majority required to change the constitution of the country.

It was this franchise for which many British people thought their soldiers were dying in the Anglo-Boer War, believing Rhodes's and Chamberlain's promise of 'civilised rights for every civilised man', so speedily abandoned at the Peace of Vereeniging.

The Cape franchise stuck like a fishbone in the throat of Jan Smuts but he could live with it. It was, however, more a cancer than an obstruction to every Afrikaner Nationalist who wanted the old Voortrekker constitutions back.

The Chamber of Mines, only interested in cheap migrant labour, had never been interested in constitutions, or, for that matter, in racist legislation. Now that the reserves were becoming rural slums from which the inhabitants were fleeing to try to become townspeople rather than migrants, the acquisition of more land for Africans had become a vital necessity.

The basic proposal was simple enough. If the 'Cape Liberal' MPs would surrender the African vote, the government would, within five years, purchase an additional seven and a quarter million morgen of land (about sixteen million acres) for African occupation. In addition, a different kind of franchise would be granted. In the Cape, the blacks would elect three white MPs and two Senators to represent them and in the other Provinces, two white Senators, one for Natal and the other for both the Transvaal and the Free State. There would also be a Native Representative Council with purely advisory functions, consisting of twenty-two members, of whom twelve would be elected.

The Cape Liberals put up some resistance, but it was the token one of virtue ready for seduction. The African chiefs and their headmen swallowed the bait as it was thrown to them by every missionary and negrophile of any importance. They saw the Bills as a wonderful deal by a government at last concerned with black welfare and better race relations. The majority of urban Africans were not interested in the franchise, and, having abandoned the reserves, were not interested in the land question either.

It was only natural that the elite Cape African Jabavu family and their newspaper, the *Imvo*, should be the first to sound the alarm on behalf of the voters who would be ousted from the common electoral rolls. They had been on friendly terms with white liberals, both in South Africa and in Britain, and even with men such as Rhodes and Smuts. They knew (not least from their own experience) how quickly the best grade of liberal resolution can melt when the heat turns on.

Once the Bills were published in full it did not take long before the Communist Party understood their small print. Its African officebearers aligned themselves with the Jabavus in setting up an All-African Convention of black leaders to meet in Bloemfontein, the capital of the Orange Free State, to protest and declare a boycott of future elections when the Native Representation Bill became law.

What was wrong with the exchange of seven and a quarter million morgen of land for a few thousand votes on the common roll of a single province? Never was the classical warning about fearing the Greeks when they come bearing gifts more timely or apt. The Greeks now to be feared were two Boer Generals with a gift-horse made of legal parchment, and the invaders hidden inside it were armed with the sharpest and cruellest weapons so far invented by white supremacy to destroy the rights and security of the black population.

A few votes in the Cape could determine the attitudes and fate of many liberal-minded candidates able to prevent constitutional changes. The seven new representatives would not be enough to replace them and would not even be properly elected. Four of them, the senators, would be the nominees of chiefs and electoral committees largely under the influence of naive missionaries and very largely under duress from local native commissioners (many of them Nationalist Afrikaners).

There was no guarantee that the extra land would be bought. There was provision for a sum of ten million pounds to be set aside for its purchase. But what if the white owners refused to sell? What if prices rose and the money allocated proved inadequate?

General Hertzog could give the worthless franchise and the worthless parliamentary and Native Representative Council seats, but could he give the land he promised? It seemed as if he and the mines were in a cleft stick. If sufficient land was bought to make rural life tolerable for blacks, labour recruitment would suffer. If it were not, tribal overstocking and erosion would become such that wages would have to increase to augment the migrant workers' subsistence agriculture in the reserves.

But these shortcomings and ambiguities were of little account in comparison with a faintly-concealed menace in the new Land Act. Its name was to be the Native Land and Trust Act. The original legislation of 1913 had frozen the amount of land under African ownership. Now every inch of land was to be vested in a trust, with the government as trustee. It would, in fact, be taken away by turning every black tribesman in South Africa into a tenant of government, and hence as much at the mercy of its policies about where they should live as urban people were at the mercy of municipal authorities. From 1936 on, African labour was to be a reservoir as fluid and manageable as water, and could be driven into any channel. The main channel, of course, would lead to the mining compounds.[3]

At that time, there were about seven million Africans in the country: roughly one third in the urban area, one third in the native reserves, and one third labourers on white farms or rent-paying 'squatters' on white-owned land too poor for any other use. These three categories were, on paper and in the brains of lawyers and legislators, analogous to reservoirs. In reality, they were human beings of flesh and blood who could not and would not accept such a fate.

During his student years, when his chief interest was in people who wrote, Basner always thought of Paris as the capital of the world because Balzac, Zola, Baudelaire and Verlaine had lived there. But his imagination also spent a lot of time in Ireland, where poets, playwrights and mystics mourned and day-dreamed over the Celtic past.

Even then, behind such luminous figures as Yeats, Lady Gregory and AE Russell, he often caught a glimpse of a tall, stern man who kept his compassion for Ireland encased in the chainmail of political realism. This was James Stewart Parnell, Protestant leader of Catholic rebellion against the neglect and tyranny of Westminster.

Later, when Basner's interest had shifted to politics, he read everything about Parnell that he could lay hands on and by the end of 1935 when the All-African Convention leaders were shouting 'boycott' against the Hertzog Bills, Parnell moved right into the foreground of his pantheon.

What was Kitty O'Shea's lover doing in a Marxist's pantheon? He was not there because he loved her more than his chance of an alliance with Gladstone (although that helped), any more than Tom Paine was there because he loved brandy better than being acceptable to Jefferson and George Washington. Parnell was there because he was a great parliamentarian and Paine was there because he wrote *The Rights of Man* and *The Age of Reason*.

It was Parnell, above all, who taught Basner to believe it idiotic to talk about 'parliamentary idiocy'[4]. If by that Marx meant parliament as an institution, a majority of mankind has considered that in one form or another there is nothing better. Anyone who applies that term to electoral systems, though, has forgotten the ancient Roman truism — when you corrupt the best, it becomes the worst.

Now, while the African leaders were crying 'boycott' at the All-

African Convention of 1935, Basner had no standing on the conference floor to tell them what Parnell had always said — in the land where Captain Boycott was born and bred — that an electoral boycott is a stupid and dishonest manoeuvre because it can never be totally effective and therefore always plays into the hands of the opposing party.

There was nothing to stop him, however, during the evenings of meeting the Communist delegates and his personal friends, from telling them that the lone and unheeded voice of the old militant from Natal, John Dube, was speaking the truth — the chiefs, who with their bloc votes would have the largest say, would believe the government's promises to buy more land, and would in return vote for any candidate favoured by the Native Affairs Department. What, then, was the point in a boycott?

Dube had been the sole important leader to stand in favour of the Hertzog Bills and from a dozen angry throats had come shouts about treachery, and murmurs referring to 'Uncle Tom'. His case was sad, but the accusations were not true. His was an honest voice, speaking for many misguided people — misguided in thinking that the pursuit of good race-relations, not politics, should be their concern and would carry more weight than the wordy, superficial indignation about the betrayal of the Cape Liberal MPs that had been expressed at the Convention. (The term traitor could never be applied to John Dube, and the term Uncle Tom — a vulgar inversion of the sentimentality in Harriet Beecher Stowe's story — discounts the humanity which can transcend race or nationality.)[5]

Mofutsanyana and Marks could speak with considerable authority to the delegates. They were both on the Convention executive as Transvaal representatives of the African National Congress and stressed what Basner was convinced of as strongly as they — that the African people would not be quiescent and their leaders not lack followers if the issues were put to them in simple terms of 'increased repression and insecurity on the land'. The Convention could accomplish nothing by discussions based on legal premises and the production of high-flown, elitist resolutions and cries of protest.

A feature upon which all three remarked, although none of them could explain it fully, was that no one seemed ready to give serious consideration to organising popular resistance to the Bills, as had been done at the time of the old Land Act of 1913, when tremendous political energy had been released and had given birth to the Congress. There was also a vital element missing from the Convention — there was only the barest sprinkling of women, yet it was women, except in the most backward tribal areas, who were to help mount real opposition once the Hertzog Bills became law.

There were some obvious causes for the change in mood. First, the earlier Act had taken away rights to land, but Hertzog's Native Land and Trust Bill promised to provide new land. Secondly, in 1913 the Congress had failed in its main purpose and was now badly in decline, under the presidency of the irredeemable Dr Seme. And thirdly, there was now dissension and competition between several national bodies, which included Congress, the vestiges of the ICU, the Communist Party and the new All-African Convention itself.

Yet even personal rivalries and ideological disagreements could not explain the strange indifference which greeted every appeal for real action against the Bills. Everyone recognised the loss of the Cape franchise as a disaster and few people in the conference hall (where there were few, and those too well-educated to be representative) believed that the government would really supply the promised land. Although the state had done little enough to further black education, twenty-three years had passed since the Congress had come into being, and in that period many Africans had acquired sufficient of it to add modern political understanding to their natural intelligence. In fact the land was added very slowly. By 1939 only 1,5 million morgen had been purchased and further additions were suspended with the outbreak of war. With further resettlements of ex-squatters, African farmers could reasonably expect less land, not more.

Basner was cynical enough about the boycott decision, predicting that the Jabavus and many others would soon be supporting white candidates for Parliament and contesting seats for themselves on the Native Representative Council.

He would have done better to reserve some cynicism for the white politicians. The African leaders at least waited six months before their resolution cracked and they rushed to stand for election. The whites did not waste more than a few weeks before scrambling to the troughs where the funds for land purchase were being mixed with 'inside information'.

No sooner had the Land and Trust Act passed through all its stages than plans were leaked showing in which areas farms had been set aside for Native occupation. Some of them even pinpointed the farms themselves. In no time, speculators had taken out options. Prices rocketed, so that when the buyers from the Lands Department came along, they found themselves (because there was no provision for compulsory purchase at a fair valuation) paying inflated sums which exhausted their funds long before they acquired their quotas.

Many of the farms were earmarked for the northern Transvaal, where the need for land was recognised to be the greatest, and most of the options on these were taken over by one speculator in Pietersburg, the capital of the area. This person happened to be a client of a firm of solicitors there, Naudé and Naudé. The main partner in the firm was 'Dop' Naudé, a brother of the MP for the district, Tom Naudé, who had not only been a Minister of Native Affairs, but a member of the influential Native Affairs Commission.

The scandal was too much even for some members of Hertzog's own party. A commission of enquiry was eventually called for, but talk of it was still rumbling on eight years later when Basner reached the Senate. By that stage he saw no reason to become involved in pressing for official unravelments. What proof is an unfortunate coincidence whereby a smart fellow who guesses what places the Native Trust will want to buy also happens to be the client of the brother of a Member of Parliament who is in a position to obtain information?

Tom Naudé later became acting State President of South Africa and therefore supreme chief over all the African chiefs, and so can be said to have been deprived of land himself by the dealings of his brother's client.[6]

10

THE POLITICS OF THE NONPOLITICAL
(1936)

Political corruption involving the land rights of helpless indigenous peoples had been common enough in many places and was no novelty in white South Africa. But a new form of corruption, more insidious and of a peculiarly local kind, was openly revealed when the second meeting of the All-African Convention was held in Bloemfontein in June 1936.

With the Native Representation Act now law, the politics of the nonpolitical entered the scene — those of the Joint Councils of Europeans and Natives, the South African Institute of Race Relations and all who said that political activity was not good for blacks and should be conducted by whites on their behalf.

In such a country as this, with an evangelic tradition and a history of oppressive racial discrimination, it was neither wrong nor remarkable that there should be a number of white clergymen, academics and philanthropists anxious to 'do something for those poor natives'. It was not strange that they should ask their African, coloured and Indian counterparts to join them for a cup of tea and a chat over what should best be done to make the status quo more acceptable and how to avoid unpleasant challenges and painful strife.

It was also not strange that leading white liberals and moderate-minded black politicians should respond to the appeal of Dr JK Aggrey[1] who proposed — on a visit from the United States in 1921 — that such interracial meetings should become formally constituted and attract enlightened businessmen, administrators and other white functionaries. Aggrey, the great Ghana-born educator, orator and apostle of racial appeasement, had been horrified at the spread of the radical black exclusiveness expounded in America by Marcus Garvey. He quoted his successful experience in combating such ideas, as well as his own famous simile about the piano which produces lovely harmonies only when both the black and the white keys are played upon.

So 'Joint Councils' of 'Europeans and Natives' were established in a large number of towns, and became very energetic in the middle twenties, when Kadalie was a power in the land. From the start, their attitude was that the ICU might do much good if Communists and other militants in its ranks could be excluded.

Among the fifteen white foundation members of the Johannesburg Joint Council were HM Taberer, General Manager of the goldmining companies' Native Recruiting Corporation (NRC) and Howard Pim, the accountant who had done so much to appoint Charlotte Maxeke as Prisoner's Friend. Its secretary was a Welsh liberal, JD Rheinallt Jones.

By 1929, the councils had become appendages of a new body, with headquarters at the University of the Witwatersrand — the South African Institute of Race Relations. This had been launched on funds donated by various people (including, directly and indirectly, the goldmining industry)[2] which were administered by Howard Pim. Its adviser and, later, Executive Director, was JD Rheinallt Jones.

Who were Pim and Jones? Basner's interest had begun to quicken. He knew from Mrs Maxeke that African chiefs and intellectuals, having consulted him, would go to one or the other afterwards, as if to reinforce his advice and that this dual traffic met with her approval. He did not ask his clients why they did this because they never mentioned it.

Pim had professional connections with the mining houses and the Stock Exchange and was active as a Quaker and in many African charities and recreational organisations. These were not odd or unworthy concerns for a man to have but the striking thing about Pim was the apparent limitlessness of the money at his disposal to give to wayward black individuals, just as much as to homes for the blind or to debt-ridden football clubs. Basner was inclined to conclude that no accountant, whatever the size of his practice, could afford such amounts, and that his office must be a conduit from more important sources.

Taberer, who was responsible for the yearly recruitment of huge numbers of blacks to work the mines, also made generous donations but was not known as a giver of handouts to impecunious political agitators. Pim however, was ready to help the deserving and undeserving alike, until the day of his death in 1934.

If Howard Pim's role and financial reserves were mainly in the twilight, Basner was beginning to decide that there was nothing very obscure about Rheinallt Jones. The latter (unlike his compatriot Lloyd George), professed a great distaste for politics, and declared the purpose of his institute to be the promotion of good race relations through reasoned discussions with white officialdom, using arguments buttressed by meticulous sociological research.[3]

The Institute of Race Relations was also buttressed by the weightiest African newspaper, *Umteteli wa Bantu* (The People's Voice), owned and financed by the Chamber of Mines; and by the most readable of them, the *Bantu World*.

The *Bantu World* was owned by two white businessmen, BG Paver and IJ La Grange jointly with a company controlled by the Chamber, and had been started in 1932 with the help of a small amount of capital provided by Howard Pim. It was edited by the best African journalist of his time RV Selope Thema, (who had at one time been editor of the now defunct Congress paper, *Abantu-Batho*).

The only journal with which either of these really had to compete was the Communist *Umsebenzi* (The Worker). As this had coloured and Indian as well as African readers and was shunned by the church-going sector of the black population, it is doubtful if, of its circulation of two to three thousand, even five hundred copies reached those Africans who made up the vanguard of the existing political organisations.

The *Bantu World* had particular influence among teachers and students. Its editor was a drunkard, but drunk or sober, the brilliant Selope Thema could turn out copy with a sparkle which made Eddie Roux and the other writers for *Umsebenzi* seem very pedestrian.

On various occasions and over some years, Kadalie had repeated a rambling story to Basner about how Ethelreda Lewis, an author (and friend of the novelist Winifred Holtby), had approached him in 1926 with offers of financial and technical support from the trade union movement and other Labour Party affiliates in Britain if only he would get rid of leftists in his movement.

For a variety of reasons he had agreed to this. The Communists were bossy, they pressed for change in the ICU's aims and management, they were not particularly popular as individuals and funds were always running short. Kadalie was later to blame the eventual dissipation of the energies of the ICU, riven as it was by factional disputes, on the Joint Councils and the Institute of Race Relations (of which the formidable Mrs. Lewis was a member).

It all sounded too Machiavellian — that a group of academics and pious liberals should do the job which the police had failed to do for years and that the British Labour Party, the Fabian Colonial Bureau and the TUC should connive in such a plot. Basner also had reason to suspect that Ballinger had come too late to do anything, good or bad, for the ICU. Even after being a Communist for some time, he was sceptical and inclined to be brusque with Kadalie, and scarcely listened to his muddled laments which always ended with a touch for five shillings, obviously intended for the nearest shebeen. The ruin of a fearless and gifted leader upset him more than the tales of intrigue.

But now, in June 1936, he suddenly felt there were grounds for thinking, indeed for feeling certain, that Kadalie was telling the truth. The second meeting of the All-African Convention confirmed Basner's views on the sinister shrewdness of the Hertzog-Smuts legislation. It brought to full light the corruption which was seeping out of the Chamber of Mines to infect all South African politics, and especially, African politicians.

At the Convention, RV Selope Thema, who had fired some opening shots in the *Bantu World*, followed them up with some remarkable speeches. For him the loss of the Cape Native Franchise, with Africans voting for white MPs, did not matter. The new Act would give them the right to elect black men to a Native Representative Council, who would receive a salary of ten pounds a month (a considerable sum in those days), be exempt from the pass laws and have free passes on the railways to travel when and where they wished. They would be free to tell the government whatever they wanted to tell it.[4]

The white Cape Liberals were no loss either, according to this argument, because they were elected on a common roll, whilst the three new members of Parliament and four senators would be picked by Africans only, to vote and speak as the African voters in all four provinces directed.

These views were political nonsense, of course, but were now general, believed because the African leadership wanted to believe them.

The Native Representative Council was a useless, misleading innovation because it had no legislative powers. It was an advisory body in which only twelve of its twenty-two members would be elected, and whose advice no one needed to take. The twelve would be elected, not by individuals but by chiefs, councils and boards in no way obliged to give heed to public opinion, and in every way obliged to pander to authority.[5]

Only the three white Native Representatives in the lower House of Assembly would be voted for directly and the four senators would be chosen in the same manner as the members of the Native Representative Council (MRCs), and be just as much vetted and put forward by white Native Commissioners employed by the government as they.

It was a political swindle which could deceive nobody and depended for its acceptance on a contemptuous appraisal of the moral fibre of its victims.

No sooner had Selope Thema announced that he did not believe in boycotts any more and would himself stand as an MRC, than the rush began. Like a charge of dynamite demolishing an abandoned mine shaft came an announcement from Thomas Mapikela, a builder, lay preacher, old Congressman and the political boss of Bloemfontein's largest location. He too had changed his mind, he said, because of a message he had just received — that Rheinallt Jones and Dr Edgar Brookes, Principal of Adams College in Natal, had both decided to bid for seats in the Senate. The large demonstrations in favour of boycotting the elections, which he himself had led in Bloemfontein only six months before, were forgotten. The session fell into confusion, and, on the motion of Selope Thema, adjourned immediately, never seriously to meet again.

Within a fortnight, many influential leaders were proclaiming that they were candidates or supporters of candidates. The only man who had a right to do so, John Dube, was among the first as was AM Jabavu, the editor of *Imvo*, who should have been the very last.

The Communist Party found itself in difficulties which would not have arisen had it listened to Parnell's warnings as transmitted by Basner. If its leadership had joined Dube in rejecting a boycott in favour of organising the electorate in 1935, they would be reaping the benefit now. As it was, in a panic at being left behind, they put forward Edwin Mofutsanyana for the NRC in the Transvaal and Free State, and accepted Basner as a candidate there for the Senate.

It was over five years since Basner had begun to practise law on his own, and two since he had joined the Communist Party.

Despite the fact that some clients had left him when he became a Communist, and despite his being best known as a criminal lawyer, there were still many chiefs who put their legal affairs in his hands. So, too, did the heads of several prosperous independent African churches. He was consultant to the Transvaal and Orange Free State African Teachers' Associations and many of the Advisory Board members in and around Johannesburg remained with him, together with almost every burial society and group of small traders in the big locations along the Reef.

Though his remunerative petty offenders in Johannesburg were nearly all dispensed with, there were more and more criminal cases in remote country *dorps*.

In addition to his politics, his professional work had become such that he hardly spent two days together in Johannesburg itself. With his driver, a powerful and able man with whom there was no fear of breakdowns or accidents, he began to enjoy travelling many miles through the night into the veld far beyond Johannesburg, equipped with a pillow and blanket at the back of a big old Dodge car.

He would appear on one morning in court in Messina, near the Limpopo river where it forms the northern border of South Africa, and be in Kroonstad, some five hundred miles south, on the next.

They would usually arrive at the town or village of their destination just before dawn, and go to its hotel, where only the night watchman was on duty, making up the stove in the kitchen or sweeping the cement floors of the verandas lining the yard. After a bit of talk, the driver and the watchman would quickly become friends, and the white customer would then get coffee, the key to a room, and a basin of hot water for a wash and shave.

There would be time to change, have an early breakfast, and make a quick dash to the local prison or police station to see his client before going to court. There would be little time to consider the facts or read up the law; everything had to be done trusting to wit and chance. There was no point in applying for a postponement because the accused — unless he was a successful *dagga* smuggler or professional thief — seldom had the money for a second visit.

Basner became so used to night travel and being awake before sunrise that the habit of it always remained with him. Sometimes it stood him in good stead, as in tropical Ghana; sometimes in European winters, it plagued his family and friends. He firmly believed that people who only get up in full daylight live mutilated lives, sadly deprived of the morning star and the touch of the little winds that move around at dawn. He also may have kept to this habit in other places and later times to remind himself of the marvellous landscape of South Africa, which he had only begun truly to discover when he was thirty.

He could not be the lawyer for the teachers' associations without meeting many teachers or for the trading associations without meeting traders. He met educated chiefs and educated commoners. In time he felt he was on the track of the mystery which had puzzled him ever since he started thinking seriously about South African politics. And it was his clients who gave him his clues.

It was all very well to accept that tribal and factional rivalries, political ignorance, drink and police action had destroyed Congress and the ICU. But great movements with a mass following and deep-seated grievances do not disappear almost overnight because of persecution, or quarrelling and incompetent leaders. People always find new leaders, and persecution only drives popular parties underground. Why did this not happen in South Africa? Why had the blacks lost all impetus?

The explanation lay somewhere in conversations with a chief who had once been an ardent Congress supporter or with a headmaster who had encouraged his teachers to work in the ICU. They had reverted, or been converted, to the belief that political action was useless and destructive and that civilised intercourse between blacks and whites would improve matters peacefully in due time. They may have needed Buntings and

Basners to fight a racially unjust administration and its laws in the courts, but they relied on Pims and Joneses to combat racism itself.

Although he would sleep on those long night drives over vast distances, Basner also had time to think.

What would have happened to his country if it had been fortunate enough to escape the discovery of diamonds in Kimberley and of gold on the Witwatersrand? It could have developed its great natural resources and human potential to become rich agriculturally and industrially. This would have been unavoidable in spite of ignorance, backwardness, lack of ambition or chauvinism on the part of both Boer and Bantu.

Why should the goldmining industry consider it necessary to have majority shares in every important English-language newspaper, control the main distributing agency and have a hold over Afrikaans papers through shared or complete ownership of their printing presses? Why did it own *Umteteli* and control *Bantu World*?

Imagine the brewers of Britain or the armament producers of the United States setting out to acquire a monopoly of the news media in their countries. Of course it would be foolish not to expect great combines to use their finances and advertising clout to influence editorial policy whenever possible, but the total control the Chamber of Mines aimed at in South Africa was something different.

There was nothing unsophisticated or uninformed about the Chamber. It had a corps of private intelligence agents in the white and black trade unions, as well as an excellent political library that included the works of Marx and Engels, with files said to have been assembled by Harry Haynes, a former Communist Labour MP and trade unionist.

If its main arm among the blacks was the non-political Institute of Race Relations, this stemmed from a shrewd appreciation that the gold industry would inhibit a real industrial revolution in the country for a long time. With that, it would inhibit the growth of an African middle class. Without such a middle class, it might one day be confronted with a solidly united black population, and so had to devise means to capture and render harmless those elements which could provide a leadership. Chiefs and their families, petty traders and journalists, teachers, clerks and clergy were not a 'black bourgeoisie'. A true bourgeoisie would have had not only substantial reasons, but powers, to discourage popular insurrection. But most of these Africans had scarcely any possessions to protect and plenty of reasons for sharing in the passions of those with less standing than they.

So — Basner was convinced — the task of the Institute of Race Relations and its Joint Councils was to tame, if not to castrate, black militants and potential militants. The eunuchs had to be reassured with promises, bribed with little privileges and flattered with hospitality at tea parties (and they had better like tea), with white professors, ministers of religion and progressive businessmen. Dr Aggrey's piano, its black and white keys resonant with harmony, could provide background music to a bass-viol accompaniment of extremely well researched exposés of distressing social conditions. The chief piano player would be Rheinallt Jones.

Again, the Chamber of Mines was too efficient to rely only on local talent and the expertise that could be provided by the Fabian Colonial Bureau and other harmless anti-imperialist bodies in Britain striving to blunt the rough edges of Tory or Labour Party colonial policies.

The best expertise came from the USA, where a large black population, black churches, the NAACP and serious anti-imperialist sentiment made experiments in race relations look credible for South Africa. Such different personalities as the Rev Ray Phillips, a white liberal American, and Max Yergan, a rather more radical black social worker, came to spend many years in South Africa, organising social centres and recreation clubs for which considerable sums were raised from various well-intentioned persons (not to mention the Chamber of Mines).[6]

The moral fibre of the educated minority of Africans had wilted. Their political intelligence had been put to sleep. If they had been a middle class, economic inducements might have invigorated them into pursuing political ambitions of their own. In 1936, they were only intellectual nationalists who had been persuaded that no efforts of theirs could bring wealth for themselves or freedom for their people. As things were, most of them found it realistic to be frugally cosseted as individuals by kindly whites who also promised to do their best to lighten the burdens of the suffering masses.

11
CANDIDATES WITHOUT ELECTORATES

The whites who stood for (and eventually won) the three new parliamentary seats allotted to the Cape were interesting but not surprising. There was Donald Molteno, a sound lawyer and descendant of an old and genuinely liberal family. There was Mrs Ballinger, who, before marrying William, was Margaret Hodgson, a lecturer in history at the University of the Witwatersrand and a member of the Johannesburg Joint Council and the Institute. And there was GK Hemming, a popular lawyer from the Transvaal region, who had opposed Bunting in the 1929 election for Tembuland.

'Peg' Ballinger won the largest majority because she fought on a platform repudiating the representation embodied in the Act. She became the most respected and forceful of the 'Native Representatives' and remained so until turned out, together with them, by an unappreciative Afrikaner Nationalist government twenty-three years later. That government was unappreciative because it had more contempt than Hertzog and Smuts for liberal opinion at home and abroad. By 1950, people like herself were no longer useful to white supremacy, since it had ceased to want to pretend to resemble anything like a democracy.

The shock and scandal of the 1937 elections was the Senate candidates — supported by most of the African leaders.

In Natal, there was Edgar Brookes, a moralising evangelist who had been professor of Native Law at Pretoria University. He now expressed regret at having helped Hertzog prepare earlier and tougher drafts of his bills but was inclined to favour their present form.

In the Eastern Cape was WT Welsh, the former Chief Magistrate of the Transkei, who, Basner felt, should have been representing the South African Police rather than the African population. As Chief Magistrate, Welsh had joined the police in harassing and obstructing Bunting during the 1929 Tembuland election campaign.[1]

In the Western Cape, there was Malcomess, a wealthy and benevolent supporter of General Smuts, whose United Party would have had to find him a seat if the blacks had not.

Once the challenge of JD Rheinallt Jones was announced, it seemed that no one would come forward for the Transvaal and Orange Free State. It was almost unbelievable that this mighty champion of the non-political should enter the arena, but once the press confirmed it not to be just a rumour, that was that. Every clergyman, black or white, would be his election agent. Every black headmaster and senior teacher in every mission school would be his canvasser. Every reader of *Umteteli* and the *Bantu World* would press his Chief or Local Council to confirm the opinion of the Native Affairs Department that Jones was the only possible choice for their Senator. Even if a few political malcontents in the urban advisory boards, with their meagre votes, stood out, anyone opposing him seemed bound to lose his deposit.

Born in 1884, the son of a minister in the Welsh Calvinist Methodist Church, Jones had come to South Africa not long after leaving school, at first to settle in Cape Town, and then to go to Johannesburg at the end of the First World War. After working for some time in a bank, he had become assistant registrar at the newly-constituted University of the Witwatersrand, which later came to house his Institute of Race Relations. Since its foundation, the Institute had (and has) proved a unique source of telling facts and figures about conditions in South Africa as well as being a nursery for able scholars and well-meaning social reformers — all this very largely due to the efforts of the equivocal Jones.

Although the Communist Party had been loath to abandon the notion of boycotting the Native Representative Council, it had not foreseen, and could not now ignore, the intervention of Jones in the Senate elections. The opportunity given by the electoral laws, which had to allow registered candidates to campaign in areas normally barred to anyone remotely resembling an agitator, could not be overlooked. A Communist did not care how few votes he got as long as he managed to get the Party line across about the exploitation of the working class and the shortcomings of bourgeois democracy. Losing deposits at elections was not a measure of failure but a fair price to pay in any suitable area.

The difficulty was that the people the Party would have liked to put forward — Moscow-trained functionaries — did not have the necessary qualifications. To stand as a Senator, you had to have been resident in a constituency for two successive years and own five hundred pounds worth of freehold property.[2]

No one thought of Basner as a candidate — except himself. He was virtually a newcomer, good material for the Friends of the Soviet Union and the Anti-Fascist League maybe, where intellectuals and bourgeois sympathisers could be expected to join workers in a common struggle to defend the Socialist Fatherland against Nazi aggression. He was not trained, nor was he the 'right type' to present the Party's image as the revolutionary vanguard of the forces creating a socialist state by means of the dictatorship of the proletariat. He had, after all, only recently been given permission to speak for the Party on the City Hall steps and join in punch-ups with the Greyshirts on the Reef.

Needless to say he never shared the Politbureau's estimate of his worth and competence. Nor did he share the general opinion of Rheinallt Jones's invulnerability. The cynicism, and contempt for the intelligence of the African people, with which apostles of non-political methods of bettering race relations now hurried to fill political vacancies, wakened an anger in Basner far greater than did the iniquities of the purchasers of Native Trust farms or of those chiefs and their retainers who acted as government informers and security agents.

He had not been surprised when the Institute of Race Relations abandoned its non-political posture to urge all white liberals and black leaders to help make the new laws work. What he had not anticipated was that its Director should take off his non-political clothes and reveal his nakedness on the public stage; claiming his own omniscience together with black gratitude as the reasons whey he should be elected senator representing the Africans of the Transvaal and Orange Free State.

Behind Ethelreda Lewis's plot to curb the militancy of the ICU, Basner saw Rheinallt Jones and behind Jones he saw the Chamber of Mines.

Basner had been tilting at the machinations of the goldmining industry and the hypocritical propaganda of its liberal supporters in the puniest, most personal way; contenting himself with endless debates and disputes with his clients and fruitless discussions within the Communist Party (which paid lip-service to economic analysis but seemed mainly concerned with internal witch-hunting or street-fighting with poor-white hooligans). He had recently married. His father had died in 1933 and his personal ambitions had been confined to earning money to keep his mother in comfort as well as to maintain his wife and himself and to writing a play about Leonardo da Vinci. His political ambitions had been limited to contributing to the defeat of fascism.

In the not-so-recent past, Basner had indulged (he now thought) in intellectual snobbery as well as a too-literal interpretation of Marx, by having a contemptuous attitude towards parliaments and all their works. One of his criticisms of Bunting had been that the latter was too fond of fighting elections, but since the passing of the Native Representation Act, Basner had become more and more persuaded that participation in a fake democratic process in order to show it up could have positive value. To reject it was to leave the field open to the other side, and so leave the public with its illusions intact. In later years, he was to go further, and thought that Lenin's greatest disservice to Marxism lay in this field. 'Bolshevik' tactics may have been an excellent recipe for winning the battle for power in Russia, but were fatal in their effect of losing the 'hearts and minds' of the majority of mankind (in Communist as well as capitalist countries) to dreams about the free nature of the capitalist world.

Now, anger at the bills probably gave him the courage which a sense of responsibility alone would not have done. His widowed mother would have to wait for a better house and Leonardo's scattered bones stay longer without the flesh he envisaged for them.

So it happened that it was not the Communist Party who put him forward for the Senate but he who told them he was a candidate. At the central committee meeting to which he was called, Basner pointed out that he was the only person with the requisite residential and property qualifications, and probably the only one with a chance to enrol enough support even to be nominated. As it was, they could either choose him or support him as an independent.

Not only was his semi-ultimatum accepted, but John Marks and Edwin Mofutsanyana both felt that his candidature would reinforce Edwin in a bid for a seat as an MRC.

There was indeed no great disagreement over Basner's standing — even a fair amount of approval. But the Party was mainly interested in the class struggle and wanted the campaign to concentrate on the towns. In his and Edwin's manifestos, the black proletariat should be urged to spearhead the South African revolution, just as it should elsewhere. For his own part, Basner countered that there was a chance to reawaken the spirit which had roused the whole African population before the advent of the Land Act in 1912. If the Congress had become mighty overnight, it could do so again. There was no proletariat ready to make a revolution. There was not even a trade union in South Africa's dominant industry — goldmining.[3] Land was the key issue for two-thirds of the people.

John Marks, a coloured schoolteacher born in Johannesburg, particularly agreed with these views. Edwin Mofutsanyana's acceptance of them was much more reluctant, for all that his roots lay deep in tribal society. Since, however, Edwin was to contest a seat that officially represented the towns and *dorps* of the Transvaal and Free State, his more orthodox approach did not need to conflict with Basner's (which perforce would be to a broader audience in the same provinces).

It was strange how differently those two close friends had been affected by their education in Moscow. The one, except for his Marxist outlook, remained a simple man who could fit into the humblest of rural surroundings. The other's tastes and habits had become so cultivated that he could no longer feel really at home in the world he knew best: Sophiatown, Newclare and Alexandra, the crowded freehold townships that still remained for black occupation in or just outside Johannesburg.

After it became known that Basner was to oppose the Director of the Institute of Race Relations, William Ballinger also came forward as a candidate for the Senate. By now the ICU was utterly defunct except for a few warring autonomous branches here and there and Ballinger was managing the South African section of the 'Society of the Friends of Africa', a British organisation established in 1926 by Winifred Holtby and Arthur Creech Jones and backed by the Fabians. It was designed to promote the social, economic and political development of blacks in various parts of the continent, and paid special attention to the development of trade unions. Under Ballinger, the South African section organised trade unions in the late 1930s and early 1940s, employing Self Mampuru and James Coka. His wife Margaret had joined her husband in this society, which seemed to have aims very different from those of Jones and his like.

The new entrant made Basner hesitate, and caused him some heart-searching. With Ballinger in the field (and openly asking him not to split the anti-Jones vote), why should he stand? He was not going to campaign as a propagandist for Marxism but to disclose the futility of race relations and the hypocrisy of non-politics. Above all, he was interested in animating the African people to fight again for themselves. Ballinger was a decent man, thought by many whites (including Communists), to be far better known than Basner. He professed to be a militant socialist, and had British friends and funds behind him. It was his job to be in politics and he would not have to abandon a practice and spend his own money as Basner would. His wife had declared that the best Native Representative had to be one who could prove the wrongfulness of a form of suffrage which deprived perfectly capable people of a chance to represent themselves. It could be assumed that William would act in the same spirit.

But try as he would, Basner could not get over his distrust of the Ballingers. Was it because he was a Communist? That could not be the only answer. Basner distrusted missionaries, negrophiles and do-gooders, and had a Marxist loathing for the kind of social democracy exported from Britain for colonial consumption.

In the end, he decided to eliminate Ballinger and tackle Jones on his own in a new version of David and Goliath where the champion of the Philistines would win for sure, but at the cost of an ever-increasing headache. Kadalie would have to be found, cleaned up and given a platform. The leonine orator of Nyasaland might be hoarse, but his growl would send such support as Ballinger could muster scampering into the undergrowth.

The elimination of Ballinger was obviously a matter of some importance insofar as it would make for a clear alignment of what forces there were against Rheinallt Jones.[4] This could only be accomplished (since Ballinger was determined to stand) in the nominations which were to precede the elections and which required exactly the same procedure as the elections proper.

To ensure that the chiefs and their headmen would have complete leverage, the regulations demanded that votes (of men only) would be cast in the districts in which an African's poll-tax was allocated and not his place of actual residence. Thus the towns, including cities like Johannesburg, Bloemfontein and Pretoria which were inhabited by about a third of the black population, had only a few thousand votes between them, whilst one chief in a tribal reserve could cast twenty thousand on the presumption that he stood for all the adult males who were born there. This was not only an electoral swindle but part of the comprehensive falsehood — now known as apartheid — which claimed that Africans in South Africa did not belong to urban areas but to black tribal homelands.

There were three kinds of votes and voters. First, an insignificant number cast by the majority decision of an urban location advisory board; secondly, a larger number cast by a majority of councillors in some country districts controlled by a local council of headmen rather than by a chief alone and thirdly, a very large number cast by individual chiefs. To have any chance of success, a candidate had to win chiefs to his side or he was wasting his time.[5]

It was manifestly intended, when the Native Representation Act was drafted, that there would be no real political contests. If practically all the votes belonged to the reserves, what was the point of holding meetings in the towns? If the actual votes were cast by the chiefs or local councils, what was the point of calling public meetings in their areas to address tribesmen who had no say of their own? Since a chief could always be disciplined under the Native Administration Act if he ceased to be *persona grata* with the Native Affairs Department, what was the use of coming forward for election unless you were *persona grata* yourself?

While this was the general position in all four Senate constituencies, it was absolute for Natal where there was only one real elector — the Paramount Chief of the Zulus — and almost the same for the Transvaal and Orange Free State where a few big chiefs in the northern and western Transvaal held dominating positions. (The largest bloc in the north was held by Sibasa of the Vendas, a man reputed to be eccentric to the point of mental instability.)

The initial task for Basner was to organise his office staff to include qualified lawyers to take over during his expected long absences on campaign, and to raise enough cash to finance it. He took in two partners, selling two-thirds of his interest. Now he, Edwin Mofutsanyana and John Marks could have an extra car between them and sufficient funds for travel, publicity and their own expenses.

They started by heading for the northern Transvaal and making the town of Pietersburg, surrounded by the largest tribal areas, their headquarters.

This was to be the first of a number of excursions, most of them, electorally speaking, hopeless. All three knew how overwhelmingly the odds were against them, but Basner for his part felt sure that Jones's coming victory would be pyrrhic. Edwin had fair hopes of a response from the towns and *dorps* which were his only personal objective, and they were together now in believing that they might act as a spur towards reviving the African National Congress, even if not a popular ardour for Communism. The Party had given them a free hand, and there was more rejoicing than despondency when they met in long sessions early in 1937 to prepare for their inevitable defeat. Some effort was made on Basner's part to find Kadalie, but to no avail.

They were very light-hearted, really. Quite young, in their early thirties, and not at all what might be expected of a Marxist echelon. Though they were certainly well-read and serious about world affairs and in deadly earnest about South African politics, they were also not averse to good food and drink and were always ready for whatever entertainment came their way.

In Pietersburg location there were two men who, although they controlled only a handful of votes themselves, had much influence with the chiefs in the neighbouring reserves. The one was MK Molepo, principal of the local mission school and the other Thema, an elder brother of Selope Thema, editor of the *Bantu World*. Both were old Congress leaders, and neither had succumbed to the philosophy of Aggrey and Rheinallt Jones. Both were now politically quiescent: Molepo because he did not wish to jeopardise his position with the missionaries, and Thema in order to retain his municipal licence to trade in the location.

In spite of their assistance, readily given in the form of letters of introduction and recommendation, the trips to see the chiefs were dismal affairs. The educated ones were adamant — Rheinallt Jones was their man. The uneducated ones, who held the biggest votes, were more polite — and more evasive. They felt that the Native Commissioner, who would preside over the election, would be very angry if they chose 'le-Komunisi'. Could they be assured that the ballot would be secret?

Worse than the actual canvassing was the trouble of reaching the chiefs ... and of getting away from them. Here Jones had the advantage. If he wanted to meet a chief all he had to do was phone the native commissioner, who would send a constable to fetch him to his office. Basner's group would have to make a long journey to a remote tribal area and travel the last few miles on a stony track to a hill-top or valley where the chiefs liked to build their houses.

Should the chief feel like it, he could keep his visitors waiting for hours for an interview and, if he was kindly disposed, hours afterwards, to taste his excellent home-brewed beer and hear his problems. If he was not a Christian (which was quite often) and got drunk (which was oftener), he would insist that John and Edwin remain behind to sample his women as well. To refuse was an insult which might lead to all sorts of unpleasantness. To accept meant that Basner (as a white), would have to wait in the nearest *dorp* hotel for his comrades to return, sometimes more than a night late, as courtesy required. He would complain loudly and bitterly, and so would they, being hungover, with clothes creased and shoe-leather scuffed on his behalf; and, of course, voteless for all that.

They were wasting their time and wrecking their already aged vehicles. (A boiling engine and ruined tyres seemed to mark every journey.) On the advice of a rare and remarkable supporter among the sub-chiefs, Frank Mogale, one of the younger ones, they decided to cut short their campaign in the north and make for the Orange Free State, where there were only two minor tribal reserves and where the ICU had left a residue of political jetsam and fossils in all the small *dorp* locations. 'The chiefs are convinced that Jones will get them land from the seven and a quarter million morgen General Hertzog promised, and you'll never talk them out of it,' was how Mogale summed things up.

They went south, then, to Kroonstad, the second largest town in the Free State after Bloemfontein, its capital. And in Kroonstad they found an old lion, Keable Mote.

Once one of Kadalie's leading lieutenants, Mote had met the end of his stormy political career when, in the early 1930s, the ICU's collapse had become complete. Brave and energetic, he had been responsible for the establishment and militant activity of numerous branches of the ICU in the Free State (as well as a few in his own birthplace, Basutoland). Headstrong and fallible, he had, in his lifetime, been accused — with some justice — of both extremism and perfidy. He had seceded, with his branches, after Kadalie's break with Ballinger, and had later vainly striven to reunite the ICU's scattered elements.

They had their work cut out to blow sparks of curiosity, then of interest, and finally of enthusiasm, out of those mostly elderly political cinders — Keable Mote and his cronies, clustered in a small, dark church hall in Kroonstad location to hear what their three visitors had to say. Then, as they grew less dispirited and cynical, they became helpful far beyond all expectations. Lists of teachers, self-employed artisans, clergy, general labourers, hawkers, in all the locations in the towns and villages of the Free State and southern Transvaal were produced. Pencilled on pages torn from a school exercise book, the names were those of men and women who had been office-bearers and organisers in the ICU or Congress. 'Concentrate on the women. Meet them first. They are the real fighters,' was Mote's final message.[6]

Basner and his two comrades returned to Johannesburg to consider new approaches and make new plans. And there, sitting in his office, Basner saw an apparition neatly dressed and cold sober — Clements Kadalie.

He was not quite the young Hannibal who had strolled down Africa from the hills of Nyasaland to conquer the only land worth his attention but his strong face, seamed from a thousand days of stress and dissipation, still had enough authority and intelligence in it to reveal a born leader of men. He was forthright in saying at once that he had not come to champion their cause or rally to it the old cohorts of the ICU whom they hoped to revitalise. At the All-African Convention, he had favoured an electoral boycott, and was still of the same mind. But WG Ballinger was entering the field against Jones and Basner. So — if wanted — he was at Basner's disposal.

He was wanted all right. Whatever his motives (or Basner's tactics, for that matter), he was capable, even now, of reminding hundreds of people that power could lie within themselves.

Also in Johannesburg were a number of other very different old stalwarts who decided to lend Basner — if not his party — their support. Among them, LT Mvabasa was both typical and particularly influential. In his passionate younger days, during the 1914-18 war and for a while after that, he had actively engaged in trade unionism through the agency of the Industrial Workers of Africa, a short-lived but militant organisation encouraged by Bunting and other white socialist precursors of the Communist Party.[7] He had been managing director of *Abantu-Batho*, the Congress paper, and in the twenties had been an enthusiast for the pan-African ideals of Du Bois and Garvey. A continuous office-holder in the Congress since its inception, he had also been a prominent figure in the recent All-African Convention.

Now, after a lifetime of participating in squabbling conferences and disastrous cap-in-hand deputations to governments at home and abroad, together with all the financial miseries of an ill-run national movement, he could best be described as a sardonic moderate. He was ageing, and professed himself to be as well-acquainted with his own shortcomings as with those of everyone else of his generation.

He was a political war-horse, however, who could not but say 'Ha ha!'

at a chance of battle — sniffing menace in white paternalism with an intuition born of experience; revolting at the thought of his people passively accepting as their representative a man capable of swallowing the double fraud of the Hertzog Bills. And he had a very shrewd appreciation of the opportunities the contest provided for canvassing on behalf of Congress.

When Basner complained about the chiefs, and how different they were from those whom Congress had recruited to resist the Land Act in 1912, Mvabasa denied it. 'The difficulties were just the same in those days,' he said, 'but we taught the people to teach the chiefs'.

How elementary! The pressure of the people. Why had it been forgotten in dealing with the chiefs? Why had the Communist Party ignored it? Why had no one referred to it at the second Bloemfontein Convention? Like other Communists, Basner had only thought of 'the people' in terms of workers in towns (potential trade unionists) and peasants in the country (bemused by missionaries or their tribal heads).

When his mind started working, it was easy enough. He would deny that the vote belonged to the chiefs and local councils — even to the advisory boards. He would maintain that it was held in trust by them for their people and must be used as their people said it should. This could turn the Africans into something other than the impersonal counters contemplated in Hertzog's Native Representation Act. A disreputable farce could even now become a real means of popular expression.

Off again they went, the three of them, to the Free State, campaigning in an election they could not win, addressing an electorate that was not there.

12

SEEDS IN NEGLECTED SOIL
(1937)

The results of Basner's campaign in the Orange Free State were as Frank Mogale and Keable Mote had predicted.

There, the black population of little more than half a million was scarcely a fifth of that of the Transvaal and its votes amounted to a negligible 70 000 or so against a total for the two provinces of some 470 000. It was quite detribalised (except for the two small reserves of Witzieshoek and Thaba Nchu), and road communications were easy. Bloemfontein, the only really big town in the province, had a relatively good native location administration and amenities existed there that were absent everywhere else. Basner and his comrades were tempted to save time and travel by summoning delegates from the dozens of smaller places to rally there.

In Bloemfontein, however, they met with a serious obstacle: not in the usual form of the white authorities, but in Thomas Mapikela — he who had so dramatically helped break the boycott of the elections adopted at the All-African Convention of 1936. Old, well-to-do and tough, he was a leading Joint Council figure and supporter of Rheinallt Jones and was now himself contesting a seat on the Native Representative Council. His position was so entrenched that Basner's local supporters found it impossible to hire a hall or find private accommodation for the influential villagers and vote-wielding advisory board members they wished to call together.[1]

The strategy they planned had to be abandoned and Basner and his local friends were forced to go into the countryside to visit as many *dorps* as they could.

Basner soon had cause to be grateful to Thomas Mapikela for elbowing him out of Bloemfontein and into the *dorps*. If the number of Free State votes was negligible, the region was bountiful in experience — experience which would stand him in good stead in the next few weeks and in coming years. Above all, Mvabasa's advice about teaching the people to teach their leaders — half-forgotten amid dreams of big meetings in Bloemfontein — began to bear fruit, if only as far as the advisory boards were concerned.

He started with towns like Harrismith, Witzieshoek Reserve (now the 'homeland' of QwaQwa), on the mountainous Basutoland border and Ladybrand, a convenient village for Thaba Nchu Reserve.

He would be introduced to a teacher, a beer-brewing widow, a carpenter . . . who would remember the glories of Congress or Kadalie but knew nothing of the Institute of Race Relations. In a few hours, arrangements would be made for an evening meeting in a little independent African church. Most of the audience would be women, crowded on benches, with babies on their backs. Only a few, elderly men would come, the others being tired from a day's work and the long trudge back to the location. The residents also needed to be careful. Their residential permits were a privilege not a right, and they might lose them if the authorities should decide that the meeting was illegal.

The superintendent, with a couple of black policemen, would be waiting at the door asking questions. Basner would produce a Government Gazette showing that he was a candidate in terms of the Native Representation Act and was entitled to enter any location or other Native area for election purposes without a permit. The superintendent would need a torch to read it, because there was no electricity and the only light came from guttering candles on a table on the platform.

By this time the audience would be shuffling its feet, singing a hymn, or calling on the police to go away and let things begin. The superintendent would argue that the Gazette referred to Basner and not anyone accompanying him and Basner would want to know how he could conduct a meeting without interpreters. He would begin to wrangle, then turn his back to get to the platform. It would not be safe for the superintendent and his constables to stop him, and they knew it.

Edwin and John could easily fit Party propaganda to the grievances of their semi-urban hearers. Passes, the laws against beer-brewing, restrictions on lodgers (which effectively tore families apart) and the high cost of transport, were the same issues everywhere. It was not hard to arouse feelings and to suggest working-class action over such matters.

Basner's role had to be different. He was a candidate for two provinces which together contained nearly half the African population of the whole country, of whom about two-thirds did not live anywhere near real towns. It was, he felt, his task to raise national issues which would expose white racist policy in terms of its fundamental aim: to supply cheap labour. He saw no reason to emphasise (to those who knew it better than he) the injustice of blacks carrying passes when whites did not, but dealt intensively with the destination to which the pass system was driving them.

'How do you approach political economy with an audience of mothers?' he wondered. 'Talk about babies,' was the answer. 'Ask how, and for what, they are being reared. Whether, or for what, they are being taught. What is their future, and why?'

He only had one speech, which he was to repeat over and over. Though it was directed at the women, the men absorbed it just as well. He told them that their children did not go to school because it was ordained that they should be menials when they grew up — in kitchens, on mealie fields, and deep underneath the ground. He scarcely needed to tell them that their infant sons would be humiliated and brutalised, that their daughters would be skivvies or prostitutes and shebeen queens serving the migrants on the mine compounds of the Witwatersrand. He told them that their husbands, fathers and grandfathers were called 'boys' because they were paid a boy's wages and not a man's. He told them they lived in municipal locations under permit so that when they and their men became too old to be of use as workers they could be sent away to die — anywhere. He ran through the gamut of their lives to explain that racism had little to do with the colour of their skins and a lot to do with starvation wages. As for the dividends of apartheid — he did not need an accountant to describe them.

It was demagogic but it was the truth, and as real to his listeners as the lightning and the rain outside the church hall on many a stormy night when the candles flickered in the draught and sobs accompanied his perorations. He would raise his voice to shout that it was time to stop crying and drive their men into Congress and trade unions and make them strong. Then they would sing *'Nkosi sikelel' iAfrika'* and *'Morena boloka sechaba sa eso'* — 'God save Africa', 'Lord save our land'.

Five years later, when he had reached the Senate, Basner made amends by vowing never again to end a speech with a peroration but now he could not afford to be so fastidious. His words had to reach ears which would not hear him unless they were repeated powerfully by those who did.

With the help of a clergyman who attended a meeting of his in

Harrismith, he was able to contact Chief Charles Mopeli of Witzieshoek in the town, and so was spared a tiresome trip into the mountains and some precious time. He found the Chief a gentle and educated man given both to prayer and drink, perhaps, but very conscious of the responsibilities of his office. Also, he was the doyen of the Joint Council movement in the Harrismith district and it proved pointless to suggest to him that, since Rheinallt Jones was against political action, it would be a shame to force him into political office.

Basner gave Witzieshoek up as a bad job, and so missed getting to know the militant headmen and people of a tribe that was to struggle fiercely against the Land and Trust Act for many years to come.[2]

In the Thaba Nchu Reserve, which came into being because a past chief, Moroka, helped the Boers in their wars with the Basotho, he had better luck.

Dr JS Moroka was a sub-chief among the Barolong people. He was a rarity in that he was a medical practitioner, considerably interested in making his own living, but also eager that his followers should become prosperous through scientific and businesslike farming and good education.

Fundamentally a moderate, even a conservative, Moroka still understood why the Institute of Race Relations was dangerous for Africans and why the policy of the Congress leadership, with its stress on elite black negotiation with the government, was both weak and wrong. In later years he would also become President-General of Congress and a member of the Native Representative Council but could never bring himself to make politics his life-work. Meanwhile, he had no more power to influence the vote from his reserve than did young Chief Frank Mogale in the north.

If the foray into the Free State would not bring in more than a few thousand votes, Basner could still return to the Transvaal feeling sure that nearly all the locations except for Bloemfontein would be for him. The second largest, Kroonstad, was his and Edwin Mofutsanyana's after tremendous efforts by Keable Mote.

In the Free State, aside from the two small reserves, the locations attached to the white *dorps* were the only homes the people had in spite of the official myth that all Africans belong to tribal areas. Here they lived (and, of course, on the white farms around them) and here he hoped that his comrades and he had left political seeds which would germinate and grow taller and stronger than those of the ICU to strengthen Congress and overrun everything Rheinallt Jones represented.

Back in the Transvaal, with the nominations for the elections-proper approaching, they continued to concentrate their energies on the towns, large and small, though distances were so great that they could not often go far beyond the Witwatersrand. At a couple of lively meetings Basner and Ballinger came together to argue their own merits as stone-throwers against the gold-plated Jones but otherwise it was the Free State all over again, except that in and around Johannesburg the locations were much bigger. Considerable crowds were ready to forgather in the open air, and these consisted of many men as well as women.

The preliminary vote took place in March. Basner did not get the support of a single chief, and if the Communist policy in his platform was of any influence, it could only have been negative. At that time, at the bidding of Moscow, the Party had abandoned its previous wholesale anti-imperialist slogans in order to persuade such nations as Britain, France and the US to unite with the USSR in combating the fascism and aggressive aims of Germany, Italy and Japan. This had made the Party very unpopular, even in Johannesburg.

Poor Mofutsanyana received one of the lowest totals, and certainly felt it was because he had stood by the Party line. Though there was much truth in this, he also suffered the handicap of being a poor public speaker. His physical health was bad — so much so that his tall body was almost cadaverous from a tubercular condition which he ignored with all the fatalism of an African peasant. Greatly respected by everyone as a committee man, he lacked the common touch in large gatherings where his sense of humour and feeling for tribal tradition concerning everything except politics failed to come across.

Jones had an overwhelming count of 305 333 followed by Basner with 77 349. Ballinger was a complete loser, with 4 757, and was obliged to retire, much to the pleasure of Kadalie, who rightly took a great deal of credit for this himself. The three campaigners now had little time, money, or indeed, energy left for battling in the reserves. They did, however, return to the north for a while, if only to take final advantage of the freedom to hold meetings which remained to Basner as the sole surviving Communist candidate.

Thereafter, they confined themselves to speaking in a few large urban areas and to sending roneoed leaflets and manifestos through the post.

In Pietersburg, which had a relatively large and well-developed location, they again took advantage of their two friends Thema and Molepo who were highly thought of in the district.

Thema, who was ageing, found it hard to move about, so most of the chiefs and local councillors from the neighbourhood who had difficulties of one sort or another would come to his house for advice. Younger men, too, from the tribal lands would visit him when their business in town was finished, to drink liquor (from which most of his income came) and listen to his stories about early political struggles.

MK Molepo, the school principal, and his wife were very active people. She was the nurse for the location, and when chiefs or their headmen came to Pietersburg, some would bring a sick child or a pregnant wife to Mary Molepo for attention. He was experienced both in politics and the skills required to cope with the psychology of whites and could also be relied on to give sensible advice on matters ranging from the problems of a rural school to the best places to buy good seed corn.

An understanding was reached concerning Thema's and Molepo's present function. Their approach would be based on Mvabasa's simple but seminal remarks about the people teaching their leaders. They would no longer press the chiefs to change their minds and vote for Basner but would try to persuade them that it was their duty, as trustees, to stage gatherings to which the various candidates could be invited to make themselves known among the tribesmen they wished to represent.

Of course the three of them knew that Rheinallt Jones and the NRC candidates who supported him would never come to such gatherings but they felt sure that, once they had an audience, their own presence and words would begin a process of political fermentation.

So successful was this tactic that they found it impossible to attend all the meetings Thema and Molepo managed to arrange.

A tribal meeting is for men, mainly middle-aged or old, who are not away working in cities or herding the cattle. Those women who come, stand well back on the fringe. There was little point in discussing babies and, since the men were mostly peasants, not much in discussing wages. Basner did not feel it important to talk about organising trade unions in the event of the men leaving their own areas to seek work in towns, though he conceded the right of his two comrades to do so. It was even difficult to speak about the goldmines because the proportion of men recruited for the mines in the northern Transvaal was not as high as that in, for instance, the Eastern Cape.

His only telling message was that the Native Land and Trust Act was a swindle even greater than the Native Representation Act. Ownership would pass from the tribes to the Trust, bringing with it cattle-culling, ploughing restrictions and limits to collecting firewood without compensation to tide anyone over. Little new land would be bought, because the likes of 'Dop' Naudé's client were already making it too expensive. What would be bought would be barren and waterless — owned by absentee farmers or by mining companies for the sake of mineral rights — and already full of African squatters who would then constitute a new impoverished population to add to their own.

The chief and his councillors would listen quietly and gravely, plainly worried. Their followers would stand up and mutter agreement, accepting that Basner spoke the truth — not so much because they believed that he knew the government's plans as because they already knew its record.

Those few meetings had an impact which seemed to reach the Native Affairs Department and the Institute of Race Relations at one and the same time. Official intimidation and obstruction became formidable despite the legality conferred by the electoral rules.

Suddenly, messages went out to chiefs and local councillors to come to the Native Commissioner's office in Pietersburg to meet the candidate for the Senate, Rheinallt Jones.

The invitations were brought by police constables — trudging or riding on horseback through the bush — on official letter-heads, in the most polite language. Every voter knew that he or his medical certificate had to arrive or his Supreme Chief, the Governor-General of South Africa, would be inclined to send a different sort of invitation.

On some of these occasions, not only the Commisioner but the Secretary of Native Affairs might attend in person. They would sit next to the beaming candidate who would unfold large maps. They would call upon him to state solemnly that the areas marked in red would be acquired by the government and handed over to the tribes.

When Basner heard the news he knew that the gods would deliver Jones into his hands . . . in five years' time. The man had become a hostage for the good faith of a faithless regime which had been treacherous and remorseless to the African people since the Anglo-Boer War. Nobody would be able to ransom him, not even the Chamber of Mines, with all its treasure.

13

BEDEVILLED TIMES

The final results were announced in the middle of 1937 and, on the face of it, the size of Basner's poll against that of Jones signified nothing but a resounding defeat: 66 234 to 404 447 — worse than in the nominations. Yet for those who were interested and knew the tenor of events, it had been a remarkable triumph. Basner was not surprised at his good showing and his various black collaborators — also unsurprised — were delighted to know that all their hard work and confidence in African political intelligence had been justified. Together, they celebrated his defeat by holding a party.

The white Communist leadership was both delighted and surprised, although they agreed for once with the Trotskyists centred in the Cape, who ascribed the support for Basner to his popularity as a lawyer. Journalists, together with those white candidates who had succeeded in the other two provinces, were puzzled, perhaps more than anything else, over Ballinger's unhappy disappearance in the early stages.

The people in Jones's camp, black and white, were better informed and more realistic. No longer able to regard Basner as a sort of backsliding David with nothing in his scrip attacking a servant of the

Lord whom he mistook for Goliath, they recognised him to be a formidable Philistine who had bespattered the temple of race relations with political droppings. Jones's victory had to be a hollow one in the eyes of intelligent men in high positions like DL Smith, the Secretary for Native Affairs, or W Gemmill, manager of one of the two vast labour recruitment agencies for the goldmining industry. They were perforce aware that Basner had gained practically all the advisory boards in the Transvaal and Orange Free State, had only lost Bloemfontein by the casting vote of its chairman, Mapikela, and had very narrowly failed to win over some of the largest local councils in the rural areas which represented nearly a hundred thousand votes. Their man, therefore, could not speak for the Africans in the towns, whose political significance nationwide was substantial. He could only speak for the captive or corrupt layer of chieftainship which kept the tribal Africans in restless and sullen submission.[1]

To Basner and his friends, however, it now began to seem no more possible to follow up their success than for their opponents to repair their fences. They had fought an election in the name of the African National Congress and Congress alone should have reaped its fruits. But its national leadership, though soon to be freed of Dr Seme, was so timid, loaded with illusions about possible changes in government policy and rendered so passive by its links with the professional white negrophiles that it appeared unable to move towards any mass formation.

They fell back to wait for the seeds they had sown to grow unattended and dispersed, pleased enough with their achievement, but unhappy and frustrated over its probable aftermath. Mvabasa returned to his parochial politics in Johannesburg (in Pimville, the oldest of its locations, named for Howard Pim), Kadalie to his favourite shebeens, Thema to his rocking chair in Pietersburg (reading with indignation his brother's editorials in the *Bantu World*), Molepo to implement a curriculum he disapproved of in the mission school of which he was principal and Basner to the sight of a desk laden with unanswered letters and a waiting-room full of anxious upturned faces.

Edwin Mofutsanyana went to rest for a while in Basutoland. Quiet as he was, and when his health allowed, he had, during the elections, shown a surprising ability to merge into a tribal background and there to wage a down-to-earth campaign more effectively than the ideological warfare for which he had been trained. To Basner's mind neither Edwin nor John Marks (fond of lively parties, strong drink and strong polemics) was ever again to be as unquestioning of Communist Party dealings with non-Party people as they had been before their shared experience campaigning away from the large towns.

John was the only one of them to embark immediately on strengthening his connections with the African National Congress. But this was the consequence of his association with a most incongruous individual.

RV Selope Thema had headed the list of twelve Africans elected to the Native Representative Council, followed by nine others who thought much the same way — Joint Council and Institute of Race Relations men who would work in harmony with the officials and government nominees on that body. An exception was AM Jabavu — like others of his family, a liberal in the old Cape tradition. Another was RG Baloyi.

Richard Baloyi was a very uncommon African, but only because he was rich: a businessman whose interests included a bus company in the freehold black township of Alexandra, near Johannesburg. During the election, in which he was a candidate for the Transvaal rural seat on the Council, he had found it useful to hang on the coat-tails of Basner's associates, but was also said to have been free with presents to a number of chiefs. He was a choleric, bull-like man, ignorant but wily, who had been a prominent member of Congress for years, though it was hard to say what he stood for there. In a poverty-stricken movement, however, with leaders little better off than their followers, Baloyi (and perhaps Mapikela) was a person who could be turned to for funds in personal or organisational emergencies. Furthermore, he was deemed capable of managing accounts, even if only by employing qualified persons to do so.

John Marks, who constantly had financial problems, had recently found it a matter of survival to work for Baloyi as his secretary, in addition to accompanying Edwin and Basner during stages of the election. Needless to say, this not only meant that the Communist Party's candidates were occasionally neglected, but that John's duties as a Party functionary were neglected too. He was expelled in disgrace.

What followed from this unpromising and deplorable situation was classically ironic. Loosed from the bonds of discipline, he concentrated his trained mind, experience and revolutionary temper on revitalising Congress, especially in the Transvaal.

The elections over, Richard Baloyi and Thomas Mapikela had joined forces with their own political intentions in mind. Though they were both the very reverse of revolutionaries, they both liked and respected John. They had become convinced that a well-organised national movement was the only arm which could add muscle to normally useless negotiations with government. They had energy, which would be enhanced by the freedom their election to the Native Representative Council gave them to travel freely and hold meetings legally. John was as valuable to them as they were to him.

Within six months, even Thema had become converted to the idea of re-animating Congress. It would seem that he, too, had become aware of how the wind was blowing. Similar moves were afoot in the other provinces, whose sections of Congress had always been more lively than its central organisation. Their Presidents — John Dube in Natal, the Rev James Calata in the Cape and Mapikela in the Free State, may only have differed in the quality of their conservatism, but were all highly capable men now in a mood to work. And in the Transvaal, the leadership of SP Matseke was refreshingly upstanding and radical.²

John Marks found himself in at the beginning of a painfully slow but definite improvement in South African black politics.

It was hard for Basner to settle down because he had tasted blood. (There is no better way to describe the mood of a political animal who has been as close to its prey as he — and in his first chase.) But he had other reasons for dreading a return to his former routine.

He had not become a lawyer out of respect or liking for the profession. It had been an easy way of earning a living whilst trying to supply elementary justice to a section of his fellow beings denied it by the brutal indifference of their rulers and the rapacity of incompetent practitioners. As this position changed (with an awakened sense of responsibility in a new generation of lawyers), his services were growing less necessary. His own practice, however, was growing again and habit and the need for income could take over where sentiment and social duty left off. The prospect was far from attractive.

At the same time he did not look forward to long, dreary and acrimonious meetings of the Communist Party, nor to the legal and other chores it demanded of him. The executions of Zinoviev and Kamenev had taken place in Russia during the excitement after the 1936 All-African Convention and the first Moscow Trials while he was busy with the election. He had paid little attention to their meaning. But now there had been a second series of trials and executions and he had time to brood over them and even link them with his past distress at the decision to divide the Friends of the Soviet Union into two racial organisations.

At any other time in any other country than South Africa (he later believed), he could not have stomached the moral and intellectual corruption which the Moscow regime was asking its adherents to swallow. But, if he and others of his comrades were not innocent or ignorant, they were helpless to express their revulsion without abandoning political action against intolerable tyranny and exploitation at home. The Labour Party had a colour bar and its slogan was still 'White Workers of the World, Unite'. Liberalism was not a creed for radical reform, but for betrayal. Should he resign, he would have to sit in an armchair like old Thema in Pietersburg (but reading left-wing literature), or perhaps, just for company, travel to Cape Town to join the white Trotskyists who held seminars in which they polemicised strenuously with one another, and led a rich social life amongst Malay and coloured intellectuals.

He had no quarrel with the Communist rank and file. The Africans offered courageous and devoted service in all the tasks assigned to them in the fight against racial discrimination, often at risk to life and limb in the same way as they would have done had they remained solely in Congress or the ICU. In the Transvaal, a number of young white men and women, mainly students from the University of the Witwatersrand, who had recently joined, really cared about practical matters such as organising factory meetings, confronting the Greyshirts and conducting night classes for black illiterates. These new members were largely middle class (and so in some cases looked tentatively towards Basner for a lead) but there were also Afrikaner workers from the secondary leather, garment and distributive trade unions, who were on perfectly happy terms with both Africans and middle class English-speakers.

Basner's difficulties — which were shared by many people in the Party at that time — were with the leadership. It numbered no more than a dozen individuals at the most — arrogant, dogmatic, aloof and dictatorial. Some of them were newcomers to the country who seemed neither to know nor to want to know about local conditions. Others, having returned from study periods in Moscow, had come back with commissar complexes. They all lived simply enough but acted and talked as if power within the Party was the most desirable and important acquisition open to a human being. They were not elected but were chosen abroad and no one except themselves knew by whom. But they were The Party — as Basner had to explain to some African members who wanted him to join them in forming an independent South African party. They spoke in the name of the Comintern, the world-wide authority of the Communist movement. If they expelled you, you were *out*, no matter how much local support you commanded. If you set up your own movement, you would end up (like others who had tried it in the United States) frustrated and a nuisance to the working class.[3]

The United Front policy of the Comintern, so stringently followed by the leadership in South Africa, had caused so many failures and so much heartache that, by 1938, even Edwin Mofutsanyana's faith and principles were shaken. He proposed that the Party should divide along racial lines — a sad mirror-image, it might seem, of the style of the Friends of the Soviet Union, but this time the reason was to avoid the need for black members to be inhibited by the toning-down of USSR anti-imperialism from acting on behalf of their own people. His proposal was turned down but, as the culmination of a painful situation, it was in part the cause of a decision to move the Party headquarters in the following year from Johannesburg to Cape Town — a thousand miles away — and so relieve internal tensions in what was now the country's political centre.[4]

The Greyshirts were more evident in the streets every day, preparing to celebrate the centenary of the Voortrekkers: not so much to honour the past as to hail the future of the First Reich of Apartheid. During that time of rising tempest throughout the world, there could be no place for him, Basner felt, except among his quarrelsome comrades. He spent many hours exercising his brazen lungs and foghorn voice on the Johannesburg City Hall steps and in public squares in country towns like Bethal and Standerton in the highveld of the Transvaal, where the Greyshirts assembled. There was very little opportunity for a carry-over from the electoral campaign, and his legal work gradually became confined to cases arising from the Native Land and Trust Act, with his partners undertaking more and more of the rest.

His notable showing against Jones had given him a higher position in the Party, and a stature in the eyes of many who in the past either did not approve or did not know what to think of him. The 'bolshevik' faction in the Central Committee was therefore compelled to include him in its policy-making discussions. He had always been their best public speaker, but as a usefully left-wing bourgeois lawyer. Now he was billed as the main Communist rhetorician. For perks, he had the front seat next to the driver in the crowded lorries which carried the Anti-Fascist League supporters into the country, and became a popular figure at social evenings. Simultaneously, he was bored with his personal and professional life and politically confused and depressed.

At some time — probably only weeks after the 1937 election — his state of mind became such as to persuade him to go abroad, though for how long, he had no idea. What he thought he most wanted was join the British contingent of the International Brigade fighting in Spain. He dreamt of Spain and itched to put up a case to senior Communist functionaries in Britain and France for a change of South African policy. He also, perhaps, just wished for a break. But the break proved to be a very short one — two months at the end of that year.

In London he met a blank indifference from Harry Pollitt, the British Communist Party secretary, to black aspirations and problems. In Paris, he found it taken for granted that the Spanish Civil War was already lost and a disturbing meeting with Dolores Ibarruri ('La Pasionaria', the revolutionary orator) caused him to doubt Comintern motives in Spain as much as in South Africa. An encounter with André Marty confirmed his dismay. That once courageous Communist leader seemed actually deranged. Having attempted to discuss the dilemmas of the South African Party with Marty, only to be told to proceed forthwith to Moscow to do so, Basner hurriedly cabled his office in Johannesburg to cable back that his return was urgently required. (He doubtless had in mind three other, and far more orthodox, persons than he, who had disappeared when on similar excursions.[5])

The day after Britain declared war on Germany in September 1939, the 'Fusion' government in South Africa split. Hertzog was for neutrality and Smuts for war and the House of Assembly voted by eighty votes to sixty-seven in favour of the latter, who duly became Prime Minister of a government tough enough to keep the local Nazis under control. Twenty-six days later, Russia announced its pact of friendship with Hitler and invaded Finland.

Soviet troops goose-stepping through the mists towards Helsinki cleared Basner's head of mists which had been swirling in it for some time. He had swallowed Stalin in Moscow and the bigots in Johannesburg as disciplinarians and André Marty and Harry Pollitt as Comintern colonial experts. He had swallowed the expulsion of militant and honest black and white comrades for right-wing and left-wing deviations. He had been prepared to swallow anything to save the socialist fatherland.

Even now, he needed no Red foreign minister to advise him that Chamberlain and other western leaders would mark time in a phony war in the hope that Hitler would deploy his full strength eastward. He needed no Red marshal to instruct him how important the terrain of Finland would be in the defence of Leningrad. But a socialist fatherland that could trade terrain for the honour, courage and solidarity of the whole working class of western Europe and of all decent people everywhere, was one which could not be saved unless Hitler's own madness destroyed him. There was no longer any point in accepting the Russian brand of communism for strategic reasons, it had to be judged in terms of individual conscience. Basner's conscience dictated a letter to the Johannesburg *Star*, severing his connection with the Communist Party.

This did not mean that he ceased to believe in class struggle and the necessity for socialism — provided it was not high-powered, dehumanised state-socialism as in the Soviet Union and its satellites, or charity state-socialism as the British Labour Party sees it. Furthermore, he came to believe that anyone who leaves the Communist Party, even for the best of reasons, and joins its opponents in order to assail the corruption of its leadership and dogma, will end up deep in the opposite camp. In time, the CIA will get him, or the Church.

Things were to change a great deal before the Party in South Africa was declared illegal and dissolved in 1950 under the Suppression of Communism Act imposed by the Nationalist government of Daniel Francois Malan. In the nineteen-thirties the Party resembled the Soviet one of the Moscow Trials, ideologically if not in terms of power. By the late forties, a new, younger generation had taken over — still Stalinist, but more active and more knowledgeable about local conditions and readier to encourage the growth of a genuine black national leadership.

By that time, however, Basner had already been out of the Party for more than ten years and away from Johannesburg for several of them. Another ten years, and further changes took place within it of which he was not fully aware until the events following the massacre at Sharpeville in 1960 brought him once more into contact with its members — willy nilly — in Pretoria Central prison.

14

SPARKS AMONG THE STUBBLE

To be detested by many of one's recent political comrades as an open renegade is not pleasant, but more unpleasant to Basner was his realisation that a period spent in active politics weakens both the will and the capacity of an individual for any other kind of occupation. Besides (with a wife and small daughter to support), his living was earned in a profession which he found increasingly detestable.

Enlistment in the army could have been a respectable excuse for quitting both politics and law. Plenty of men were volunteering to fight Hitler and Mussolini, to defend their white motherland or Empire, or simply to seek change and adventure. An experienced drill-sergeant, however, would quickly have marked him down as a barrack-room lawyer going on for forty and consigned him to the cookhouse rather than combat abroad.

Later, in 1942 while in the Senate, he was naïvely (and to his great amusement) offered a colonelcy in the South African Army's 'Native' Military Corps. Since this body was not permitted to bear any arms, he could not contemplate supporting its recruitment despite his (and the ANC's) support for the war.

Meanwhile, a struggle had developed at home which occupied Basner's whole attention. The cases which had begun to dominate his practice had intensified the fury aroused in him by the Hertzog Bills. Alone among white radicals, he became deeply involved on a daily basis in 1941 in the terrible problems of the two-thirds of the African population who lived on the land.

Educated black conservatives were at one with orthodox Marxists of whatever race in putting a dose of something like contempt into the pity they lavished on the peasantry. The former, as Christians committed to British concepts of civilisation and democracy, deprecated pagan customs, clannishness and the manifest political weaknesses of tradition-bound chiefs and their tribesmen. The latter used different language to say the same thing but added to it the credo that revolution could only be initiated from within an urban proletariat.

It will be recalled that the second of the Hertzog Bills became the Native Land Trust Act in 1936. Predictably, its negative provisions were promptly enforced and its positive ones hardly at all. (When a South African government measure is called a Natives Land Act, it means 'no land for Africans', and when it is called a Native Trust Act, it spells perfidy.) A year later, it had been complemented by the Native Laws Amendment Act, designed to restrict the urban black population to those required for labour at any one time. The Act instituted municipal industrial censuses and gave the Minister of Native Affairs the power to order the removal of 'surplus' blacks from any town.

It would need biblical imagery to evoke what ensued.

There had been several years of great drought and with it, locusts to consume what the drought had not withered. In 1937, swarming after them, came tax-gathering police, armed with forty thousand summonses for failure to pay poll-tax in the starving Pietersburg district alone. Hunger and mindless harassment, even on such a scale, were not unfamiliar to the people in the Native Reserves, but the next affliction to strike them was something new: In 1939, the taskmasters descended upon them — 'Agricultural Officers', empowered by the Act to decide how many cattle could be owned and by whom and where and how much ploughing could be undertaken.

There was nothing inherently wrong in the stated aim of the Act: to vest all African land in a Trust to protect it against soil erosion caused by over-cropping and over-grazing. Tribal Africans (like most Afrikaner farm-folk), had not taken kindly to intensive methods of tillage or stock rearing and acute rural over-population and poverty did not improve their efforts. There was much to be said for appointing experienced agriculturists to take over the duty, hitherto assumed by Chiefs and their headmen, of defining and allocating arable fields and areas for pasturage.

There was nothing inherently wrong with the idea — if the Trust had been a real one and not merely yet another scheme to drive the peasantry into migrant labour. The land was shockingly eroded and needed rest and remedial measures for it to be saved but meanwhile, without alternative space being provided in which to grow food, how was a man to support his family? The cattle were poor scrub-beasts, over-many and destroying the soil; but if herds were to be cut down in a drastic manner, what substitute could there be for them in a society whose very basis was a cattle economy?

With sufficient extra land, expert assistance, tactful official behaviour and a true determination to be of service, there is no reason to believe that the government could not have achieved its professed aims. But there was no desire to effect a transition, only a desire to force as many cheap black individuals as possible into white employ, leaving their families behind them in the reserves. As long as their work was required, poverty would oblige them to go. As soon as they became redundant, the law would chase them home again.

If this sounds far-fetched, another portion of the Act must be mentioned. This provided for the compulsory removal of black tenants — 'squatters' — from white-owned land which the Trust did not intend to buy.

Miles of property in the vicinity of the reserves had been rented out to generations of Africans by absentee owners (largely mining companies), who had found it too unrewarding to merit exploitation by themselves. Among active white farmers, however, this practice had become a major grievance. They were chronically short of labour because of the miserable conditions and treatment they offered, and because of the value even the most indigent of squatter or reserve families placed upon their independence. Promises by government to buy more land for blacks implied an increase in such independence, and so were an additional threat to the labour-hungry farmers.

A sop for the farmers, therefore, had to be handed out by the Act, and this was to the effect that 'white' land occupied by blacks could be proclaimed as being for white occupation alone.

No one could have imagined that this step would be taken before the promised land became available, but so it was. District after district was proclaimed, and tens of thousands of squatters found their only refuge gone. Useless farms which whites would not cultivate and so had rented out were depopulated by eviction orders carried out by police. The Urban Areas Act of 1923, now fortified by the Native Laws Amendment Act, was invoked to forbid the men, women and children who lived there to move to, and find housing in, the towns. They had only two alternatives: to accept servitude on white farms or stream into the already crowded nearby reserves.[1]

Even with more and better land available, the agricultural innovations incorporated in the Act would have caused tremendous dislocation in tribal custom and ways of life in the reserves themselves.

In the past, when chiefs and their headmen allocated the mealie fields and parcelled out the grazing, disputes were frequent and fierce, but tended to be settled peaceably in tribal councils. In the circumstances of 1938 and after, with no extra land, an influx of evicted squatters and the appointment of ignorant and callous agricultural officers, the new regulations created havoc.

Nine years before the Hertzog Bills, the Native Administration Act had been passed, which began with these words:

> The Governor-General shall be the Supreme Chief of all Natives in the Provinces of Natal, Transvaal and Orange Free State, and shall . . . be vested with all such rights, immunities, powers and authorities in respect of all Natives as are or may be from time to time in the Province of Natal.

English-speaking Natal was the best model for the legislation then considered necessary, being as it was the *fons et origo* of really effective control over non-whites. Neither of the old Afrikaner Republics had anything as comprehensive or as suitable for the use of white supremacy as the Natal Code of Native Law, initiated by Theophilus Shepstone in British colonial days; and having been retained there after Union in 1910, it was extended to the whole country (except for the Cape) in 1927.

The Supreme Chief did not need any formalities, such as the rule of law flowing from Parliament, to govern nearly six million people:

> The Governor-General, as Supreme Chief, shall exercise all powers, authorities, functions, rights, immunities and privileges which according to the laws, customs and usages of Natives are exercised and enjoyed by any Supreme or Paramount Chief and which shall be deemed *inter alia* to include . . . powers to punish disobedience of his orders or disregard of his authority by fine and imprisonment or both fine and imprisonment.

In case it is imagined that the Governor-General thereupon started to travel in state through his various domains, holding *indabas* or *khotlas* (tribal meetings), the next section must be read:

> The orders and directions of the Supreme Chief may be carried into execution by the Secretary of Native Affairs, the Chief Native Commissioner, any Native Commissioner *or any other officer duly authorised by the Supreme Chief or the Minister of Native Affairs*. Any such person . . . shall be regarded as the deputy or representative of the Supreme Chief. (Author's italics)

In fairness to the legislators of old Natal and to the Parliament of 1927, including the Labour members of Hertzog's cabinet of that time, it must be pointed out that no deputy of the Governor-General was given the right to order one of his subjects to jump off a cliff or be impaled on stakes (Shaka's customary punishment for petty offences among his Zulus)[2]. Without a proper trial no one could be executed or imprisoned for more than three months at a time and the deputy could only banish a person from his home for life untried, or impose an individual or collective fine. It must also be said that as a purely administrative procedure only banishment was resorted to under Hertzog and his successor Smuts (a kindly tradition not followed by the prime ministers who succeeded them).[3]

The assumptions of the Native Administration Act provided the ambience in which the Native Land and Trust Act was to operate.

The agricultural officers assigned to the Trust by the Native Affairs Department turned out to be poor-whites, political supporters of extreme Afrikaner nationalism and failed farmers taken off the overseeing of road-mending and railway construction gangs. Made into super-chiefs, they pegged out boundaries, fixed cattle quotas, limited the amount of firewood to be cut, displaced settlements — behaving as if they were feudal lords on their own property (and provided with ample opportunities for bribery and favouritism to boot).

A poor-white, having lost the status he claimed as his birthright, would brook no nonsense from any black. Dissident tribesmen quickly found themselves in handcuffs and the real chiefs, who had also lost their status, were as indignant as the kinsmen who had quarrelled with their decisions in days gone by. Tribal backwardness had made for misery tempered by humanity; the new system was racially arrogant and the misery inhuman.

In many places, euphemistically described by officialdom as 'betterment areas', as little as four and a half acres of thin and stony soil were set as the maximum permitted per family for ploughing. Cattle were ruthlessly culled (often to the profit of the agricultural officers), which meant not only economic hardship but the wreckage of hopes of marriage for young people obliged by custom to obtain them for dowry.[4]

Arrests and imprisonment followed every trifling incident. Chaos was added to considerable inconvenience and a natural resistance to social change. From 1939 on, defiance and outright rebellion accompanied the Trust regulations wherever they came into operation.[5] Police raids, gunfire, threats of aerial bombing when squatters refused to leave their villages, protracted mass trials for assault and public violence all became a matter of routine throughout the northern and eastern Transvaal. The worst places were Sekhukhuneland, the white-owned farms in the Lydenburg district and Vendaland in the Zoutpansberg area, but the scene was little different wherever African tribes had been quietly established in the Transvaal and Free State since the Anglo-Boer War.

The Natives Land Act of 1913 had chastised the people with whips.

The Native Land and Trust Act of 1936 chastised them with scorpions.

From 1941 on, Basner became an itinerant defender in one mass trial of tribesmen after another in nearly every outlying district of the Transvaal and on the borders of the Free State. Some of them lasted weeks, and at one period he was away for months, with each of many cases immediately succeeded by another. He became a denizen of dismal hotels, surrounded by dreary commercial travellers. They at least went home for weekends, but on Saturdays and Sundays he was mostly in the local prison taking statements from prisoners, or consulting with their kinsfolk in the car, since naturally they were barred from meeting him on 'European' premises and their own homes could be miles from a negotiable track. Sometimes, when a very urgent matter demanded his presence in Johannesburg, he would brief a young barrister whose minimum fee, nearly twice as much as his, could not be charged to people seldom able to collect as much money to pay what he himself had to ask.

There was no solace in the bar of an evening, because it would usually contain a few drunken farmers, aggressively hostile to the citified attorney defending 'those bloody kaffirs'.

It was a miserable period, and once the novelty of learning how the Trust and its officers functioned had worn off, it was unrewarding in every sense of the word. True, he was far from impoverished because he had partners who earned well enough for themselves and him together. His name still brought plenty of custom to the firm even if the partners resented both his personal unprofitability and his absence and his clients complained of his failure to defend them in person. Implications and aspects of the Land and Trust Act which neither he nor Rheinallt Jones and the negrophiles had foreseen became tormentingly apparent. To rob Africans of their land had required no more than parliamentary draftsmen with a good education of Oxford or Leyden and experience in legislative double-talk, but violation of trust needed a police force and troops with guns, backed by magistrates who could skip through legal loopholes like trained circus poodles through hoops.

His physical discomfort in rural dorps was trivial enough, but the mental stress engendered by what he saw and heard there was not. Expression of his indignation and disgust in court, together with a forensic skill which occasionally led to acquittals, in no way relieved him of his sense of the futility of his efforts; rather they exacerbated it.

Just as he had on occasion in Johannesburg, he would try to dissuade the representatives of a community from wasting their all on cases which, even if won, could never release them from their tribulations. He would put it to them that the pains of further resistance could in the long run be more worthwhile. But the penalties to be faced by the accused were too harsh even for people who had been driven by despair. The longing for justice and for a mouthpiece to voice their wrongs, if only in a mean little courthouse, was too strong.

By 1940, all leading Africans and virtually all their sympathisers, including Jones, had recognised how total was the fraudulence of the Hertzog Bills. The ten million pounds voted for land purchase was nearly gone — into the pockets of the speculators, who had forced prices up as much as fivefold. The outbreak of World War II had given the Smuts government an excuse for freezing whatever funds remained and for postponing indefinitely the provision of more. Less than a quarter of the promised land had been bought — all of it stony and dry and already occupied by 'squatters'.

These general facts were known to liberals and leftists alike and became the subject of foreseeably fruitless remonstrances, taken to the highest official quarters.

The specific facts about coercion and revolt in the reserves, the 'new' already populated land and the farms in process of depopulation were known to the people who suffered there, but to hardly anyone else who might be expected to care, including Basner, who only learnt the full truth late in 1941.

The dearth of publicity was remarkable even for the South Africa of those days, where virtually the entire press ignored events among blacks unless they had significance for whites.

A small town like Pietersburg could be important enough as an administrative and agricultural centre to have its own newspaper, plus a stringer for a leading one in Johannesburg. Resistance to harassment by thousands of Africans in the neighbourhood of such a place, however, was no more likely to be headlined than the pressure of blades of grass against the tread of passers-by.

War news and the wartime shortage of paper certainly did not deprive the English or Afrikaner Nationalist press of all space for unimportant matters, but journalists were scarcely encouraged to interview blacks directly about anything at any time. If informants were required they would naturally be whites whose business it was to maintain suitable contacts. Since these could never be Reds, they had either to be officials or welfare workers of various kinds and in the countryside, those categories boiled down to police and employees of the Native Affairs Department on the one hand, and missionaries on the other.

As in all countries, the authorities, high and low had every interest in minimising disquieting events in their territories. In South Africa the missionaries, even though genuinely humanitarian, may similarly have hesitated to advertise ungodly recalcitrance in their flocks.

It must be kept in mind, however, that Smuts and his followers were at that time finding it much harder to control powerful and openly Nazi Afrikaners than helpless African menials. All whites professing themselves to be democrats and in favour of the war had reason to confine their concern to what was, after all, a vital matter of internal and external security. Perhaps, therefore, rural black turbulence, being of even less than usual consequence to editors and their readers, may just have been disregarded 'for the duration'.

So simple an explanation for so pregnant a silence seems hard to accept, but may well be true. How otherwise can one account for the ignorance of the whole spectrum of literate opinion in South Africa? The two conservative black newspapers in the Transvaal make no reference to the troubles in the north. The Institute of Race Relations publications are just as empty (and the more shamefully so because their avoidance of the subject cannot be put down in part to nervousness, as can that of the *Bantu World* and *Umteteli*).

The Reds had a press of their own, small and hard up though it was. It was not subject to racist inhibitions, credulous acceptance of government news handouts or timidity. Even so, Baruch Hirson, a painstaking researcher, has been able to find no more than seven articles in left-wing papers of those days giving evidence of the effects of the Trust Regulations on the reserves and the farms surrounding them. Only one of these articles appeared before 1939, and that was by a man named Alpheus Maliba, who, curiously, since he was then a loyal Stalinist, had it printed by the little Trotskyist paper produced in Cape Town. Of the remaining six, which came out in 1941, 1943 and 1945 in two Communist Party publications, three were by him. What other revelations there were came from Basner[6] and he, it would seem, could do no better than wait until March 1943, when he was able to speak in the Senate.

The Communists had gained considerable experience from the 1937 elections but could still only apply what they had learnt to the industrialised towns, and even there did not recognise that most of the blacks were only half-urbanised migrants. They had stepped up their efforts to form trade unions but could make few recruits among the temporary workers because they did not study or understand the background to many of their grievances. Only John Marks and Edwin Mofutsanyana had managed to discard enough dogma about proletarian dictatorship to listen with sympathy to tribespeople living in Johannesburg who complained of such matters as the ruinous effect of stock-culling on sons needing cattle to find wives. But Edwin was restrained by his party, and John by his involvement with general Congress politics and the formation of the African Mineworkers Union from taking any direct interest in rural affairs.

Alpheus Maliba was the solitary leftist who proved determined enough to dedicate himself to battling against the consequences of the Land and Trust Act, and he was someone uniquely at home with, and knowledgeable about, the society which the Act was despoiling. He was a Venda, from the remotest, largest and most backward of the Transvaal tribal reserves, encumbered by an old and degenerate chief and surrounded by farms filled with threatened squatters.

Born in 1901, Alpheus Maliba, like thousands upon thousands of others, had come from the country to the Witwatersrand in his twenties, to seek work. There, when he was already over thirty years old, he learnt to read and write at a night school founded by Eddie Roux and in the year the Hertzog Bills became law joined the Communist Party.

Even had its leadership been convinced of the worth of the formidable and dangerous task he was ready to undertake, lack of funds and of members capable of being useful to him would have set limits to the Party's collaboration. As it was, after bitter internal argument, some help was found for him, if only a little office space and clerical assistance, and, very occasionally, transport. He was thereby enabled, but only as late as in 1941, to gain really practical and whole-hearted backing from amongst those of his own and other northern tribespeople who lived in and around Johannesburg.

The backing came from an organisation innocuously called the Zoutpansberg Cultural Association. With its support he was able to strengthen the Zoutpansberg *Balemi* (Farmers) Association and a trade union which he had managed to establish, centred in the small towns of Messina and Louis Trichardt. These places, sixty miles apart, together dominated an immense stretch of country in the far north, but his activities extended hundreds of miles further — south-west to Pietersburg and south-east again to the Lydenburg district.

He and his supporters led demonstrations, strikes and passive and active resistance. Men ploughed their land where ploughing was prohibited. Squatter families refused to move. Women marched in protest against being obliged to plough and herd cattle because their husbands and sons had been driven away by the need to earn cash to support them and pay taxes.

Maliba was arrested several times, imprisoned and banished — as were innumerable and nameless brave and desperate people throughout the Transvaal — and after 1943 it became impossible even for him to continue.[7] Police and troops had been used to overwhelming effect. Hopeless trials arising from their resistance drained the meagre resources of the tribes just as the necessity to earn in order to exist drained them of their manpower.

Little was to happen in the Reserves between 1944 and 1948, but this was for a reason additional to the crushing repression the people had experienced in the previous years. The Smuts government became conscious that the war effort required some let-up in the administration of the Trust — if only to make South Africa more acceptable as a participant in the international anti-Fascist alliance. And, more important than such political wisdom was economic pressure. The war had opened new vistas for the expansion of secondary industry and there were indications that the Witwatersrand goldfields were petering out. Hence there was a certain relaxation of migrant labour policy and talk by Smuts and other white politicians about 'Christian Trusteeship' of the blacks. This comparative peace lasted in the countryside until the Afrikaner Nationalists took power in 1948, and in the wake of the discovery of huge new gold deposits in the Orange Free State. Then disturbances in the reserves began again, in some areas worse than ever.

To Basner, as to the people of the north, Alpheus was a truly heroic figure. Their paths often met, and they came to mean much to one another: Maliba, the stocky peasant, his round, very dark face brimming with intelligence, humanity and charming laughter in the midst of every hazard; Basner, the intellectual urban Jew, his naturally ruddy complexion the redder for the explosive temperament that tussled within him against his trained mind.

They could joke together, travelling through the endless thornveld, sometimes in the heat of the day, heading for a meeting or a trial, often at night on similar errands, or in order to steer Alpheus clear of the police.

Perpetually beset by the law himself, or helping others to contend with it, Maliba was both a consoler and a teacher. Basner could be persuaded that there was value in the skills his hated profession had given him because someone he so respected considered they were needed. Besides, apart from his expertise, his role as a white lawyer (and eventually as a Senator), enabled him for a while to give Alpheus easy access to people in prisons, locations and distant huts, since he could claim him to be an interpreter-cum-clerk. Later, when Alpheus became a marked man, hunted and ever in hiding, all that was left to them was the ultimate sanctuary of the motor car.[6]

In return, a special access of his own was given to Basner — to the thoughts and feelings of men and women belonging to a culture alien to him, who treasured skinny cattle for deep traditional reasons of self-respect and whose lives were passed in scrabbling for sustenance in sterile soil which they treasured above all because beneath it lay the bones of their ancestors.

15

CONSENSUS IN A POLITICAL WILDERNESS
(1941-1942)

With no new land and their followers (swollen by unwelcome squatters) reproachful or downright mutinous, the chiefs were enraged. Though only a few stood openly and bravely against the Trust regulations, they all had the same private object of wrath — their unfortunate map-peddling representative in the Senate, Rheinallt Jones. Basner felt it his duty, trying not to sound smug, to tell those who asked him that it was possible that, despite his warnings, Jones had been misled by the promises of the Secretary of Native Affairs and his officials.

But was he misled through natural stupidity? Or was he betrayed because it was part of his job to be betrayed? Was he a Simple-Simon-Doctor-Pangloss Jones? Basner never liked him enough to be sympathetic. If the Institute of Race Relations had not been a by-blow of the Chamber of Mines, and if the Chamber of Mines had not been a structure built on the groundwork of Cecil Rhodes and bolstered by

Lord Milner's Kindergarten and Campbell-Bannerman's Liberals, Basner might have softened sufficiently — in view of Jones's present and apparent misery — to believe him to be both a simpleton and an egregious optimist.

Even when he tried, Basner could not exonerate Jones for being foremost (together with Professor DDT Jabavu) in urging the Cape Liberal MPs to abandon the black franchise for the Hertzog Bills. He began to think, and with relish, of fighting the next election. For that, old allies had to be gathered together again and new ones enlisted.

When, many years later, Basner came to question what drove him to deal so harshly with people like Jones and William Ballinger, he wondered whether it was merely personal ambition combined with a Machiavellian flair for political strategy. He would have denied both at the time, he knew, but felt that he could not then have explained his denials as clearly as he could after close experience of Tanzania, Ghana and the problems of African unity during the 1960s. His own instincts, he believed, had told him in the thirties that what Africa needed was to generate and evolve its own political direction, and that the imperialist powers would wield every economic carrot and subversive stick to combat the rise of indigenous political consciousness and organisation.

In 1937, even the Communists and many of his trade union friends had been shocked when he proposed using Clements Kadalie to eliminate Ballinger from the elections. He had justified doing so on the grounds that William and his wife (for both of whom he had personal liking), preferred to be professionals in African politics rather than in the white sector where they could have been more usefully employed. But a deeper objection lay in their connections with the Fabian Society and the Labour Party in England. These two agencies, he considered, had proved as disastrous for the British working class as for the colonial world they purported to help but had only succeeded in manipulating to the advantage of more powerful interests. It took him ten years to modify his attitude towards the Ballingers. There was no doubt that Margaret Ballinger was the fiercest and ablest parliamentarian the liberal forces had produced. Her career had moulded her husband's to such an extent that when Basner resigned his Senate seat in 1947, he was ready to help William win it.

He also came to wonder whether the anger against Jones that still survived in him forty years later was an unjustified reflex that had lasted far too long. He would have liked to believe this to be so without falling back on *nil nisi bonum*, which he considered a practice as silly in recording the past as locking the stable door when the horse has gone. But he had always found the combination of moral rectitude and liberalism repellant, and in Jones he found a measure of both. By moral rectitude he did not mean religious faith and by liberalism he did not mean the midway position between conservatism and socialism. He simply had

Pharisees in mind, like those who troubled Christ or those Liberals in Britain who brought down Charles Stewart Parnell.

He had no objection to people saying, 'We of the Liberal, Tory, Labour, Communist political parties . . .' but *we liberals . . . we* conservatives . . . *we* socialists . . . *we* communists . . .' made him want to spit in their eye. A political position is one thing, he would maintain. Belonging to a sect — 'we chosen ones, enlightened ones, upright ones' — is another.

He swore he never heard Jones take up a straight political position, for the simple reason that he could not.

As for his own role, Basner wanted to see himself not as a leader but as an entirely temporary stimulator and spokesman. Not being inclined to underestimate his own ability to give impetus to others and represent them whilst they were gathering it, he thought this was possible. His aim would be to win a seat in the Senate; hold it for no more than a five-year term and in the process persuade his constituents to make him, and others like him, unnecessary. How far he succeeded in these aims, which would seem to have required a remarkable combination of arrogance and modesty, each reader may judge. Being an astute interpreter of politics, and therefore all too familiar with both the relevance and irrelevance of individuals to the texture and flow of political life, Basner eventually claimed for himself, with some arrogance, a modest degree of success.

The lunatic fragmentation of South African society makes for an equally lunatic fragmentation in the existence of every individual who lives in that country. Basner was no exception. He enjoyed sex and was not very happy in his marriage, but did not even contemplate having an affair with an African woman because, if casual, it would smack immediately of exploitation, and if serious, would spell utter ruin for both of them. He liked good food and comfortable living, but was aware that neither of these tended to be available to blacks. Even professional people and traders were out of touch with such amenities as delicatessen stores, being compelled by law to live in slums or concrete municipal pill-boxes and subject to insult in white shops. He was fond both of card games and of backing a likely horse, but never happened to meet a poker-playing African he wanted to win from, and punters on the race-course were as segregated by skin-colour as bathers in the sea and urinators in urinals. Classical music and play-going meant much to him, but concert halls and theatres did not even contain segregated seats (like parks and railway stations), perhaps because their offerings were assumed to be pure white by nature. Nothing pleased him more than to spend a few days watching game in the bush of the Kruger National Park, but even if any African family he knew shared the idea of such a holiday, there was no accommodation for them in the charming fake-primitive huts provided for white visitors at the cost a few shillings a night.

So, for what may be lumped together as the amenities and diversions of life, he made excursions into the white world. There, especially in his Communist Party days he could find a few men and women friends who tended to be more literary and musical than political by inclination. He also had some boon companions and knew a fair number of well-to-do intellectual hostesses (apt to consider both him and his opinions morally dubious but interesting), who invariably had well-trained black cooks.

To say he made excursions into the white world may sound odd of a man whose wife, child and home were in a white suburb, who stayed in white hotels when out in the country, whose kin, schoolfellows and professional colleagues were white, who spoke scarcely a word of an African language, and whose thinking was rooted in Europe. But it was so — and so also for the minuscule number of other whites whose lives resembled his. The great majority of his close friends had come to be black, and by far the greatest part of his time was spent in their world. (And very cheerfully too, despite its deprivations and the cumbersome and sometimes risky mechanics of getting about in it.)

They were, of course, political people, and men, because political women like Charlotte Maxeke and Josie Mpama were rarities in their society.

Because of his friendship with Mrs Maxeke, he had met teachers and clergymen of all persuasions, together with the tiny handful of doctors, lawyers and educated chiefs that then existed. Because of his membership of the Communist Party he had met revolutionary Marxists — a different breed entirely. Perhaps because of his own middle-class background, he thought he had been able to maintain a foothold in both camps. For that matter, most African Communists, unlike white ones, were able to do the same in their own world.

There had been a difficulty to overcome during their first campaign under the Native Representation Act in 1937. Election addresses and literature in the name of the Communist Party would have had no impact on the chiefs and mission-educated intellectuals who controlled the so-called vote. Issued in Basner's name only, they would be regarded as the impudent efforts of an ambitious thruster. He had to have a committee of Africans of different shades of opinion behind him, if only to break through the morbid film of non-political thought clouding the judgement of the unfranchised majority.

In their councils of war in Johannesburg, he, Marks and Mofutsanyana had wished above all for the support of Congress leaders of the stature of John Dube and the status of Seme's successor-to-be, the Rev ZR Mahabane, but knew it would never come. For a while, they had doubted if anyone would come.

But people had come, and without being called. They had come from the large locations of Johannesburg and the minute village ones of the Orange Free State and eastern Transvaal, from Pietersburg, Kroonstad and Harrismith, from the orange plantations of Zebediela and the remote hills of Sekhukuneland. They were old men who had never forgotten the enthusiasm and confidence with which Africans flocked to the standard of the Congress in 1912 and younger ones who remembered how, only a decade before, white supremacy had been shaken by the tread of the detribalised workers marching out of factories, dockyards, packing-rooms and kitchens at the call of Clements Kadalie.

Once the cry had gone forth that the vote was a trust and the ballot to be fought for on the lines of real election, offers of support had so flooded in that the only question was who to include in the campaign committee.

Another committee would have to be formed which would not only support him, but would include some candidates for the NRC.

Elias Moretsele, born in Sekhukuneland, and Treasurer of the Transvaal branch of Congress, was self-educated, and when he and Basner first met in about 1936, was about forty. He was the owner of the Bantu Restaurant, at that time the only African eating-house in Johannesburg, where numerous black politicians of the city had their meals. It was the centre of the radical element, just as the Bantu Men's Social Centre was the gathering-place for all the 'non-political' intellectuals. Basner could only use an Irishism to describe Moretsele — he was a 'darling man'. Shrewd, gruff and frank and yet the least abrasive of individuals, Moretsele would tell him — and anyone else if he felt so inclined — not to 'play like a child and talk nuisance'. Basner never heard him express anything but his real feelings, never knew him refuse to help anyone in trouble or make a political observation which did not have sound, mature sense in it.

An important addition to their circle — for it had become a circle — was Paul Mosaka. When he first appeared among them, they saw a clever young man, successful in business as a trader and the director of a burial society at an early age but giving no indication why he had been successful, too, in achieving the comparatively high political honour of election to membership of the advisory board in Orlando, Johannesburg's biggest location. First as a teacher and then as a store-manager, he had been a protegé of Dr Moroka of Thaba Nchu, after graduating in arts at the South African Native College of Fort Hare.

Mosaka — born in Johannesburg's Pimville in 1911 — had been too young to play a part in the important days of the Congress or ICU, and they knew he had been interested in the Institute of Race Relations. Only slowly did he reveal the fiery temperament and energetic, strong intellect of a leader of outstanding worth. After 1942, when he became a member of the Native Representative Council, he was to distinguish himself as the most powerful speaker in that assembly of powerful debaters and, almost overnight, as a national figure, recognised as such by the English medium as well as the African press.

Only much later, when they became almost daily companions, did Basner learn that Mosaka had been a diabetic from childhood and needed regular injections of insulin to live. His death at fifty-two came as no surprise to Basner, since his state of health was a sorrow he had had to get used to long before that event.

LT Mvabasa and Mweli Skota were given pride of place on the new campaign committee, especially because they were veteran members of the advisory board of the oldest (and smallest) Johannesburg municipal location — Pimville. As two canny and pragmatic Congress leaders at a loose end with the decline of Congress, they had long recognised the political possibilities of the board elections. Although Pimville was so small, it was probably, thanks to the sturdy character given it by the pair of them, the most influential force in the annual Conference of Advisory Boards, which had become a buoyant feature in the sluggish stream of African politics since the collapse of the ICU.

The pattern set for the creation of an advisory board in Pimville had been followed in most urban locations: three or four members were elected by the residents, the same number nominated by the local authority which also chose the chairman, who regularly disregarded the Board's advice. The Board had no powers, and was, as its name indicated, advisory only.

Among the chief failures of the Communist Party, Basner felt, could be counted its slowness in recognising the importance of the board elections. By the time it entered this field, reactionaries like Thomas Mapikela had become too entrenched for their machines to be ousted. The failure could be put down, ironically enough, to the colonial status to which the Comintern relegated the South African Party. If its policies had not been determined by Moscow-trained functionaries, there would have been shorter debates about a 'black bourgeoisie' and 'kulaks' and longer ones about creating militant advisory boards in the towns and militant local councils of headmen in the tribal reserves.

Old Thema came in from Pietersburg. He was not as able as his younger brother, Selope Thema, but was deeply respected for his political integrity. With him came Molepo, now a candidate for the NRC — who, in the years since 1937, had ignored his own security to stand by his peasant kinsfolk and support Maliba's organisations in their struggle against the Trust, taking loss of his headmastership and the right ever to teach again as his eventual due, and knowing that banishment from his birthplace would follow.

Also from the north came a somewhat shy local councillor, Abel Rangata, who would not be denied, and two Mahlangus, Ndebele clergymen from the Pretoria district, blood brothers, but completely different — one as solemn as an owl and one as lively and noisy as a grasshopper. There was freckle-faced little Gaur Radebe from Alexandra Township on the outskirts of Johannesburg, cheekily enduring one of two or three well-merited periods of expulsion from the Communist Party. And, lumbering up onto the bandwagon, was the inevitable

Richard Baloyi (no longer John Marks's patron, because the Party had by this date wisely been quick to forgive and reinstate a sinner of Marks's manifest loyalty and political calibre).

Two relative newcomers to politics represented the largest single section of the educated population. They were JJ Lesolang, the President of the Transvaal African Teachers Association, cautious, thoughtful and earnest and David Bopape, brave, provocative and fervent, a teacher from the mining town of Brakpan on the Reef. Each of them, so different in temperament, typified the changed mood of the teaching profession in the five years since the passing of the Hertzog Bills.

The committee also included in its ranks two bishops: Lekganyane and Lion — the wealthy and autocratic heads of independent African churches which they ran as agricultural communities in the rural Transvaal.

There were rich men and poor men, some beggar-men (but not many) who needed the few pence they could get as canvassers and distributors of leaflets, and indubitably, one or two thieves. In short, they represented a cross-section of the population. The Communist Manifesto had been amended to read: 'Everyone in Africa has chains to lose'.

Basner and the whole of his committee wanted sponsorship from the African National Congress. That still could not be, because its latest President Dr AB Xuma was, as it were, strongly neutral on the side of Rheinallt Jones and was, although occasionally critical, a leading member of the Institute of Race Relations.[1] The ANC's central executive committee was evenly split and eventually decided that Congress as an organisation should maintain a boycott of the elections, with individual members free to support whichever side they chose.

Dr Xuma maintained public impartiality. The now lively Transvaal branch, with Moretsele its treasurer, endorsed Basner, Paul Mosaka and MK Molepo, who were standing for the NRC[2]; and RV Selope Thema, a member of the national executive, continued to be Jones's chief election agent. It was a ridiculous and shaming situation, showing how successfully the strategy of race relations had reduced to impotence the largest and oldest African political movement. Yet it opened the door for the cry 'Reorganise Congress' and the companion cry 'The vote is held in trust for the people'.

Moretsele was a tower of strength. It must have been a great strain for him to serve under a man like Xuma, who, between 1940 and 1949, was to hold on to the leadership by dividing the opposition and whose timidity in every crisis was atoned for by a great display of militancy when it carried no risk of a clash with, or even reproof from, the authorities. Basner considered Xuma the most powerful of all supporters of the Institute of Race Relations, and the most dangerous, because he never disclosed his true position and followed a passive, non-political line whilst at the head of the Africans' main political organisation. Elias

Moretsele stuck grimly to his uncomfortable post. You did not 'play like a child' with the office of a treasurer in Congress and when Basner left South Africa in 1961, Moretsele still held that office, happy under the presidency of that true Christian militant, Chief Albert Luthuli.

16

ENDING A BEGINNING

The embryonic signs of new thought and action that first appeared in 1937 had begun to develop. The association of such disparate characters as Matseke, Thema, Moretsele, Marks, Baloyi and in due course, Mofutsanyana, in revitalising the Transvaal section of Congress, had led to a more general acceptance of the idea that the national movement itself could again become viable.

Even Dr Xuma, who was to be so dismal in the role of commander of the forces of liberation, was proving useful as a bringer of some order into Congress's structure and finances.[1] From the Cape had come the first effort to unite the coloured, Malay, Indian and African communities in a Non-European United Front.[2] And the first unanimous drive was being made, under the sponsorship of Congress, to create a black mineworkers union, with Matseke, the Transvaal President, as its chairman. The foundation of that union alone was as crucial to the future of South Africa as any political movement.

By 1942, preoccupied though he was with the coming elections, Basner's personal life and political intentions were also beginning to take new shape. His criticism of the Ballingers and other liberals for their professional and individualistic concern with internal black affairs could well apply to himself now that he was no longer in the Communist Party. His problem lay in finding a political home. The Labour Party was as unblushingly committed to the perpetuation of white supremacy as ever and on the far left, the Trotskyists (as well as refusing to support the war) were even more sectarian in outlook than the Communists.

The black world, particularly in the countryside where his political experience was deepening daily, absorbed his immediate attention. It gave him every cause to expect to win the Senate nomination poll in September and the election proper in November.

Despite the tacit or open support still given to his opponent by people with the influence and standing of Xuma and Thema, Basner and his committee were to discover that they had little need to concentrate on deflating Jones. However, Basner recollected having at some stage made or written a statement to the effect that the funds for the Institute of Race Relations and its Director's own election expenses stemmed largely from the goldmining industry. Jones apparently replied to the allegation by saying *'Non olet pecunia'*, 'Money has no smell — when put to proper purposes'.

Basner, who may not have claimed to be a prince of pamphleteers (as Bernard Shaw said of Trotsky), did not consider himself a commoner either. His response was a broadsheet about the stench of gold in non-political politics which caused black noses — justly more sensitive than others — to wrinkle in recognition. No trace has been found of this document, but it was probably in the style of an exchange of insults between Jones and himself that suddenly erupted at a very late stage in their contest.[3]

It was clear that Jones and his Institute were already too discredited to put up much of a fight. The Native Affairs Department was now the force to be contended with since it had become alerted to a danger the Hertzog/Smuts government had not anticipated: the use of the electoral machinery to gain access to urban locations and rural reserves, which strangers were not allowed to enter without permits. Permits were not given to left-wing politicians.

In view of this, Basner's committee changed its strategy, and more or less ignored Jones and his 'good boy' supporters. They made no effort to visit the chiefs, but invited them to meetings outside those areas where Native Commissioners and police could question their right to be present (and could themselves attend, and by means of their presence alone, intimidate).

Fortified by the clamour of their followers, the chiefs (except for the most backward ones, who held the most votes), were very ready to come as were numerous local councillors.

Although the provision for establishing local councils covered the whole Union of South Africa, these were a feature peculiar to the province of the Transvaal. To some extent a democratisation of the chieftainship system, they were mainly designed as a measure to help the Native Affairs Department in its supervision of the big, remote, tribal areas. Where the chief was mentally defective or positively insane, a drunkard or inordinately corrupt — and there were sadly many in those categories — it would have required a permanent army of policemen and officials to administer and keep order. To obviate this, the tribe could choose to be ruled by a council of headmen, and would elect a number of them to take over the chief's duties. He could then be left to his *ngakas*, wives, beer and certain traditional ceremonies, but would not try cases, be concerned with allocating land, or handle the finances and business concerns of the tribe.

If genuinely elected, and if not meddled with, the local councils could have become powers for real democratic control over tribal affairs. As it was, the native commissioner in the district would pay the salaries, veto the candidature, conduct the election and supervise the proceedings of the council (which were always held in his own office when important matters were discussed). Sometimes a man of real worth fought his way through to become a councillor, but the majority were the nominees and agents of the Department.

Among the country places where it was possible to hold meetings without hindrance were the lands of men such as Bishop Lekganyane who was literally the proprietor of a very large church of his own: the Zion Christian Church, which occupied several farms in the Pietersburg area.[4]

The Ethiopian movement which started in the 1890s had, in its break with the white missionaries, marked the beginning of African national consciousness. Since that time, independent offshoots of recognised Christian denominations had proliferated, among them a new phenomenon: groups of 'Zionists', as they came generally to be called. Their leaders were not so much pastors as prophets, inspired to administer divine healing to the soul and bodies of their maltreated people. The fount of their idiosyncratic beliefs was the Bible. Their interpretation of its message incorporated many elements of the creeds of various north American and European fundamentalists but imbued them with a special quality of relevance to the uprooted and ravished culture to which they themselves belonged. Above all, their common dream was of Mount Zion in the Promised Land — that unearthly land which has such intense meaning for those who on earth have no place to call their own. There was a tendency for many of these people to try to find a temporal as well as a spiritual home for their congregations and in the northern Transvaal this was given particular impetus by the expulsion of the squatters from the white-owned farms (which was an upheaval on so large a scale as to have important side-effects, not the least of them being upon religious institutions).

Collecting believers around him whose joint resources were sufficient for the purpose, an individual prophet would take steps to purchase one of the handful of farms which remained available for black occupation. To do that, of course, he would have to get permission from the Native Affairs Department and worm through a tangle of red tape. The very few who succeeded in doing this had to be people of a temperament capable of reconciling God-intoxication with more than considerable hard-headedness. Among these, Ignatius Lekganyane was particularly determined and competent. Because he had been vouchsafed the power to obtain land — that most precious of worldly treasures — rather than because his doctrines were more attractive than those of other Zionists, he gained an enormous number of followers. They turned out to be excellent farmers, so much so that they became economically as well as numerically strong.

Solomon Lion was a man of similar abilities, who, on coming to the Transvaal from Basutoland together with a number of adherents of the Zion Apostolic Faith Mission Church which he had inherited from his father, attracted others and set up a substantial community at Klipgat, near Hammanskraal, about twenty miles north of Pretoria.[5]

The ruthlessness shown by these successful leaders in accumulating property was comparable to that of high Roman clerics in the past and to that of Indian and American purveyors of short cuts to bliss or unction in our time and their churches and farm settlements, registered in their own names, were financially inextricable. Their congregations prospered, however, under a rule reminiscent both of Robert Owen's paternalistic socialism and of traditional tribal co-operativeness and fealty.

They and their people ran their affairs so well and were so law-abiding and so little trouble to the authorities, that they were even looked on with favour by the Native Affairs Department.

But of course, they were Africans. As Africans, they had national aspirations, and their churches were not inhibited by the same considerations and disciplines as those imposed, say, by the Anglican, Catholic or Dutch Reformed Church missions. They were remarkably independent psychologically as well as materially and legally and never fell under the influence of the Institute of Race Relations and the muted harmonies of Dr Aggrey. Self-appointed bishops and chiefs at the same time, Lekganyane and Lion were inclined to support the African National Congress more wholeheartedly than the average black intellectual or trade unionist simply because their cults were profoundly national and, equally simply, because they were not very interested in political organisation as such.

The aberrant fervours, business methods and personal presumptions of the Zionist leaders could not but be repugnant to the majority of orthodox African clergy and to Congress office-holders such as Dr Xuma. Even Chief Albert Luthuli, for all his tolerance and broad humanity, could never feel quite at home among people in whom it was as easy to see ignorant ranting, crass materialism and tribal atavism as it was to find artless piety, practical efficiency and nostalgia for a venerable past.

To Basner and his associates standing for seats on the Native Representative Council, Lekganyane and Lion were invaluable for the facilities they provided to make contact with the minds of people of every rank and way of thinking in the rural areas.

The few Zionist bases could not however, be anything like enough to cover the vast hinterland of the Transvaal (strategically placed though they were on the fringes of the northern and western reserves). The *dorps* still had to be the main foci whence messages could spread through the surrounding countryside.

There were Ethiopian and Zionist congregations in each *dorp* location. Some of the former were quite large, and though they tended to be consciously respectable and theologically conservative, they were also consciously independent and black. Some of the latter were so tiny as not even to have a rickety little church of their own, and held their services of praise and healing in their leader-prophet's shack, or made their way, robed in white, to a nearby stream, hymning joyously to the beat of drums and their own bare feet, to hear the Word, pray or speak-with-tongues, or give witness to a baptism. Women always made up a majority, though as leaders they were rare. No matter what the size of these groups, they and the Ethiopians, together with members of white-run churches, all had connections in the reserves, ranging from humble fellow-believers to sympathisers and kin in chieftainly circles.

Each location had its mission school, whose teachers, in their turn, were at home to colleagues on mission stations in the tribal areas, where the chiefs relied greatly on their advice. The years since the Hertzog Bills and the 1937 elections had wrought great changes in the attitudes of these men and women. Their Transvaal Teachers' Association was now led by determined personalities like Lesolang, Molepo and Bopape, who reflected the political sentiments and awakened professional demands of people formerly rendered passive by hopes of white liberal uplift.

The ICU and Congress old-timers were still around, regaling the younger generation, as parents and grandparents are so inclined to do, with oft-told stories of days long dead; but now, perhaps, not so much boring their descendants as exasperating them into political thought.

Those country locations, large and small, looked, and were, the same, no matter what the shape of the land or the product of the soil. They were always just out of sight and mind of the dusty and silent white settlements that made use of them and consisted of huts and herds and patches of cultivation.

Each one, according to its size, would have its little quota of teachers, pastors, petty traders and clerks, plus perhaps, a trained nurse. Most other people would be virtually illiterate, though nearly all understood at least one language besides their own.

By lamplight, the literate read to themselves or aloud to others from the Bible or from newspapers, political leaflets and dog-eared school textbooks passed from hand to hand. Though the infant death-rate was high, there were many children and there were few old men and women.

Most of the inhabitants were manual workers, who swept and cooked, nursemaided, dug, watered and weeded, laundered, hauled grain sacks and sewage buckets, delivered goods and mended roads in and around the white *dorps*. A minority of them worked night-shift to earn something extra or to make more use of their talents as burglars, brewers, artisans, *ngakas*, preachers, musicians and, now and then, as political agitators.

There were also many men who, having failed to get passes and so find employment among whites other than on neighbouring farms, had no permits to stay, and were therefore lawbreakers, obliged to live on their wits as illicit sub-tenants. They frequently included the offspring — once they had reached the age of eighteen — of registered location dwellers. The number of small-town blacks, including those living in their employers' own backyard premises, always equalled or exceeded the total of whites.

In the big urban areas and country *dorps* of the Transvaal and Orange Free State, the campaigners called meetings suddenly and late at night, and proceedings would be completed before the location superintendent and his police were out of their beds to claim them to be unlawful. They noticed that far more men attended now and the tiredness and timidity of the first election were over. But they failed to realise that most of these men were not residents but illegal lodgers who feared nothing because they had no security to lose.

The absence of one very small group of people was scarcely noticed: the new young intellectuals[6] who, despite all odds, were graduating from Fort Hare and the universities of the Witwatersrand and Cape Town. Too cynical to see a future in liberalism, communism or Congress as it stood, they would give significant new direction to the coming years.

In the end, Jones was defeated and Basner became a Senator, thus acquiring a constituency more than three times the size of England and Wales, with a black population of nearly three-and-a-half million — more than a third of that of the country's entire population and half that of its African people. In the same two provinces, Mosaka and Moroka gained urban seats in the Native Representative Council. Baloyi, for better or worse, retained the rural seat he already held, but Molepo failed by a narrow margin to oust Selope Thema from the other. Maliba, Marks and Mofutsanyana, who had all been put forward by the Communist Party, also failed, which might not have happened had they been able to stand on their own as notable Congress office-holders rather than as representatives of their party.

Charlotte Maxeke

Picture courtesy S A Institute of Race Relations

J D Rheinallt Jones

Picture courtesy Africana Museum

Clements Kadalie

Guardian

Lorries were lent by sympathetic employers to help transport workers during the Alexandra bus boycott.

Inkululeko

Edwin Mofutsanyana

Inkululeko

Alpheus Maliba

Sidney Smith

Margaret and William Ballinger

Picture courtesy Africana Museum

J B Marks

Picture courtesy Bailey's African Photo Archives

Elias Moretsele

James Sofazonke Mpanza in action.

Picture courtesy Bailey's African Photo Archives

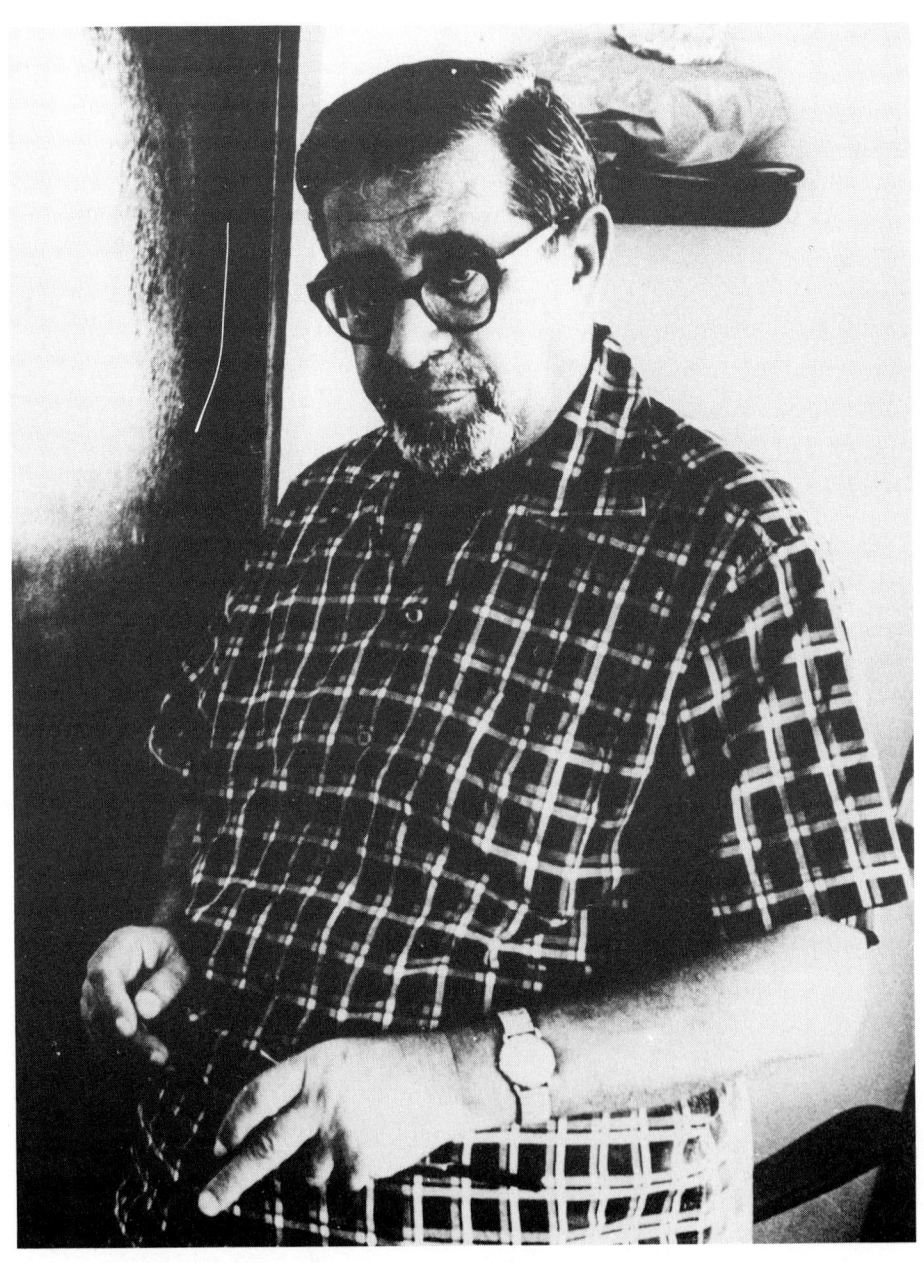

Picture courtesy Bailey's African Photo Archives

H M Basner in Ghana.

The electoral picture was very similar in the Cape and Natal insofar as the black candidates were concerned. It only differed in that since no white militants contested seats in Parliament there, there was no indication that negrophilism had lost its credibility.

In 1935 and 1936, it may be recalled, Basner had found the deliberations of the All-African Convention a depressing experience. All the same, it had been exciting, even electrifying, for him to meet and listen to so many outstanding personalities assembled at a single gathering. He found it no wonder then, that from 1942 onwards the powerless Native Representative Council should present a challenge of logic, informed opinion and eloquence so great as to oblige a future government to abolish it (in 1951) if only because it might harm white parliamentary prestige.

There were probably only two men in South Africa's wartime cabinet — Prime Minister Jan Smuts, and his deputy, JH Hofmeyr — whose capabilities were equal to those of the Rev John Dube, RH Godlo, BB Xiniwe, Professor ZK Matthews, Dr J Moroka and Paul Mosaka. For natural eloquence, there was no one to touch Dube, and for eloquence combined with intellectual excellence, no one to touch Mosaka. The Native Representative Council was readier and far more competent to set up the machinery for a conventional democratic government than any other group of politicians in the country and it would have been a government able to hold its own in legislative and administrative procedure against that of any long-established Western state.

Before the balloting for the Transvaal and Free State Senate seat had finished, rumours were already circulating that the votes at local council meetings were not being properly recorded, together with stories of threats against those of their members liable to tip the balance in favour of Basner. In the end, Jones managed to retain the support of nearly half the huge 'tribal' electorate — that is to say, those chiefs or their councillors who were more afraid of the Native Affairs Department than of their own followers. It is not contradictory to add that their choice required a good deal of courage: not only was a voter's standing in the community imperilled if he came out for Jones, but his skin could be as well. In five arduous years, Basner and his committee had convinced the rural commoners, just as much as the town workers, that the vote belonged to them and not to their officially deputed spokesmen.

Basner received a clear enough majority — 58 percent of the poll (he received 332 798 votes to Jones's 237 919) — to make it plain that the mood of the people had changed. To his mind, however, the backing he obtained, together with that given the radicals who were soon to dominate the Native Representative Council, was never seen in its true light by white Marxists. The latter, who had (and still have) important influences as analysts and interpreters of the South African scene, should have been more knowledgeable. Although they certainly recognised that popular sentiment was far more unanimous than the electoral count had indicated, they did not appreciate how much it represented an informed response to the dire effects of the Land and Trust Act. They seemed unable to give proper recognition to the subservience of white liberalism to the political requirements of the goldmining industry and minimised the significance of the black rural majority as a potential political force. Hence they failed to grasp premises which great numbers of Africans — countryfolk and townsfolk, literate and illiterate — had now come to consider self-evident. Above all, they failed to understand how far the elections had served to crystallise African public opinion in favour of communal militancy, trade unionism and broad nationalism under the insignia of Congress.[7]

It would be pleasing to say that a great day then dawned. Certainly, and inevitably, it did not, as the chapters which follow will indicate.

At least, however, it may be said that a very simple and age-old lesson had been reread and relearnt by the African people at large: the Gods help those who help themselves. Two phony elections had communicated the lesson and grim experience had forced its acceptance. The interpretation of that lesson in terms of competing ideologies, and therefore of political strategy and tactics, was to become a prime concern during the next five years.

17

ANOTHER PLACE
(1943)

The parliamentary session in Cape Town — South Africa's legislative capital — began in the middle of January. At that time of year, there is no more popular place for affluent whites to visit than the Cape Peninsula. It is full summer, but heat and humidity are more than offset by the magnificent beaches that fan out beneath the mountains on the shores of the Atlantic and Indian oceans. Parliamentarians, together with their families, enjoyed a nearly free annual stay at the seaside. This, more than any other emolument of public service, gave them special reason to be grateful for their seats, as well as extra anxiety about keeping them.

As if to stress the holiday mood, in those days neither the Upper nor the Lower House met until after lunch and always adjourned in good time for dinner. Parliament, as Basner knew it until his resignation five years later in 1947, only sat for four to five months of the year, and during the first week or so of the session functioned more actively as a club than as a deliberative assembly. The real work of governing the country was, and is, done in the Transvaal, in Pretoria's Union Buildings, an enormous and handsome edifice built by Sir Herbert Baker, architect of the Bank of England and the tomb of Cecil Rhodes, and co-designer of imperial New Delhi. Here, all the ministries, government departments and official records are housed and every December, long trainloads of civil servants, with their wives and children, typists and their typewriters and filing cabinets and their contents, are hauled a thousand miles to Cape Town, to be hauled back again when the session is over.

An expensive charade for an elaborate facade, but worthwhile, if only to present South Africa to the world as a democracy.

South Africa's Parliament in no way revealed the arbitrary and psychotic nature of the state it represented. On the contrary, an appearance of democracy, fiscal responsibility and the rule of law was maintained with a dignity which certainly equalled that of the Mother of Parliaments in Westminster.

This appearance disguised reality so well that it required a well-informed mind and alert conscience to appreciate the kind of legislation it turned out and the type of administration it provided for. Police raids and baton charges on a military scale, hundreds of thousands of men and women passing through or rotting in prisons, hordes of underfed, uneducated children in slum yards and barren fields, were all utterly remote from the small palace in Cape Town that stands at the head of an avenue of majestic oaks and charming flower beds.

In a rented morning suit with striped pants, Basner participated decorously in the opening of Parliament, and was much impressed by what the colonial offspring of the Mother of Parliaments had learnt from her.

Together, the descendants of the Voortrekkers and their English-speaking opponents of the Anglo-Boer War had eagerly taken what they needed for political deception from her imperial dressing-rooms. There they all stood, in the fierce sunlight of the Avenue, awaiting the arrival of the Governor-General, whose coach and greys could have come straight from Buckingham Palace Mews. George VI would probably have worn the simple white tropical uniform of an admiral, but his Majesty's deputy — whose plumed hat gave him no shade, for all its snowy spread — was broiling like a kipper in his scarlet coat overlaid and thickened by gold braid and rows of medals and decorations.

After the Governor-General came the forty-four Senators: huge, bearded farmers from the Transvaal and the Free State in greenish frock coats and top-hats; lines of sinewy sugar planters from Natal; stout growers of wool, wheat and vines from the Cape; tanned old country attorneys, all of whom constituted the equivalent of the House of Lords. Only three of them were under sixty years of age: Brookes and Basner, Native Representatives, and Smith, a Labour Party man.

The Sergeant-at-Arms, in silk hose, rapier at his side, knocked for admission. The Speaker entered, together with the Mace and an array of haughty attendants, and was followed by the Members of the House of Assembly ('the Commons') — who deferentially lined the walls of the Senate Chamber.

Next came prayers. These took a long time, since it was necessary to ask God for guidance in both official languages. Then, the King's Speech, short and dull. The government, in the midst of World War II, had no plans for important legislation, and intended to continue ruling mainly by means of gazetted war measures.

An amused journalist described Basner on that occasion as looking like a juvenile lead in a Greek chorus of greybeard Boers. Graphically speaking, this was accurate enough, but wrong as dramatic and political comment. Whatever attention he attracted was in a Shakespearian role — as First Murderer. He had come there over the prostrate body of Senator Rheinallt Jones, and so was a sinister figure in the eyes of the white public (if not in those of his black electors, who were more level-headed). What did the white section know of the struggle on the Trust Farms, of the betrayal of the chiefs, of the polemics between the 'good boys' and the reawakened political elders?

The official luncheon in the Members' dining-room, with Prime Minister Jan Christiaan Smuts — taut and trim in Field Marshal's uniform — acting as host, was as long and excellent as the speech he had submitted to Parliament through the Governor-General had been brief and uninteresting. *Sosaties* and *bobotie*, beautifully spiced dishes introduced to the country by Malay slaves, reminded Basner how much civilisation the early Dutch settlers had brought with them. The brandy was superb and made him consider what an acquisition the seventeenth-century refugee Huguenots had been for the Cape.

The meal found him seated at a table reserved for the Native Representatives and Labour Party members of both Houses. The conversation at that table, with Margaret Ballinger at its head, was lively and serious in turn, and gave Basner an opportunity to get to know five of his six colleagues — three MPs and three Senators — none of whom, besides Mrs Ballinger, he had met before.

He was interested mostly in Donald Molteno and Edgar Brookes. The former was a barrister and a member of one of the Cape's oldest and best known liberal families. Basner had read his speeches in the House of Assembly over the past five years and had been greatly taken by his radical approach and grasp of the economics which had dictated South African racial policy since the Act of Union in 1910. He was taken aback, however, by Molteno's subdued and constant deference to the ebulliently optimistic views of Margaret Ballinger. Brookes, in his own style, was as effective as she. He was a scholar and educationist of note, very eloquent in a quiet way, devout, and as a former Hertzogite, a repentant sinner. He was worldly and, thanks to his membership of the Institute of Race Relations, crammed with statistics.

It was all very stimulating, but for some reason, Basner began to feel depressed. What was spoiling his lunch? Could it be spontaneous jealousy of the radiant 'Peg' Ballinger, greeted with genuine affection and respect on all sides, and kindness itself as she introduced him to everyone who stopped at their table? Perhaps the idea of the delegated representatives of the African people celebrating the opening of Parliament as if they were tobacco-growers or part-time company directors was too much for him? It was not in his nature to think it immoral to enjoy good cheer. Had the Communist Party made a 'bolshevik' out of him despite himself? Maybe he was neither envious nor a prig, but becoming creepily aware of the dangers of seduction.

Obviously, the seductions of Parliament as a comfortable club, as a career for talented men and women and an honoured social niche for lazy ones, were incomparable to anything another sphere of life had to offer. Basner was married, verging on middle age and still had ambitions to be a writer, given the means and leisure. How could be summon up the energy and, above all, the ruthlessness, required for a campaign against his friendly and civilised colleagues and the whole dignified and presumably powerful facade before him?

They rose, and he took himself off, flushed with food and liquor, to sit under the oaks near the entrance to Parliament. His last visit to Cape Town had been fifteen years before, on his return from the United States. Then the whole world still seemed open to him, but with everything in it apparently out of reach. Now his world had shrunk to the size of South Africa, and nothing seemed beyond his reach should he but stretch out his hand.

But had he come here to stretch out his hand to anything? That — like a concealed mouse — was the question nibbling away at the back of his mind all day. He had arrived convinced he was in the Senate for no other reason than to make it clear that a white representative of black electors under white supremacy was either a knave or a fool and that anyone deferring to the terms of Hertzog's Representation Act was literally furthering black disenfranchisement. And if this was what he had really come for, his first day's experience of Parliament gave him no good omens for the future.

It was true that Basner had never intended to divert attention from real issues by ridiculing parliamentary masquerades. He felt he resembled his father in finding deep human sense in old traditions. He had, however, planned a public denunciation of his fellow Native Representatives. In that way his role as First Murderer could be emphasised and his main promise to his electorate could be fulfilled.

But now these tactics seemed trivial and an actual abandonment of political realism within a Marxist framework. The main opponent had to be the Chamber of Mines, and his sights had to be fixed there and not on personalities. He would have to establish some reputation for reasonableness, try to be comprehensible to whites as well as blacks, and speak mainly on economic, not racial issues.

The mental effort required for such complicated reactions could not cope for long with the hot day and the lunch which had induced them. He fell asleep, and woke, still somewhat dazed, to catch the late afternoon train to the small holiday resort and fishing village of Kalk Bay where he was staying.

Next morning, sitting on the veranda of his hotel, with a cool breeze blowing in his face, eating pawpaw (the inevitable fruit on white South African breakfast tables), he could look quite placidly down at Kalk Bay's little beach and sail-filled harbour. He could see no reason to reverse his decisions of the day before, so much so that the seaside could now delight him just as much as it did any other parliamentarian. He had revised his strategy for the session in the sensible manner of any other old hand.

He was going to relax for a while, which was not easy, and keep quiet, which was even less so. In the mornings he would keep himself occupied in the Senate library, learning the rules. (A lesson from Parnell: to give parliaments trouble, know their procedure better than the Speaker.) He would also do some research into the shareholding and interlocking directorships of the companies owning the main newspapers of the country.[1]

However, it took a very short while for him to reverse these cool resolutions, beginning with his maiden intervention — in a debate on the report of an interdepartmental committee concerning Africans in urban areas.

Though strong enough, his speech was no more than a spirited condemnation of governmental and municipal treatment of blacks in towns. Only recently, during a demonstration against appalling living and working conditions in Pretoria, sixteen men had been killed by police and eleven thousand unemployed had been rounded up from the Reef alone within thirteen days under the notorious powers of Section 17 of the Urban Areas Act of 1923. While describing the general plight of townspeople, he also dealt briefly with that of labourers on white farms, since it was such as to impel them to flee from the land and seek preferable affliction in city slums.[2]

His approach to the latter theme served to confirm senatorial preconceptions about him — and in a way that no other argument could have done. The Senate, even more than the House of Assembly, was dominated by representatives of the white farming community, bitterly complaining of their mostly well-merited shortage of black labour.

His apprehensive liberal colleagues, however, were relieved, if only by the tone of voice in which he had spoken. From the first — and probably advised by Mrs Ballinger — they had been as considerate and nice to him as possible, trying their best to shepherd him into their fold.

Their relief, however, was made too apparent. Their open pleasure at his respectable behaviour was counter-productive. The result was to restore him to his normal spirits.

Who was Margaret Ballinger to think she could parade him as a tamed wild man in her parliamentary circus? Five years before, she had coined a slogan Basner envied: 'The only good Native Representative is one who has no belief in such representation'. In her first speech in the House of Assembly she had been so eloquent and so knowledgeable on the subject of African wages that the whole House had cheered her and since then she had never ceased to be formidable and rational in debate and entirely uncompromising in opposition to racial discrimination. In other words, Basner considered, she had done all that could be expected by white South Africa, the Chamber of Mines and Parliament itself to show that there was a democracy in which the whole population could have its say.

So a few weeks at most sufficed to disappoint the hopes of his colleagues. No time at all passed before an overwhelming majority of senators gave open expression to their disgust about the noxious interloper in their midst and Basner reacted with equal disgust to the behaviour of those whom he had chosen to confront. He had been quite aware of the passions he would arouse yet had not anticipated the resentment those passions, in their turn, would engender in him.

Eventually, time and experience were to sober his mixed feelings about Parliament. It even mellowed the human — if not the political — sentiments of a number of elderly Afrikaner senators, who actually grew rather fond of him. Their dull days were enlivened by his provocative presence. His diatribes against the hypocrisy of Smuts's followers gave them much sly pleasure and his attacks on their own dearest beliefs gave considerable exercise to their tongues, if scarcely any to their minds. He came to be convinced that there was a decline in the senatorial death-rate during his five years as a Native Representative, and an increase in the thickness of the volumes of published reports of Senate debates.

A detailed description of Basner's speeches in Parliament is beyond the scope of this book. In any case, to accord them much space would conflict with his own assessment of their political significance. Without some indication of their style though, and of the social and political atmosphere in which it was displayed, the account of him and his times would be incomplete.

Two months after that maiden speech and contrary to established custom, he tackled a major theme — the one which had preoccupied him so much during the preceding two years. He did this in the form of a motion calling for a commission of enquiry into the administration of the Native Land and Trust Act of 1936.[3]

His presentation of his case was as exhaustive as the debate it occasioned was crude. He supplied, and was challenged about, almost all the information he had collected concerning the operation of the Trust.

The brief extracts from the Senate record which follow are given for flavour rather than as the factual meat of the debate as a whole:

> Mr. President, I move the motion standing in my name.
>
> I feel that I should not start without offering this House some apology and some excuse for tabling in my first session a motion in so comprehensive a form that it seems to embrace the whole of the future of South Africa. I can only plead that I, in this House, am the sole representative for three and a half million people, one half of the total native population and one third of the total population of this country.
>
> I want to say that the condition of the people whom I represent is such, they are so hungry, they are so landless, they are so lacking in elementary democratic rights, that even if it was not my wish, it is still my responsibility not to show any false modesty, and not to show any spirit of seeking for popularity, but to tell this House exactly what they want this House to know ...
>
> ... I cannot, however, start without referring to my first entry into debate in this Chamber, in Senator Dr Brookes's motion on the Interdepartmental Committee's report ... I expressed what I thought were the thoughts and feelings of the people whom I represent, and the truth about their position. At the conclusion of my speech, I was met with such a spirit of hostility in a certain section of this House that I do not want it to mar this discussion.
>
> ... The attack on me was such that I could find no justification for it in anything I had said. I can only say that there were two elements connected with it, one, the racial element, which I shall treat with contempt, and which I shall not refer to again. The other, and the more important aspect of the matter is ... that the day after my election the organ of the Nationalist Party, the *Volksblad*, came out with an editorial in screaming headlines, "This Jew Communist will now spread his anti-Christian and anti-European and anti-white doctrines in the furthest kraals."

On another occasion ...

> ... I do not want to give the Opposition the satisfaction of using me as one of their election planks ... and therefore want to put on record something which I would not have referred to otherwise. I want this House to understand, before it considers this motion, that I am in no way connected with the Communist Party ... and that this motion was framed and

designed, not from the point of view of furthering any political doctrine or the interests of any political party, but from what I consider to be the interest of the country as a whole.

He then dealt with the effects of segregation — that is to say, apartheid — on South Africa:

> The doctrine of Segregation started not today or yesterday. It started when Jan van Riebeeck came to the Cape in 1652 . . . and told his sailors and soldiers, 'You are not to mix with the native population'. It has proved so successful in the last three hundred years that we have today nearly a million coloured people in this country.
>
> The legal and economic doctrines of Segregation took longer to formulate, but they were in one way or another put into the statute book and into practice over a great number of years. We must examine, for our own sake, for the sake of the Europeans in this country, what has happened to us (since) . . .
>
> We are a population of two million Europeans, and of these two million, we have half a million poor-whites, or one in every four. But take the most favourable figure, which the Government takes, of one in every five. That means that for every five Europeans, one is a poor-white, without any hope at the present moment of rising, or of his children rising, above the condition of poor-whites . . .
>
> . . . And what have we done to the seven million non-Europeans? Is it necessary . . . to go over the report of the Interdepartmental Committee? Is it necessary for me to go over the report which you heard from the Minister of Public Health? Is it necessary for me to state, except in broad terms, that the whole native population is starving, is ruined, is in misery, its health declining, being ravaged by disease and malnutrition?
>
> So what have we done with the ten million human beings that live in our country? The whole of the non-European population, we have degraded, as well as a quarter of the European population . . .
>
> . . . I do not say we have done that deliberately. I do not say that members of this Hon. House or the European people as a whole have done that, but I do say that it was done out of stupidity by one section of the population and out of devilish cunning by another section. It was done by those mine owners who needed cheap native labour, and who could use the racial

psychology of this country in order to further their own interest. It was done by a few land-owning companies, and by what I call the upper strata of the population — whom I do not call the farmers, but who are, and have been, and cannot forget that they are, feudal landlords . . .

The average white middle class of this country does not benefit by the conditions which we have imposed on the native people. On the contrary, we are holding the country back as a whole, and we are holding it back, not for the sake of our racial pride or for our racial domination, or even for our racial security. We are holding it back . . . for the benefit of one big industry which needs cheap native labour, and for a small section of the population which wants to make big profits . . .

My appeal today is this — and I must be understood at the present moment not to be suggesting that you close down the gold mines — we have got to say to these people, 'Either you let go the reins which you have imposed on this country, or those reins will be taken out of your hands, either by the European section in a democratic form, or — and I say . . . again, that I am representing three and a half million people, and I live among them, and I know the lines along which they are thinking — the reins are going to go in an unconstitutional form .

. . . What is happening in our large towns today is not something which is peculiar to South Africa. It is something which happened in England . . . and it happened in almost every country which was industrialised. But is there any need for us in 1942 to do what was done in 1842? Surely we have learnt. Surely we have advanced from that stage. Surely we do not have to go through the conditions which created those terrific slums in London and Manchester and other towns of the world. We ought to be intelligent enough to learn. Unfortunately . . . we do not think in those terms . . .

. . . We do not think of those natives coming into the towns as rural people coming into an industrialised environment. We think of them as tribal savages, as tribal natives who are visiting a place where they do not belong, a place where they are going to stay for a little while. We think of them as coming in as temporary residents, for a temporary purpose, and that they will go back to the Reserves . . .

. . . My Hon. friends on my right are perfectly consistent, but they do not go far enough. The leader of the New Order in

Another Place is a highly intelligent man.[4] Unfortunately he has certain infantile tendencies, but I think he is a highly intelligent man. One of the things which he said — and he is the only consistent segregationalist in this country — was that we must remain a raw-material-producing country. That man is a Fascist. He wants racial domination. But at least he thinks straight . . . He is perfectly consistent. If you are going to be a gold-producing country, a base-metal-producing country . . . that is perfectly consistent, except that you come up against the human factor.

But you are not dealing with robots . . . I submit that you are not dealing with machines that you put for six months of the year here and for six months somewhere else. You are dealing with human beings; and those human beings may not be satisfied. They may not be satisfied to remain serfs and helots while a few people . . . remain the producers of raw materials.

The debate arising from Basner's proposed motion, which mainly concerned the specific effects of the Land and Trust Act, provoked a predictable set of exchanges (many of them omitted from the printed record because they were hardly dignified). Afrikaner Nationalists and English- or Afrikaans-speaking supporters of Smuts's United Party of course considered themselves to have sharply differing viewpoints about the maintenance of white supremacy in the nineteen-forties, but today it is hard to discern the difference between Piet van der Byl (the Minister of Native Affairs), Senator van Niekerk (a member of the Opposition), and Senator Welsh (appointed by the government after failing in 1942 to be re-elected as their representative by the Africans of the Transkei[5]).

Senator Basner: That land given to the native is not land on which he can live and on which he can stay. That land is given to him so that his wife and children can stay and cultivate it, but, if he wants to live, if he wants money to pay his poll tax and rent and money for his shoes and clothes and money for his children's needs, he has got to go to the mines to work, and to the farms to work.

Senator PW le R van Niekerk: That is fairly sound policy.

Senator Basner: The Hon Senator says that is a fairly sound policy. But then we must say so openly. If the Government says to the native people, "We are buying the land for the Trust in order to give the native a place in which his wife and children can live while he goes and works elsewhere and then comes back," then I will go to the native people and say to them, "I am wasting time. This talk of trusteeship is just so much hypocrisy. They are not buying this land to help the natives. They say they are buying the land to help the farmers and the mine-owners . . . the Government is buying land so that we can subsidise the wages of the Chamber of Mines and the wages of the farmers . . ."

. . . Today, as I am speaking now, probably the magistrate in Pietersburg is sentencing ten poor wretches for ploughing the morgenage (acreage) which they ploughed when the Trust farms were bought . . . The Department (of Native Affairs) feels exactly the same way as the Minister (of Native Affairs) did when he clenched his fist on Friday, and said: "we are going to take drastic steps against these people". Against whom is the Minister taking drastic steps? Against desperate criminals? Against savage saboteurs? Against dangerous revolutionaries? Or is he standing here and clenching his fist at ignorant, poor and helpless human beings who are fighting for their existence, who want enough land to plant their crops for their wives and themselves and their children? . . .

. . . I know the temper of the people. I know how they feel . . . What is going to happen is that a few of them, perhaps an isolated few of them, are going to attack one of your officers and there is going to be bloodshed.

The Minister of Native Affairs: Who eggs them on to do it?

Senator Basner: Nobody. Hunger eggs them on to do it . . .

. . . I am asking the Minister today . . . not to fall into the habits and mentality of the Native Affairs Department, the people who rule by proclamation,[6] the people who are in the habit of saying: "Just do as we tell you, not as you think" . . . I am not blaming the Native Commissioners . . . It is the system which makes certain individuals rule over other individuals by proclamation . . . We have a dual system in this country, a system of democracy for Europeans, whom we rule by statute, by ordinance, by Acts; but when it comes to natives they are ruled by proclamation, and there is no appeal."

Senator Welsh: Doesn't it benefit them?

Senator Basner: Whom?

Senator Welsh: The natives.

Senator Basner: I do not think I can seriously, especially this afternoon, meet the argument when I am asked whether the absence of democracy benefits any section of the population.

Senator Welsh: You are hedging again.

After that first parliamentary session, every recess, for the next four years, was punctuated by African strikes, demonstrations, violence by police and workers; so much so that the sittings in Cape Town became for Basner both restful seaside vacations and guilt-ridden, frustrating periods of idleness (punctuated by futile senatorial speechmaking).

18

TREMORS UNDERGROUND
(1943-1944)

Returning to Johannesburg after his first parliamentary session, Basner could only be sure that, with Mrs Ballinger as Rheinallt Jones's more capable and independent counterpart, his role as a destroyer of 'race relations' in Cape Town was useless. All further efforts in that direction would be no more than reassertions of his own integrity.

During the elections, the younger Africans on his side had seen him as neither a defender nor a leader, but as someone able to define and communicate their burgeoning sentiments, both within and outside their silenced society; and the older war-horses had heard him as a voice which bade them gird up their loins and come back into the fight. With the new Native Representative Council and the new mood it reflected in the rising generation of intellectuals, further efforts on his part to reawaken African political consciousness were, he knew, not only needless but impudent. And if he still saw himself as a political trumpet, neither he nor any of his supporters expected him to produce such a blare on their behalf as would cause the walls of white supremacy to crumble.

The people who took Basner's election really seriously were the pro-Nazis in South Africa. The Greyshirts, although now proscribed, were active underground, but had become outnumbered by a rival and more open organisation, the *Ossewa Brandwag* ('Ox-Wagon Guard'). This group, founded during the Voortrekker Centenary celebrations in 1938, differed from them very little, except in successfully pretending to closer identity with Afrikanerdom and its National Party than with Hitlerism pure and simple.

The attitude of both movements towards Basner was hardly surprising in view of his activities against them before the war as a Communist and speaker for the Anti-Fascist League, but was interesting because it reflected a division within the National Party itself. When he came to the Senate, his advent was frankly welcomed by Dr Dönges, the shadow Minister of Finance, a conservative, able and bitter member of the elitist secret *Broederbond*[1]. This was because Basner, as an English-speaking opponent of imperialism, could cause trouble for Smuts. To the *Broederbond*, the crude storm-trooper mentality of the *Ossewa Brandwag* (which was composed mainly of workers and poor-whites), had become more an embarrassment than a useful weapon in the struggle for future power.[2]

Soon after the session ended, Basner received a message to go at once to Pretoria to see Colin Steyn, the Minister of Justice. When he arrived it was to be told that information had been received about plans to assassinate him. He should take care. 'Do you have a revolver?' the Minister asked.

'What about police protection?' Basner wanted to know, upon which an irritable look came over Dr Steyn's usually cherubic face. 'This is a matter of security which does not concern the regular police — and we haven't enough of them to look after everyone under threat,' he said. He probably did not know how many of his own subordinates were Nazis themselves, and had reason to be just as frightened of being assassinated as Basner. The latter left the Palace of Justice, wondered whether the best thing to do was go to bed until the war was over, and borrowed an ancient and overweight revolver (with complicated safety-catches which he never got the hang of) which was to remain undisturbed in the cubby-hole of his car for the 'duration'.

Smuts's measures to deal with vulgar domestic subversion were very effective. This was because everything he did when he was really interested, he did well. His security service[3] was the most efficient section of his administration because, even in peacetime, one of his main concerns was the suppression of unruliness — among whites as much as blacks. No one of any importance was murdered, and the victims were a few individuals whom the Nazis regarded as informers — all Afrikaners, naturally. Basner survived, thanks to Jan Smuts, rather than Colin Steyn or his dubious firearm (which was as likely to explode in his own face as send a Greyshirt to Valhalla or an *Ossewa Brandwag* man to Calvinist perdition). He even survived five years in that other Circe's paradise — the South African Parliament — better than Smuts himself.

In 1948, when Smuts's United Party was defeated by the Afrikaner Nationalists under Dr DF Malan in a general election, Basner happened to be in London, and wrote an article for *Reynold's News*, explaining a result which to the *Times, Telegraph* and *Guardian* seemed as amazing as it was shocking. How could they know what *Broederbond* infiltrators had been up to in the higher reaches of the South African civil service to make price controls and other regulations under War Measures intolerably Draconian and corrupt.[4] How could they understand how thoroughly Hitler's ideas had spread through a population whose sons were facing Rommel's and Badoglio's guns 'Up North' in Libya and Egypt? Smuts, too interested in the grand strategies of Britain's War Cabinet and in founding the United Nations, did not know. Why should London's editors be better informed?

Throughout his life Basner could unfailingly be provoked by the imputation that he was popular, and hence elected to the South African Senate, because Africans are peculiarly partial to lawyers. He would hotly maintain this to be a racist slur on the part of individuals who would never dream of giving genetic reasons for the presence of disproportionate numbers of professional mouthpieces in European and North American legislatures.

He did, however, agree that lawyers, thanks to their experience, tend to make competent parliamentarians and understood all too well the need among blacks in South Africa for politicians expert in the law.

Back in the Transvaal, he imagined himself free for a while to take back his legal hat and put off his parliamentary one, but as things turned out, the two hats came to look pretty much the same. Instead of coping with the pile of cases that had mounted in his office, he agreed to appear before the Witwatersrand Mine Native Wages Commission — both in his capacity as a Senator and as legal representative of the African Mineworkers Union.

The South African government gave no statutory recognition to black trade unions, but these had in time come to be informally accepted by a fair number of white employers. The Chamber of Mines, however, had been implacably opposed to such a notion ever since its inception in 1899. During and after the First World War, Bunting and Jones's International Socialist League, the ICU led by Kadalie, and Transvaal Congress personalities like Mvabasa, could all claim some progress in encouraging the growth of unionism among Africans on the Witwatersrand — but never on the goldmines.

There had been three notable strikes on the mines (all broken with ruthless efficiency) between 1913 and 1920, but all were quite spontaneous. They certainly did not result from a breakdown in communications between an organised workforce and management, simply because there was no organisation and no communication in the trade union sense.

In 1913 the Communists had tried to penetrate into the gold mines but had failed to make so much as a pinhole in their ramparts, and it was eight years before another, and this time more effective move was made. A white trade unionist and Trotskyist from the Cape, Max Gordon, outwitted the mines police, and organised the distribution of hundreds of leaflets in a few of the compounds.

Black miners lived in heavily guarded, fenced enclaves (compounds) together with thousands of their fellows, speaking numerous dialects of half a dozen different languages. They slept on concrete bunks in concrete dormitories with up to forty other men from their own districts. Their diet, though plentiful and nutritionally adequate, was monotonous and repulsive: daily mounds of porridge and anonymous stew scooped out of vats. They trudged and queued for hours both above and under the ground to get to and from the stope where they broke and loaded rock at a depth that could exceed five thousand feet. In addition to the arduous labour in cramped, swelteringly hot and dangerous surroundings which is the lot of miners everywhere, it was normal for them to be abused and common for them to be assaulted by their white foremen. Under the terms of their indenture, they were forbidden to leave the compound without permission, and managements tacitly accepted homosexual activity in preference to giving their employees full latitude to go to the brothels and shebeens outside, where they were often attacked and robbed or arrested for causing drunken disturbances and tribal faction fights. The only large-scale recreation organised for them was 'war dances', which was hardly enough for men separated from all normal life for ten months and more at a time.[5] With tinder like that, Max Gordon's first pamphlets and converts sent flames licking through many compounds within a few months of the outbreak of the Second World War. Meetings began secretly at night in the dormitories and in the day in the yards outside them. Despite all efforts by the *indunas* (African overseers) and company police, it became impossible to keep trade union ideas from the huge multitude of peasants from all over southern Africa herded yearly into the gold mines of the Witwatersrand. The *indunas* were chased away and suspected spies beaten up.[6]

Although South Africa had entered the war against Hitler and Mussolini with one arm tied behind its back as it were, a new spirit had managed to reach the land. The government could not bring the country into a world-wide alliance against fascism without using slogans and making promises about a better and freer world which would include the whole of humanity, not just the white race. Word of this had obviously reached the remotest kraals, and hence had tunnelled into the bowels of the gold-bearing Reef.

By now, too, the most obstreperous South African Nazis were being interned and their sympathisers reduced to sullen silence and conspiracy. The English-speaking whites were becoming as liberal as their Tory counterparts in Britain, and many young Afrikaners, especially in the armed forces, were becoming truly liberal. It was all very momentary — but intoxicating while it lasted.

In 1941 the Communist Party re-entered the mining field. The prime motivator of the move was Gaur Radebe, strongly supported by John Marks. Gaur, together with James Majoro, a non-Communist mine clerk and one-time labourer underground, began to contact and instruct small groups of recruits.[7]

Within a year (in August 1941), it was possible to inaugurate a miners' union. To that end, the Transvaal Congress called a conference in Johannesburg which included a large number of black political and trade union leaders, and which was actually welcomed by some white trade unions in other industries, as well as by radical members of the Institute of Race Relations. This happened a month after Germany's invasion of the USSR, which transformed Churchill and Stalin, and therefore, Smuts, into brothers-in-arms.

The African Mineworkers Union had at last become a reality, even if a reality still unrecognised by the authorities (unless habitual alarm mixed with equally habitual contempt amount to recognition). Its president, SP Matseke, the upstanding but ailing president of the Transvaal branch of Congress, was soon to be succeeded by John Marks. Its secretary was James Majoro. It had a name, a committee made up of Communists and others, and an office.

There was little need, however, for fearless agitators, typists and stencilling machines. Word-of-mouth voicing of grievances and solidarity was enough, and the miners' response had a momentum of its own which fitted no conventional pattern of industrial action. Here, rather, was all the pent-up surge of a peasants' revolt.[8]

A year and a half later the restlessness in the compounds became too great for the mining companies to ignore. They recommended, and the Smuts government accepted, what all sensible governments turn to when pushed to do something but obliged to do nothing: the appointment of a commission of inquiry.

With loudspeakers at big assemblies, the Chamber of Mines made the good news known on all their properties, and, for good measure, throughout the reserves and beyond.

Although its title was the Witwatersrand Mine Natives Wages Commission, the inquiry's terms of reference were wide enough to cover not only wages but conditions in the compounds and on the tribal lands. It was headed by Mr Justice Lansdown from Natal, the highly respected author of South Africa's standard textbook on criminal law. From the judge's reputation and the terms of reference, it was hard to tell whether

Smuts wanted a genuine inquiry or a whitewashing one, but as things turned out, there was very little whitewash. The commission performed quite another function. It succeeded (as Bismarck would have said), in drowning the country's basic problems in ink. The black miners were kept quiet for the months during which it sat, the months during which it came to its conclusions, and the months before Smuts came to a real decision. By that time, the war and the restraints it imposed were over.[9]

The Communists on the executive of the African Mineworkers Union were hardly keen on having Basner present its case to the Commission. Basner felt this was not as much out of personal animosity as because, like Smuts, they were in something of a cleft stick. What they really wanted was a showdown. But a showdown between striking miners and the gold industry would interfere with the war effort, no matter how desirable its other consequences might be.[10] Failing that, he believed, they wanted vigorous protests to be made against the colour bar and the privileges it gave the white miners but did not want to offend the white working class. They wanted fierce criticism of the Chamber of Mines but without stressing that the Bank of England and the US Department of the Treasury (inter alia) were as much responsible for its paltry wages and callous manipulations as South African racist greed. They could not be sure that Basner would observe the subtle distinctions between a policy necessary to a Kremlin in league with capitalism and the urgent desires of an oppressed section of humanity to cast off at least some of its chains.

Pressure in favour of his appointment was so strong from the non-Communist miners' leaders, the Transvaal Congress and others, however, that no one else was really considered. He knew the history, the conditions, the difficulties and duplicities of the goldmining industry better than anyone else except perhaps his opposite number: William Gemmill, who was to appear for the Chamber of Mines.

In this, the most important public inquiry for many decades, the governing body of the goldmining companies' association had not chosen, as might have been expected, any of its top managing directors or legal experts, but Gemmill, assisted only by his son.

Gemmill, a giant Scot packed with brains, charm and knowledge — a very Rolls Royce of a man — was probably the most able official at the Chamber of Mines, though his post was ostensibly a secondary one.

As head of the Witwatersrand Native Labour Association (WNLA), he was responsible for the recruitment of about 150 000 men yearly, mainly from the then Portuguese East Africa, Northern Rhodesia and Nyasaland. Until 1937, Gemmill had also been in charge of the Native Recruiting Corporation (NRC) which operated on behalf of the Chamber in South Africa as well as in the British High Commission Territories of Basutoland, Bechuanaland and Swaziland (which were, in all but administration, the equivalent of very large native reserves). He had, however, relinquished his leadership of the NRC in order to extend the activities of the WNLA northward, and so lessen the ever-troublesome dependence of the mines on South African labour.

A great deal of his life had been spent in bush shirt and shorts travelling to establish and supervise the recruiting camps and offices that lay scattered from Port Elizabeth in the Cape Province to Fort Hill near the Tanganyikan border, to places close to Angola and the Belgian Congo.

The Commission expressed its surprise when Basner, in his opening address on behalf of the miners, referred to a labour force of a million men. (The judge had no doubt heard of his reputation for immoderate claims and exaggerations).

Gemmill came quickly and smoothly to the Commission's assistance, explaining that the gold industry preferred a black miner to work for an optimum period of no more than fourteen months and then go home to rest (unpaid, of course) for another ten or so. In effect, therefore, up to a million workers were indeed required every two years — if the coal mines were included — to maintain an establishment of about 400 000.

Mr Justice Lansdown, a shrewd and experienced man, understood why Gemmill had intervened and explained that figure of a million men before an array of journalists. He knew that Basner would have put the point differently, not saying 'the Chamber of Mines likes to send its people home after fourteen months at most', but 'the heat and toil underground are too much for the strongest of them after fourteen months, and the rock dust begins to wreck their lungs'.

Basner would have taken the opportunity to describe vividly the cement bunks, the unsightly and unvaried food, the distaste for sodomy and the assaults by white miners which management had tried vainly to curb. He would also have disclosed why it took the miners ten months to recover, because 'home' — at least for the slightly more than 42 per cent who came from the South African reserves[11] — was a denuded rural slum whose thin soil yielded thin crops, thin cattle and thinner milk, and had, in their absence, to be ploughed by women and old men.

Of course, all this evidence was brought out later, through the government's own reports, through medical and veterinary officers, not missionaries and clergymen and the Institute of Race Relations, and through Congress and the testimony of the black miners themselves. But a dramatic outburst on the first day would have been newsworthy, unlike the slow accumulation of damning facts which was to fill the coming weeks. Facts worried Gemmill far less than press publicity, so tactically speaking, he had won the first round on points. Strategically, the Chamber of Mines and Field Marshal Smuts could now wait, to win the second round three years late by a knockout and through the barrel of a gun.

All those facts amounted to nothing, really, when considered against the history of wage deterioration.

In 1943 the average black miner was receiving exactly the same money as he had in 1896: two shillings and threepence per shift — slightly under three pounds a month. Allowing for inflation, this was more than 15 per cent less in real terms than he had earned forty-five years before.[12]

The white miner could claim that his real earnings had risen very little in that period, but he still received ten times as much as the black's cash wage, food, lodging and hospital treatment put together. Since whites constituted about a tenth of the total mine labour force, the total wage bill for them came to about the same as that for the entire complement of blacks. In addition, they were paid a good deal more as miners than they could expect as factory workers whereas Africans employed on the mines were getting half as much as those employed in the manufacturing industry.

In the restrained prose of a modern economist, '... the imperfections (in the labour market) that enabled the goldmines to maintain their policy of collusion lay in legislation that enabled them to isolate their labour resources from the competing sector.'[13]

In other words a whole apparatus of government had been set up to channel hundreds of thousands of men into mining and pay them half the going rate in secondary industry.

The great difficulty about wages was, of course, the price of gold, a commodity whose selling price is not the concern of its producers but of international financiers acting through governments, reserve banks, national treasuries, currency requirements and currency speculations. All these are linked by invisible yet unbreakable threads with thousands of share manipulators in hundreds of mining and investment companies on all the main stock exchanges of the world. It must be presumed that the Chamber of Mines and the government of South Africa (mostly through its fiscal powers) had an influence in determining the gold price, but by no means an important one.

It was claimed that the low price plus high taxation and production costs made profitability so small that the decrease in wages was inevitable. As often happens in South Africa, the explanation made some sense on the face of it but was basically sheer falsehood.

Superficially, an increase of even one shilling per shift on a goldmining labour force of over three hundred thousand would mean an annual increase of more than fifty-five million pounds, which the industry would at that time have had difficulty in finding. Actually, the argument was nonsense, because the government was taking a very large share of the profits in taxation in order to give the white population a living standard, social services and subsidies it could not possibly otherwise afford. The government also obliged the mines to continue employing, for overtly political reasons, an unnecessary and highly paid force of white miners. The remaining profits paid dividends on shares whose worth was calculated, not on their face value, but on their stock exchange quotations, in many cases five — and sometimes twenty — times their face value.

Try as hard as he could, Gemmill could not destroy the case made for an increase in the black miners' wages. The chairman of the Commission himself seemed unhappy and uneasy at the overwhelming nature of the case, and could only try to persuade the union to modify its claims.

Gemmill did not panic and did not seem half as worried as Judge Lansdown, though Basner and the African Mineworkers Union knew that an attempt had been made through an Anglican bishop to stop certain clergymen from giving evidence, and that the mining industry's police, black and white, were intimidating other witnesses. These efforts were not very rewarding, since they could be publicised, as Basner managed to do in an attack on the mines police at the New Consolidated Gold Mine in the person of their chief, Colonel Trigger — alleging spying, infiltration into trade unions and harassment. Unlike the mass of accurate details about miserable conditions and rates of pay this made good newspaper headlines, especially when Trigger replied with a suit for slander, which caused a great sensation (and which he failed to win).[14]

In spite of Gemmill's rosy description of the fruitful Bantu homelands producing crops to augment the miners' earnings so that a living wage was enjoyed by all; in spite of his photographs of happy tribal warriors dancing their war dances every Sunday; in spite of his dire warnings that even a penny a day more on wages would spell ruin for the industry, the Commission had to recommend an increase of over twenty percent, amounting to between fivepence and sixpence per eight-hour shift.

That recommendation was made in December 1943. They were great heroes: Basner the Senator, the Communists and non-Communists on the Union's executive, the Congress leaders, the white clergymen who had braved their bishop, even the judge who proposed wages that would now equal those of forty-five years earlier. The news spread wildly in the compounds. There were whistles, chants, stampings of feet in victory.

In April 1944, the government announced its approval of a rise of fourpence to fivepence, to be paid for by a remission of mining taxation. Then came two years of quiet until August 1946 when Smuts was ready to respond to the challenge of the African Mineworkers Union — and did so with a knock-out.

19

OH, WHAT A BEAUTIFUL HARMONY...
(1943)

In 1943, while the Mine Wages Commission was successfully defusing black dynamite underground, the African population as a whole continued to flicker, heave and occasionally give vent to explosions, but seemed as unready as ever for resistance of a systematic kind. In the middle of that year, though, something happened which was as little foreseen by black leaders as by white theorists of every political persuasion.

This happening related to a superficially minor and local issue, affecting an urban community which was neither typical nor celebrated for its discipline: Alexandra Township.

A busy and efficient dual carriageway, Louis Botha Avenue, ran out of Johannesburg towards Pretoria, passing through several miles of white suburbia before crossing the city limits and reaching open country. Off it, an untarred road led to the crest of a rise, beneath which Alexandra lay, spread out like an enormous and dirty checked apron.

Called a 'township', it housed about eighty thousand people. No one had seriously tried to count them, and none of them was keen to be counted. It was divided into two and a half thousand quarter-acre stands, each with a tin-roofed house or so, some quite substantial. The standholders owned their property in name, but very few were free of loans at fearsome rates of interest. Every owner had lodgers, not only in his or her house, but in mud huts and shacks cluttering its yard: working people; invalids and aged couples; children playing and crying; drunkards brawling; women squatting on the ground over fire-tins to do their cooking.

Alexandra was nominally managed by a small 'Health Committee' of provincial officials and appointed or elected blacks and whites. It resembled Johannesburg's municipal locations in that it was undrained and had no electricity, but it outdid them in general squalor. Its water came from occasional standpipes and it had a single and pathetically inadequate clinic. Alexandra's criminal gangs were ferocious, and early any morning the sight of a corpse in a gutter caused no surprise and no one passing by looked at what it was safest not to notice. Horrible liquors were brewed in its yards, with horrible effects, of which not the least were the police raids which sought to destroy them. In winter, the wind would send smoke, dust and rubbish swirling, and summer rains poured mud and water down open ditches to drown children, dislodge foundations, swamp shanties and turn craters into stinking ponds.

A dreadful place? Yes, and no.

Alexandra was the largest of the few freehold townships for blacks in the neighbourhood of Johannesburg and had been laid out and acquired by Africans before the Land Act of 1913. Situated in the midst of farmland, it was one of the few footholds that remained for an established — as opposed to migrant — urban population.

The importance of a place like this lay not only its value in the sense that it provided homes, but in the fact that it enabled blacks to live near a city without permission from the municipality and without having to work for a white person. Living in Alexandra was almost equivalent to being a free citizen in South Africa and was a spiritual as much as a practical matter.

Those who wanted to be tailors, or mechanics fixing old jalopies, or *ngakas* selling herbal remedies — any occupation in which it was not necessary to serve a white man — could not live in a location like Orlando (now part of Soweto).

Well-known political agitators, trade unionists or others carrying on activities which did not please the authorities had no chance of a house in a location.

Alexandra was home to burglars and shebeen queens and to refugees who had lost their right to stay in Johannesburg because they were disabled, unemployed or widowed. It provided opportunities for thrifty professional men, petty traders and retired mine clerks who found an outlet for investment there. People let rooms and rackrented mercilessly, subject to no more moral condemnation than a hungry barracuda in a shoal of sardines. Overcrowding, there and elsewhere, put a premium on living space, and the price of land doubled and quadrupled yearly.

All these multifarious people represented only a part of the main body of Alexandra which was made up of steady, ordinary men and women who queued for buses every day to go to work in the factories, shops and kitchens of Johannesburg. They went to work on a slice of bread and a cup of strong black tea, taking no sandwiches with them, nor even a spare slice of bread. Bread and porridge had to be left behind for the children and the old.

They would start lining up in the dark between three and four o'clock in the morning, and wait for two hours and more. Of course the buses were packed as tightly as possible. Of course there were arguments with drivers and conductors and frequent breakdowns of worn-out vehicles. Police were seldom in evidence, although, especially on paydays, pickpockets were — some of them murderers highly skilled in the silent use of sharpened skewers (inserted into the spines of passengers).

These were the people who were asked, in 1943, to pay two extra pennies a day — one to go and one to return — on each fourpenny single bus fare.

Because their township did not belong to Johannesburg and because its very existence was contrary to government policy, Alexandra's commuters were not supplied with public transport. The buses belonged to a number of private operators (all whites except one) who naturally wanted to make as much money as possible.

The bus users naturally wanted the fares to be as low as possible. As regular customers of a service essential to their livelihood, they felt it a grievous hardship to be called on to pay almost as much per mile as the white workers using the Witwatersrand's transport system, who — in decent comfort — had shorter distances to go and earned at least five times as much as they. The war had inflated costs: petrol and spares on the one hand, and food, clothing and rents on the other.

The people refused to pay the penny increase. Instead, they decided to boycott the buses and walk. Walk they did — twenty miles daily to work and back — for nine days. At Basner's urging, their leadership organised itself into the Alexandra Emergency Transport Committee.

On the morning of 1 August, and in direct response to Basner's suggestion, made at a meeting of 5 000 people, a tremendous phalanx of men and women formed itself in the darkness to move out of the township, leaving the buses to stand empty. As the sun rose, they marched into Louis Botha Avenue, filling the roadway from pavement to pavement, tramping past garden gates and shops and blocks of flats and into the city. On a long banner stretched in front of them was written 'We Will Walk Until Our Fares Are Fourpence'.

Estimates of their numbers ranged up to fifteen thousand, but their march was not just prodigious in itself, the prodigy was that so robust a growth should have sprouted from the yeast of Alexandra.

They won. The owners capitulated and the fare remained at fourpence. (It was to stay so for a year. In November, 1944, they had to walk again — not for nine days but nine weeks — before they could win once more.)[1]

During the bus boycott an episode occurred which only just failed to be a major one. For Basner, it chiefly served to underline the implications of his interview with Colin Steyn at the Ministry of Justice — that the police were as much an arm of extreme Afrikaner nationalism as the open Nazis — and to harden his feelings about his own profession.

The boycott and march had been launched thanks to a ruling by the provincial Transportation Board that the bus owners were entitled to the penny increase. This was fair enough because of the steep rise in costs, but since the commuters' wages had not risen and tuppence a day meant just so much less in slices of bread, the obvious course for the officials on the Board was to recommend a subsidy from the Johannesburg muncipality or the Transvaal Provincial Council. If this had been done, one or both of those bodies would have been obliged to find the necessary funds.

Such a solution, however, was not what the officials, as good *Broederbonders*, wanted. Tension and protests in Alexandra, black workers demonstrating and disrupting city streets and inevitable racial clashes and racial insecurity for the white voting public, could always yield good electoral dividends for the National Party.

Picketing to stop dissenting passengers from using the buses began at about four o'clock every morning and went on until sunrise, by which time all the marchers would be assembled. Sometimes things got rough, but mostly there was more noise than physical hindrance and the bus owners did not call for police assistance because they knew the likely consequences of a confrontation.

Foiled by the owners, the Native Affairs Department decided that Alexandra's excited scene was a favourable one into which to send small squads of black constables to demand poll-tax receipts (and, incidentally, passes). A violent reaction was inevitable, and was what the white police and Native Affairs officials were waiting for. The African organisers of the boycott were well aware of this and asked Basner to come to the township early every day to keep an eye open and help control the crowds.

He managed to be there well before dawn on each of the first four days but was late on the fifth, when he arrived to find over two hundred men lined up against a fence, some of them handcuffed. Many, he later discovered, had stood there obediently in bitter cold since three, when the constables guarding them had begun to arrest everyone who was not carrying papers or whose papers were not in order. A huge throng of residents, some with sticks and some with bricks, was milling about them, screaming death to the police if the prisoners were not released. There was no chance of pacifying anyone, so all Basner could do was push his way through to speak to the constables, feeling fairly confident that there would be no attack if he was seen to be parleying.

There were only four policemen. Their leader was a sensible person who quickly got the point that armed reinforcements would arrive too late to save him and his fellows if they continued to hold the arrested men. It needed only a few moments for the handcuffed ones to be freed whilst the rest melted away.

Relieved of one danger but now becoming apprehensive of another, the constables persuaded Basner to drive them to their station to explain to their superiors what had happened and the crowd, first bidding them farewell with mixed hoots and cheers, resumed its noisy but harmless jostling around the doors of the empty buses. Feeling rather noble, Basner was glad to get home to his breakfast.

About noon that day, two white police officers looking very grave came to his office to see him. They had a warrant for his arrest for the statutory crime of inciting prisoners to escape from lawful custody.

What might have been a traumatic experience for most white citizens, and probably for most lawyers, was a matter of such familiar routine to Basner that his shock was only momentary. Even during the short walk to the magistrates' courts, he could figure out what had happened.

As soon as the officers had heard the story he and the African constables had told them, they had realised it was a godsend. Basner could be alleged to have headed the mob and to have exhorted the prisoners to run. Whether the constables had resisted this version at first, he could not, of course, know but at best he could not imagine their gratitude to him holding out for very long against their superiors. And the charge was well chosen, since it carried a mandatory prison sentence on conviction which could automatically lose him his parliamentary seat.

The activity between six in the morning and noon must have been terrific for sufficient perjured affidavits to be prepared to convince the Attorney-General in Pretoria that there was a case to answer. Basner was, after all, a member of the Senate of the Union of South Africa, and its status had to be respected in his person, even if he had only become a Senator through an embarrassing historical accident. He could imagine what pressure had been put on Colin Steyn, who must have been responsible for the courteousness of his arrest, followed by an immediate appearance in court and immediate and unconditional bail.

That afternoon, back in his office, he discussed the case with Vernon Berrangé, a radical lawyer known throughout the country as an

Oh, What a Beautiful Harmony . . .

outstanding specialist in criminal law.[2] Basner's instinct was to conduct his own defence and so make a real political trial of the matter but he could not dismiss Berrangé's warning: the old adage that a lawyer who acts for himself has a fool for a client.

Berrangé was later to propose that Donald Molteno (as distinguished a barrister as he was an MP) lead the defence. He himself would then be at liberty to give evidence. As he happened to be an elected white member of Alexandra's Health Committee, he was in a position to give an authoritative description of the current mood of crisis in the township, and the kind of impact that mass searches under the detested poll-tax and pass laws could have on its inhabitants.

A few weeks later, the three of them strode (more or less together) into legal battle. Outside the court, over a thousand Africans — mostly women — took the trial as an opportunity to demonstrate, carrying banners inscribed 'Stop Poll-Tax Raids'.

For their pains, Basner's two expensive, but this time feeless, legal eagles flanked an ungrateful client who kept audibly interrupting them and grumbling that they were wasting their time on technicalities when they should be proving that the police had been sent to provoke an incident which could justify a massacre.

Mr Eyles, the magistrate, who indicated at the outset that he did not approve of poll-tax or pass raids when a place such as Alexandra was in a state of turmoil, asked counsel therefore not to press the point. Their acceptance of this reasonable request left Basner spluttering with indignation. Even the righteousness of his indignation had, however, to be reduced when Mr Eyles hinted that if the defence could only show the accused to have freed the prisoners in order to save the lives of the police, a verdict of guilty would merely bring detention until the rising of the court (which the Senate could hardly equate with imprisonment).

The magistrate was one of a breed of fair-minded men which existed in South Africa before the generation indoctrinated by the *Broederbond* invaded a considerable part of the judiciary and the whole civil service. He also had no more belief in political trials than did his brethren in other portions of the British Commonwealth, so in no time he contrived to reduce the case to a simple question of whether the witnesses on this side or on that were telling the truth. Basner was obliged to sit quietly — just like one of his own clients — watching the scales of justice as they swayed gently up and down.

It was hard for Molteno to prove that the police were lying. The constables had clearly been rehearsed with great care. 'Senator Basner was in front of the crowd. He shouted to us that we had no right to arrest the prisoners, and that we'd all be killed if we didn't free them. He shouted at them to run, and they ran.' That was all they remembered, and, word-perfect, stuck to it.

It was touch and go, but the balance finally tipped in Basner's favour.

Summing up, Eyles declared himself particularly impressed by the evidence for the defence of Witness X. Witness X, he felt, had supported the accused with a remarkable combination of forthrightness and precision, and had persuaded him that a verdict of 'not guilty' was in order.

It was a wonderful day for justice — ending with hurrahs duly accompanied by official thumps and calls for silence in court.

Down in the street outside there were more hurrahs from sympathisers streaming up with congratulations.

Basner's secretary paused on the steps for a moment to watch the scene. She had recently spent a great deal of time on interviews with eyewitnesses wishing to testify to what had in truth happened at that now-famous bus terminus. Volunteers had been very numerous, which had meant a lot of typing of statements for her employer and his counsel to choose from.

A man passed by whom she recognised. It was Witness X, on his way home, unnoticed and unthanked, she thought, so she called out to him. Here was an opportunity to compliment him on the magistrate's remarks about his testimony and perhaps suggest that Basner, too, would like to do so.

He smiled cheerfully. 'Madam,' he said, 'I'll tell you something'. His voice dropped a little as he began to describe how he had chanced to be away in the Reef town of Boksburg when the boycott started and had stayed there until it was over and the buses were running again. 'You see,' he explained, 'when I came home and heard what had happened to Mr Basner, I thought to myself 'What that man needs is the very best quality help. That's why I gave my evidence . . . even though I wasn't there'.

All she could think of was a quick getaway . . . and made it. Her distressing information gave Basner a few moments of panic, but the effect of X's efforts on his behalf lasted a lifetime. Morally and legally his situation was clear enough. A helpful rogue had saved him from hostile villains out to destroy him, and all he had been told of this was hearsay. There was nothing he could or needed to do except echo the wisdom of Ecclesiastes: 'Be not righteous overmuch . . . wherefore shouldst thou destroy thyself?'

But what about Eyles, whose days were passed in the ironclad belief that he could mete out justice on the basis of his powers of observation of the demeanour of witnesses? What about Berrangé and Molteno, with all their professional skill and personal dedication? What had they done to free an innocent man, compared to that clever and audacious liar? What about the shallow and meretricious techniques with which the search for truth goes on in courts? What about the actual crimes, committed by the police, which had been so studiously passed over by upright defenders and an upright judge?

Basner could not say that his disenchantment with his profession commenced with Witness X's successful perjury on his behalf and the conduct of the trial in general. It merely strengthened a dislike which had started when he had first met Cicero at school.

Outwardly, urban areas set aside for African occupation resembled camps for displaced persons rather than communities. They were made up of people gathered from all ends of the southern half of a continent, diversified by language, past history, religion and custom, and liable to be shifted back again at any time.

Inwardly, though, they had much to share. If very few of them were officially accepted as town dwellers, nearly all regarded themselves as such. All resented the gross legal insecurity in which they lived (because they were black) even more than the daily material and social hazards they faced (because they were the poorest of the poor).

The Alexandra bus boycott revealed the unity that can underlie diversity and its leadership typified it. Of the many people notably concerned with the boycott, it will suffice to describe only six.

There was Gaur Radebe, one of the founders of the Mineworkers Union, thrown out of the Communist Party as a 'spy and provocateur' in the hyper-revolutionary days of 1931, readmitted only to be rightly chucked out again for 'petty bourgeois' behaviour late in 1941. Now back in the Party once more, he had spent months collecting evidence for the Mine Wages Commission, and was running a lively branch in Alexandra. In later life he would join the black racist Pan Africanist Congress, be forced into exile, and there make fruitless efforts to reconcile his new party with the African National Congress which by that time was Marxist inclined. He was quick and energetic, muddle-headed and all too human, humorous and brave.

There was Lilian Tshabalala who lived in a filthy yard, in a room she scrubbed clean with the same ferocity as she attacked anyone daring to cross a picket-line. Small, with a plain, squashed little face that could at any moment burst into laughter or loud command, she seemed to have sprung from nowhere, born young-middle-aged, minimally educated and firmly topped by a tight-fitting black beret. It was she who created and led the Alexandra Women's Brigade during the 1943 boycott. The Brigade consisted of formidable church women and beer brewers who made themselves responsible for the township's solidarity and good order especially among faint-hearted or riotously disposed men.

Self Mampuru, like Gaur Radebe, had been on Basner's committee in the preceding year. As a thirty-five-year-old assistant to William Ballinger in the Friends of Africa, he had intimate contacts with old ICU militants, yet also had credentials respectable enough to allow him a place in a municipal location. No political heavyweight and certainly no firebrand, Self had a sound understanding of the principles of trade unionism and was an able committee man. Rather staid, he could be wryly amusing, especially on the subject of the British. As a student at

Durham University College some years before, he had discovered himself to be a rare and exotic African bird — so rare in those days that his popularity one winter in Edinburgh amazed him until he learnt of the Scots belief in the good luck it brings to have a black man 'first footing' it through your door on New Year's Day.³

Who but Richard Baloyi could contrive to be both a champion among bus boycotters and a bus owner? Treasurer General of Congress, he had probably been appointed to that position because of the money he made from being the sole black among all Alexandra's bus owners. Was he as fiery as Gaur Radebe the Communist merely because he saw where his political bread was buttered? Or was he aware that it was the white besiegers of his Alexandra who owed him his penny on the fare? Five years later (accused by Gaur), he was to be ousted from his post in Congress for endorsing Afrikaner supporters of apartheid seeking election as Native Representatives in Parliament.

Finally there were Mr and Mrs AEP Fish, who owned a little printing press from which they earned a modest living by cranking out funeral notices, dance band advertisements and church announcements. Very active and determined organisers of the Alexandra march, the two of them were indispensable as instant producers and distributors of information in a place where eighty thousand people had no daily paper and certainly less than a dozen telephones. It was their smudged leaflets which told the place and time of meetings, exhorted everyone to stand firm (and, incidentally, advertised for witnesses to the near-riot at the bus terminus in which Basner had been involved).

When the boycott was over, the Fishs printed a calendar for 1944 and mounted it on a photograph of the township's army on the march. The caption they gave it was, on the surface, a simple expression of local hope and pride, but it contained a far from innocent message to black political leaders throughout the country: 'Oh, what a beautiful harmony, when saying and doing go together.'

20

MUCH SAYING, LITTLE DOING, SOME THINKING

If very few residents of Alexandra were dues-paying members of the African National Congress, far fewer were disposed to deny it emotional allegiance. In spite of differences in temperament and political outlook, all those who belonged to the Emergency Transport Committee which organised the bus boycott thought it natural to be supporters of Congress. Just as naturally, they wished their exertions to be made in its name, or at least under its patronage.

In the past, African men and women all over the country had tended to feel social identity only with their kin and quasi-feudal home territories, and perhaps with people who spoke their own languages. Now, they not only regarded themselves as belonging to a huge repressed class numbering about seven million within the South African body politic, but to a class which constituted a nationality, and a nationality which in turn constituted the very substance of the South African nation.

Congress, despite its manifest decline from the peak it had so swiftly and dramatically reached at the time of its inception, symbolised much more than a political party with claims to represent specific sectional interests and attitudes.

Unlike the ICU, and certainly unlike any other organisation (including the All-African Convention), it symbolised the potential parliament of a subjugated land.

It had been powerless to stem the spate of noxious legislation which overwhelmed the black population after the establishment of the Union of South Africa in 1910 and the chiefs, originally its most substantial backers, became both estranged from politics and personally degraded in consequence of the Land Act of 1913. They and the peasantry ceased to furnish the mainspring of public protest.

The leaders who subsequently occupied the highest positions in Congress were people who had become painfully familiar with the workings and capabilities of a modern authoritarian state. This was because they were increasingly better educated, urbanised and enterprising and because the fulfilment of their modest professional or commercial ambitions demanded exceptional perseverance and ingenuity. They gained status — and retained it — for those reasons, but the process they had been obliged to pass through in order to comprehend and manipulate an alien environment served to separate most of them from full contact with their own. Their popular roots were loosened and their political growth, deprived of natural sap, was in no way stimulated by the gentle rain of white missionary and liberal thought that mitigated the harsh climate of white supremacy.

This is by no means to say that they were incapable of voicing class bitterness and national yearnings. What they failed to do was appreciate the vigour and intelligence of the human resources at their disposal and provide the organisational means whereby these could be canalised into political significance.

A largely illiterate black population remained stubbornly convinced of its need for a broad-based national protest movement, but made no concerted attempt to oust its largely spineless (and by now self-perpetuating) leaders. This was simply because those men still seemed to humbler souls to be the only available people with sufficient education to conduct the administration of such a movement and speak to their rulers in its name. Since, however, they also seemed scarcely able to do anything except speak, hard common sense led the humble to refrain from expending energy and hard-earned money until it became potentially rewarding for them to do so.

Congress therefore had a curious existence between 1919 and 1939. It had presidents, secretaries, treasurers and tens of thousands of adherents ready to demonstrate or strike at one moment or another, but for most of that time only a few hundreds actually belonged to it, and its funds were derisory. When its senior functionaries made petitions to government they could justly claim to express the discontent of an entire people but

Much Saying, Little Doing, Some Thinking 157

when asked how many paid-up members they represented, always found it awkward, and often impossible, to reply.

During the few years before and after the outbreak of World War II, popular enthusiasm for the concept of Congress, combined with individual efforts by elements of a younger generation to translate it into practicality, had engendered great hope (as well as considerable pride) in Basner, his friends, and many others. But in the months following the election of 1942, their ebullience was forced to subside and at the time of the Alexandra march it finally shrivelled into froth.

The rumbling proclamations of the Treasurer General of Congress, loud on the side of the embattled township, were all too plainly those of Richard Baloyi in his private capacity. Congress itself, typified by its President General, Dr AB Xuma, did no more than deplore the plight of the commuters and suggest that it would be best for them to cease their dangerous defiance and give him free rein to negotiate with authority in a courteous manner.[1]

Dr Xuma was eminently representative of the intellectual black elite which had come to prominence in the 1930s. He had neither stomach for, nor faith in, mass action and had been taught to believe firmly that if a sufficiently logical appeal against grievances could be drawn up and if it could gain access to the right quarters — that is to say, if Smuts or his cabinet ministers could be persuaded to read it — those grievances stood a chance of being redressed. Such a belief obviously made no sense, but it was also not one which would lead a respectable medical practitioner into any embarrassment — let alone arrest and imprisonment.

As a busy professional man who felt himself rightfully entitled to earn a fair amount of money and acquire a certain amount of property, Xuma had the same aspirations as any other middle class person. He had little of the passion — and none of the intemperance and irresponsibility — of Seme and all the pacific instincts — and none of the deep Christian identification with the poor and ignorant — of Dube. Basner, who had known him long and well, first as an ex-pupil and confidant of Charlotte Maxeke and then as one of his own clients, considered him a political disaster, but certainly not a mediocrity. When dealing with people willing to listen to reason, nobody could marshal an argument more skilfully or present it more forcefully than he. Although he was only elected President General by a casting vote out of a total nation-wide muster of no more than forty-one delegates, nobody could challenge him on grounds of ability.

Throughout his spell in office, which lasted from 1940 to 1949, Xuma made no real bid to organise Congress among the tribespeople in the reserves, and limited most of his contacts there to the chiefs. Decades had passed, however, since the chiefs had exercised influence, possessed any wealth or were prepared to defend themselves or their followers and the great majority of them had by now become no more than torpid minor civil servants, clad in the shreds of a traditional dignity that gave their spirits no more warmth than the rags their people wore gave comfort to their bones.

True, Xuma went to considerable lengths in the towns, travelling at his own expense to arrange public meetings and press for the creation of proper network of branches and the recruitment of 'a million' members. It is also true that Congress was not only undermanned, but in confusion, with each province jealously trying to keep its affairs to itself, and many local personalities wayward, dishonest or both. Above all, huge distances, extreme poverty, pass laws and police harassment were impediments to efficiency which only a mood of dedicated optimism in the existing rank and file was likely to overcome. Such a mood was one that Xuma was temperamentally unable to inspire.

Had his efforts borne substantial fruit, it is more than probable he would have regretted them. Since, however, they produced very little, he could continue to pay public tribute to the power inherent in the masses (for which he had as much distaste as Field Marshal Smuts) whilst finding it less uncomfortable to operate in the limited milieu in which he felt at home.

Adept at diplomacy, sharp, firm-willed and tidy-minded, Xuma assiduously canvassed the support of university-trained people like himself, sidetracked the militant and reproved the corrupt, reworded Congress's constitution in a sensible manner and tackled the hitherto impossible task of bringing order to its puny finances.

Conservatism was fortified in the National Executive. Some of the disorder (and most of the vitality) was suppressed at provincial level. Membership figures sometimes rose and sometimes fell, reaching at best something under five thousand (almost entirely accounted for by the Transvaal and the city of Bloemfontein).

Xuma was not only President General of Congress. He lived and had his headquarters on the Witwatersrand and was also Alexandra's Medical Officer of Health. When, therefore, at the time of the bus boycott and the great march, he failed even to set foot in the township, numerous people were shocked into thinking and doing what a short while before had seemed unthinkable to them.

They concluded that if Alexandra could put no heart into Congress nothing would, and so it was that Paul Mosaka and others (with a great deal more than approval from Basner), launched a new political party, some six weeks after the boycott ended. It was called the African Democratic Party[2] — the ADP — and its form and aims were essentially the fruit of the moment.

Mosaka was a staunch radical — very much in the mould of those who had agitated for reform in the Britain of over a hundred years earlier and whose commitment to the cause of social justice was as often buttressed by Scripture and John Bunyan as by Tom Paine or Cobbett, Fourier or

Owen. Like many of them, he had middle-class economic interests, educational attainments and ambitions, yet could not but champion a downtrodden and disfranchised working class, because he too was disfranchised and — certainly spiritually — downtrodden. Unlike an early nineteenth century Briton, however, he had no middle class to spring from or join, support or attack.

In the mid-1940s less than half of one per cent of seven million Africans was made up of white-collar employees of all grades, together with all self-employed individuals other than peasants. About thirteen thousand primary school teachers made up the majority of this percentage and of the couple of thousand entrepreneurs it included, most were pedlars and hawkers or artisans in a very small and insecure way of business. In the 1936 Census the grand total of doctors, lawyers and professional academics came to sixty-four and these, together with a few hundred better-off clergy, contractors and traders who had amassed enough money to live in a tolerable financial state, constituted not so much a bourgeoisie as a coterie — and a thinly spread one at that.

As a graduate and ex-teacher who had become a business manager, Mosaka's most natural backing came from teachers and small traders, but the unlettered townspeople who had pushed for his election to the Orlando location advisory board and then the Native Representative Council were well aware of the character which lay beneath his correct and spectacled appearance. When he spoke, the few who knew him to be an invalid could forget the fact under the impact of his emotional and mental force.

Close friendship allowed him to enjoy fiery arguments with Basner, whose Marxism he was only prepared to accept insofar as it exposed the elementary dynamics of the society in which they both lived, but not when it premissed the necessary abolition of capitalism and hence ultimately of private property. That is to say, he was an enlightened nationalist whose dream was of an open society in which no one could be kept under by reason of race and in which an African could become a capitalist and belong to a large and flourishing middle class like any other middle class in the world.

Mosaka had three notable allies in starting the ADP. Two of these were Self Mampuru and JJ Lesolang.

Both Mampuru and Lesolang were talented in staff work rather than agitation, but Self had been involved for most of his life in politics and trade-unionism — including the ICU — and was a well-known personality on his own account. Lesolang, much more conservative in temperament, mild-mannered and not particularly strong-willed, was a personality because of his titular position and his conscientiousness in performing the duties it imposed on him. As president of the Transvaal African Teachers Association, he represented several thousand ill-paid men and women whose influence in the African community had always been profound and pervasive and who were now casting off their old role as advocates of political passivity and turning themselves into angry proponents of protest. Lesolang's genuine enthusiasm, first for Basner's Senate candidature and then for the ADP, was the response of a loyal and efficient bureaucrat to the expressed views of his executive.

Dan Koza belonged to a completely different breed. One of the most determined and courageous black trade-unionists of his day and by far the most capable, he had been trained by Gordon (of whom, as a white, much the same may be said), and like him, was a Trotskyist. When Gordon was interned in 1940, ostensibly because of his opposition to the War, Koza, as his second-in-command, took over the secretaryship of the sizeable African Commercial and Distributive Workers Union and proceeded to organise other workers as well — succeeding most conspicuously in the coal industry.

As an orator and agitator he had nothing to learn from Basner or Mosaka. To the harsh logic and irrepressible trumpet calls of the one and the beguiling mixture of wit, feeling and reason of the other, he added his own ingredients — a sardonic humour that shamed the timid, and an urgent professionalism that disciplined as well as reassured the hotheaded.

The physical contrast between Koza, characteristically glowering down on a mass of strikers from under his shabby old hat-brim, and Mosaka, neat as a pin, mordantly rebutting senior white officials in English far better than their own, may serve well enough to contrast the pair of them politically. It serves even better, however, to stress the depth of common feeling that drove people as different as they into forming or joining the ADP.

For them the elimination of white supremacy was so essential a preliminary to the achievement of their long-range political ideals that the sight of black militancy being balked by a Congress which should have inspired and spurred it on had become intolerable. Like Basner, they were reacting against the general impotence of elitism: intellectual and hypercritical in the Fourth International, Comintern-directed and hence opportunistic in the Communist Party, and above all, high-flown and prevaricating in the African National Congress.

The ADP arose solely in order to force the hand of Congress at a time when the Smuts government was obliged to refrain from deploying its full strength against an increasingly restive black population. None of its adherents, with the possible exception of Koza, was interested in disputing the broad aims of Congress or its role as a kind of national assembly to which most of them would have been pleased to be affiliated as an organisation. Their quarrel was with its lack of militancy in its capacity as a broadly-based African *party*.

Their own militancy was fundamentally non-violent. Knowing that the government had more than ample firepower on its side, they had a natural compunction about wasting human lives but had also come to realise that Smuts was not in a mood to be blatantly violent himself. At that particular date it was inexpedient for him to over indulge in callousness — especially in cities, where too much could be observed and reported to his detriment abroad.

The South African political atmosphere in the war years between 1940 and 1945 had become such as to make orderly mass demonstrations, strikes and passive resistance seem very feasible means of at least loosening the bonds of black servitude and relieving the painful lot of the Indian and coloured communities as well.

Tactics of this kind were spontaneously endorsed by a great many Africans who had no intention of joining the ADP and had also begun to be approved by an increasing number of people belonging to other racial groups and ranging in political conviction from far left to liberal. Mosaka and his allies, unlike the lukewarm Xuma, could feel that their wholly African party ought to collaborate energetically with the Indians and coloureds and could also, if with less optimism than Xuma, think it only sensible to be on good terms with sympathetic white members of the Institute of Race Relations.

The emergence of the ADP provoked individual behaviour which can only be compared to that in a close-knit family suddenly rent by divorce or a disputed inheritance. Deep old resentments surfaced loudly. The new party was variously assailed as white-inspired or dyed in the red of Trotskyism — presumably through the agency of Basner and Koza or the pair of them — and, of course, as destructive of black unity. The Communists loyally joined in denouncing it as an attack on Congress, and were in their turn denounced by Basner as partners in an 'unholy alliance' with Congress, and were barred from ADP membership by Mosaka and Mampuru.

However — also as within a family — less intimate kith and kin who could see merits and demerits on both sides of the controversy took up positions of their own. A large majority was prepared to watch things develop — hopefully for the better, and a very small fraction determined to become a deciding influence in itself.

The majority consisted mainly of people who had matured in the thirties, but included many old stalwarts like Mvabasa and Moretsele, who, whilst understanding and even sympathising with Mosaka's ADP (and Basner's intimate support for it), could not bring themselves to appear to abjure Congress. The fraction, on the other hand, was at first made up of no more than a dozen very young men — mainly university graduates whose education had only been completed just before or after 1940. These, after spending some time disgustedly surveying and discussing the political scene from the sidelines, had quite recently joined Congress, but with the express intention of changing it from within. Their youth alone gave them hopes on that score which Basner's generation of friends (on average about ten years older) had now abandoned.

For months before disillusionment with Congress had spilled into bitterness over Alexandra and precipitated them into forming the ADP, Basner had spent much time with Mosaka, Koza, Mampuru, Lesolang and others making plans for a completely different kind of party from that which was eventually formed. This was to have been in no sense a rival to Congress, but an organisation intended to include — and present a radical programme for — people of all races and be free of the outside influences which hamstrung the Communists. In the event, of course, it had not materialised.

During that same period, and in Basner's own office, plans of quite another kind were being discussed, generally at night and on weekends, and largely without his knowledge. They were the plans of the members of 'the fraction'.

Two members of his staff — Macdonald Maseko, his clerk, and Nelson Mandela, who had recently started a career in law — were very friendly with Anton Lembede[3], a brilliant young lawyer who had gathered African intellectuals of his own age around him. They were even more dissatisfied with Congress than Basner and his associates, tended to have a more nationalistic attitude towards the white, Indian and coloured populations, were anti-Communist and held the Senate and NRC elections in contempt. Having decided that nothing would come of prompting and urging Xuma and his cabinet of tired old men, they determined to initiate what became known as the Congress Youth League (CYL). The group had elements of both elitism and racism, but by no means in a degree sufficient to stamp it with such characteristics. (Eventually indeed, they were to split on the issue of black supremacy — but it took fifteen years for that to happen).

Lembede died in 1947, at a very early age and before the CYL achieved real political weight. Of those who followed him, many were later to become prominent as opponents of apartheid — in exile, prison or death. At least two became known far beyond the borders of South Africa whilst remaining perforce within it: Nelson Mandela and Robert Sobukwe.

Early in 1944, six months after the ADP issued its manifesto, the CYL came out with its own. In the four years which passed before it could exert any visible influence within Congress, the ADP shone briefly, began to fade, glimmered for a while, and disappeared. It was only when the full ferocity of apartheid began to make itself felt after the electoral defeat of Smuts in 1948 that Congress gradually became worthy of the sufferering men and women it existed to represent. An increasingly brutish succession of South African prime ministers compelled a transformation which the militants of the ADP and CYL had not been able to achieve on their own.

21
BETTER A LIVING DOG THAN A DEAD LION
(1944)

The shifts of political opinion which had become widely apparent among South Africans of every race by the end of 1943 occurred in the context of the armed political struggle taking place in Europe, North Africa and Asia, but the directions they took were determined by the local past and local present.

White South African soldiers were fighting and dying in the name of democracy and human rights, but that was thousands of miles away. The country was no more in danger of invasion than Patagonia, and its Nazis were no longer a physical threat from within. The war did, however, have an impact on its economy that was so direct and solid as to be a threat to the very base of its political system. For that reason, new thinking and new attitudes were imposed on a number of influential whites, of whom few even thought of questioning their own right by race to supremacy.

Intelligent, hard-headed businessmen, their immediate concern was with the supply of indispensable wartime commodities, as well as with prospects of profit. In the longer term, they were concerned about the consequences of what then seemed an inevitable depletion of the goldmines — and so about how to prepare for the eventual loss of the country's prime source of wealth.

The typically colonial status of South Africa had hitherto been masked by self-government and the high living standards of the majority of its white inhabitants who were still regarded in far-off (but equally 'white') London or New York as the only noticeable human beings within its borders. Like any other colony, South Africa existed by exchanging raw materials for manufactured goods from abroad, and although secondary industries had established themselves to some extent, their financial and labour needs had been matters of little national moment compared to mining and farming.

War maintained and increased both the external and internal demand for minerals and foodstuffs, and so continued to require the channelling of more and more unwilling thousands of blacks to hew rock under the ground or till the soil above it. But the country had become short of many imports — shoes and building materials, aspirins and glassware, nuts and bolts and machinery . . . As a result, capital had begun to flood into a multiplicity of new enterprises, and with it, black labour.

Elsewhere in the world, large-scale displacement of population off the land and into cities had been a natural sequel to mining and industrial expansion. But in South Africa, that displacement had been methodically inhibited for half a century. An entirely artificial social structure, coolly imposed on the nation in the interests of gold production, was ardently supported by members of a racial minority who imagined it to have been established through their own efforts, backed by Providence, for their own benefit. It had an English name, segregation, which would later be replaced by its Afrikaans equivalent, apartheid.

Now, however, because of the war, a powerful demand had arisen for workpeople who would not be temporary rural migrants merely supplied with hands and feet, but a trainable urban proletariat neither wishing nor needing to go back to the countryside.

The new situation seemed unavoidable and even commendable to senior members of Smuts's administration and the business community (even including the mining companies) but the political problem it posed was formidable. Whites, who looked with abhorrence on the prospect of being rapidly outnumbered by blacks in their towns, could also perceive the threat to the colour bar which the specialised manpower requirements of secondary industry implied. Afrikaners and English-speakers could forget every issue that divided them and unite in hysteria at the polls, in Parliament and on the streets over any hint of a prick in the aristocracy of their skins.

It was therefore essential for the government to do everything possible to avoid provoking its electorate, while at the same time accepting the social consequences of an essential economic advance. Legislative sanction for a huge increase in the number of Africans permitted to reside in towns would be highly provocative. Extra taxation to fund the building of more houses for them would be more so. As for suggesting modifications to the colour bar regulations, that was unimaginable, especially in view of the Rand Revolt over just that question in 1922.

Such a dilemma seemed only resolvable in classic fashion — by a policy of masterly inactivity. In this, the government doubtless took comfort from the thought that it was not essential to avoid provoking the blacks. If they were perhaps inclined to get a bit out of hand now and then, they were definitely easier to control than whites. They also, of course, had no votes.

Africans could continue to get passes to seek and enter white employ in urban areas and be fined or imprisoned and then sent home if they stayed on after failing to do so within a short time. Their numbers being so great, there was a chance that with luck, or skill in stealing documents or bribing Native Affairs Department clerks, many of them might buck the system. If they found work in the industry and happened — through shortage of persons of correct colour — to gain a little skill, no harm need come to their employers nor to them. Because their competence could not be officially recognised under the 'colour bar' Mines and Works Amendment Act of 1926, both parties could profit from minimal wage rises. If a registered African employee could find no accommodation for himself and his family in a location, he could look for a hovel in some place like Alexandra. If nothing was to be had there either, he could become an illegal sub-tenant in another black's location house or on white private property, and just be careful not to be discovered, evicted and fined, or imprisoned.

All this would be at little cost in cash or serious political embarrassment to the state.

Highly placed civil servants issued genuinely indignant and truthful statements about conditions that became more appalling every day. Enlightened self-interest impelled proprietors and managers of firms to arrange for white employees to accompany their black workers to the pass offices whenever it was necessary to validate their documents. Enormous and time-consuming queues could thus be jumped, and harassed officials persuaded not to be their normally truculent and obdurate selves. Kindly white householders turned a blind eye to their servants' backyard rooms, illicitly crammed with spouses and children.

Meanwhile, the deliberately unenlightened eye of an unsympathetic government swept over a scene described and criticised in detail in the reports of its own commissions of inquiry.[1]

The year 1944, however, was one that seemed to justify hope rather than despair for the ultimate future of non-whites. While Rome fell,

Paris became free, the Germans fled Russia and the Japanese fleet sank in the Pacific, protest and resistance increased in South African locations, factories and city squares, and even continued to mutter in the tribal lands. Young white soldiers, students and priests had begun to stand in a positive way for the elementary rights of the black majority.[2] Even the bitter disputes that continued in the comfort of white Parliament and the wrangling that went on in the bareness of black meeting halls took place in an atmosphere that smelt of change.

Basner was in a position to observe all this and was greatly involved in much of it: in the Senate, the lawcourts, the company of other white left-wingers and, above all, in the African community. Although the national power structure remained as impervious to non-white public protest as a buffalo to the stings of occasional bees, the Africans, like bees, showed signs of swarming and, perhaps one day, doing more than make little punctures here and there.

The Communists succeeded in persuading Xuma and Congress to sponsor a campaign against passes that was intended to culminate in a huge multiracial petition to Parliament, combined with mass pass-burning. Although it eventually petered out, the campaign in its early stages produced some extraordinary demonstrations of popular solidarity. Twenty thousand men and women marched on the Witwatersrand and when the fiery David Bopape was dismissed from his teaching post in Brakpan for his activities at that time, parents boycotted all schools in the location and seven thousand men refused to go out to work.[3]

Lesolang's teachers, demanding a living wage, walked through the centre of Johannesburg in a body of four thousand.

Koza's coal-heavers struck, and when they and he were arrested for doing so (under War Measure 145, which forbade all strikes), unanimously refused to be bailed. By voluntarily sitting in prison, they continued to withhold their labour . . . legally. Their union not only forced a settlement upon management, but pushed it into the unheard of process of negotiating directly with black workers' representatives.

MK Molepo became a symbol of the miseries of all tribespeople when he was summarily banished from his Pietersburg home, presumably for persistence in bringing just complaints to the notice of the local Native Commissioner.[4]

These are only examples of what was happening, and are chosen for being typical of their time. But to Basner, both then and in hindsight much later, what happened in Orlando — the newest and biggest location in South Africa — was more significant than any other event of 1944.

Throughout his career as a lawyer, Basner had been made aware of the plight of the thousands who inhabited the municipal locations of Johannesburg and its satellite towns without permits to be either tenants or lodgers of tenants. His office was filled with the files of their hopeless cases, and its waiting room with their dreadfully hopeful faces. As living testimony to the lack of housing for Africans, they had seemed to him to represent no more than tragic and bewildered individual victims of governmental inhumanity and civic meanness. By 1942, however, they had become numerous enough to begin to have a corporate existence and momentum all their own.

Orlando location had been constructed in the thirties, but further building had ceased there, and everywhere else, shortly after the beginning of the war. Hence it was as chaotic and full of illicit lodgers as other locations, while superficially appearing less neglected and better-ordered.

Situated some twelve miles south-west of Johannesburg's centre, it had its own railway station and lay very near to the largest and by far the best-run hospital for non-whites in the country. Several miles of best quality (and lofty) barbed wire fencing kept unauthorised people out of its terrain, which was closely dotted all over with little concrete boxes, each containing two to four waterless, unheated and unlit rooms. Straight untarred roads — given identity here and there by a clump of standpipes or a longish block of bucket latrines — divided Orlando into an impressive spread of rectangles.

Apart from some barracks for single men, its biggest buildings fell into three categories: religious and educational, administrative and recreational. That is, it had a number of churches, mission schools and halls. It had proper accommodation for police and proper offices for the issue or refusal of permits and passes of various kinds and it had large sheds sheltering concrete counters at which 'kaffir beer', municipally brewed, could legally be drunk in discomfort. The beer was as notorious for being a chief source of subsidy for education and other amenities as for its taste and low alcoholic content.

Thirty-five years had still to pass before Orlando's houses received electricity. When this luxury arrived, it was bestowed upon the dwellings of well over a million people living in the conurbation of which Orlando had become no more than an element: that abomination of desolation known to all the world by its ugly acronym of Soweto.

In 1944, no one could be sure of the size of the population of Orlando, but it probably did not exceed a hundred thousand. Certainly, like every other location it was poverty-stricken, disease-ridden, harried by murderous criminal gangs and filled to bursting. And it burst.

The area occupied by Orlando sloped downwards on its southern side, where it was bordered by a deep gully — a *donga* — beyond which the land rose again as empty veld. The *donga* was usually dry, but could become a river of brown water after rain.

One midnight that March, a shadowy cluster of figures formed itself in Orlando's central square and began to move. It became a silent struggle of men, women and children, laden with bags and cardboard boxes, pieces of tin and tarred paper, chicken-wire and sacking, bundles of sticks and rusty iron staples, heading for the *donga* in the dark.

There were less than two hundred of them, but once they had broken through the fence and were over the *donga*, the morning revealed them to be the vanguard of the hosts of Israel, encamped beyond Jordan. What is more, they were building an habitation unto themselves without permit from the Non-European and Native Affairs Department of the City of Johannesburg.

A few hundreds joined them on the next night. Then hundreds, succeeded by thousands, began pouring out of Orlando: grandparents, widows and mothers with infants on their backs, shebeen queens and gangsters, ragged hawkers with their donkey-carts, clerks and messengers in cared-for clothes; drunks and dreamers, blanket-clad young labourers and aproned washerwomen and their cats and dogs and goats and dishevelled fowls and pots and fire-cans and bedding . . .

They covered the hillside with shacks made of flimsy bits of whatever they could find and carry. Children were sent scavenging for brickbats and stones to repel invaders. A squad of police duly arrived, in daylight — when most of the men were away at work — and were assailed by ferocious women and obliged to scramble back down the slope, helmets awry or off, a few heads bleeding. Johannesburg's municipal councillors, at first concerned, became worried, then agitated.

The Joshua who had led the illicit lodgers over Jordan was James Sofazonke Mpanza, whose Zulu first name means 'everybody dies'; and he named his personal following the Sofazonke Party, meaning not only that he was at their head, but that they were all ready, if need be, to die together. As a young clerk-interpreter to a solicitor in Natal, he had, in 1912, been convicted of fraud. Two years later, full of drink, he had committed murder, and his next thirteen years had been spent in prison — where he became a visionary.

Mpanza was a 'prophet' in the same Zionist tradition as Lekganyane and Lion. But, unlike them, who claimed themselves bishops and were leaders of rural religious communities, he was a conscious urban politician, an elected member — like Paul Mosaka and the Communist Edwin Mofutsanyana — of Orlando's Advisory Board. Now aged fifty-five, he was psychologically unbalanced, very astute, and a powerful and dauntless personality[5].

Although he considered himself God's chosen instrument, his Sofazonke Party was not a church. To join it no baptism was required but homelessness and the only redemption it offered was a few square yards on a few acres of hard ground. Its hymn was a famous one composed by RT Caluza in 1913 after the passing of the Land Act and the foundation of Congress. *'Sikalel' izwe la kiti'*[6], it begins; 'Redeem our land, that was taken from us by strangers'. Mpanza called his squatters' settlement Sofazonke Township, but most people called it Shanty Town.

Needless to say, there was a great stirring in the locations of the Reef and beyond and a general wave of black enthusiasm. Among practising politicians, from moderate white supremacists to the non-racial far left, the reaction to Mpanza and the squatters inevitably showed great diversity, but had a considerable undercurrent of common feeling.

With the notable exception of the ADP and Basner, the nub — and the rub — of it all was James Sofazonke Mpanza himself. He just was not *reasonable*. Therefore those who believed in him were not reasonable either. Most whites could say that he and his close adherents proved how primitive and excitable 'Natives' were. Quite a few black left-wingers, as well as white ones, could be tempted into doubting the maturity of 'the masses'. Since he was both a fervent black theocrat and a fervent believer in his own prerogatives, mutual antipathy between him and many African leaders — especially intellectual ones — was scarcely surprising.

It was characteristic of Paul Mosaka, in whom rationality and sympathetic imagination were combined in equal measure, to have listened with respect to Mpanza's dream of a squatters' exodus. Mpanza, for his part, was quite ready to accept both the ADP and Basner as allies as long as it was recognised that he should have pride of place. They had been able to form a joint committee and had planned the move out of Orlando in careful detail, on the understanding that Mpanza would be its leader, with Nchee, a full-time organiser for the ADP, his deputy.

Leading Communists, whatever their race, quite rightly did not want the human flood issuing from Orlando to be contained. Unlike Mosaka and Basner, however, they refused to collaborate with Mpanza when he approached them with the idea of letting it loose.[7] Doubtless they now regretted this, since they were in consequence excluded from having any say in its control and direction. As for the African National Congress — with a Transvaal leadership broad enough to include both Communists and what may, for brevity, be called Xuma-ites — the kind of direction it visualised is indefinable. Of course no one in Congress could openly favour containment, although a handful of individuals probably had wistful thoughts about how much nicer it would have been if Shanty Town were no more than a Zion in the sky.

Labour Party councillors ruled in Johannesburg's white City Hall. Many of them were by this time, positively liberal-minded, and unhappy about the condition of urban Africans — not least because of the painful facts now pressed upon them by their own municipal officials. The latter, like the higher authorities in the government's Native Affairs Department, were beginning to speak with almost the same horror of what was going on as did Race Relations researchers and missionaries.

The use of armed forces to erase Shanty Town and scatter its inhabitants was not only impolitic at that time but went against the inclinations of nearly all the city council members as well as those of many comfortable ratepayers. Six months later, a second Alexandra bus boycott would produce the remarkable sight of well-dressed white housewives spontaneously taking out their cars to offer lifts to African marchers. Poorer or abnormally racist voters did not now seem particularly upset to hear of an incursion of blacks onto empty land that happened to belong to the municipality and already abutted on a location.

So what agitated the Labour Party was the problem of how to contain and control the Orlando phenomenon in as humane a fashion as their own mentality and that of the majority of their ratepayers would allow.

Mpanza, Basner and Mosaka could not of course be sure about the intentions of the city and government authorities, but experience taught them to prepare for the worst. The squatters had ceased to be a tight-knit little band, and within a few days had come to number as many as fifteen thousand. Could such a shapeless horde have spirit and substance enough to withstand gunfire or long-drawn-out pressure such as a siege? Their exodus differed completely from Alexandra's march. The bus boycott, determined though it was, had been in the nature of a strike, and ended when its immediate aim was fulfilled. Shanty Town's shacks might be flimsy, but were intended to spread — and endure.

To strengthen communal morale it was agreed to hold a mass meeting in the new settlement at which the three of them would speak.

The meeting was held by torchlight one dark night a week after the first move had been made. What was said by the speakers is forgotten, but surely they must have spoken with the tongues of angels, because the spirit of the multitude they addressed could have wrung eloquence from the dumb. The gathering started, as was the custom, with prayers offered by an elderly clergyman. Then came the speeches, translated (as was always essential) sentence for sentence into passionate Zulu, Sesotho and English, a litany accompanied by growls of assent from men and the traditional prolonged trill of women that excites warriors before battle. A benediction was given, followed by the two national anthems — as ever, most moving to hear, and as ever, in marvellous harmony.

And that was supposed to be the end of it. But as the visitors left to descend the hillside and reach the road below, the crowd moved with them, and from it suddenly came the first piercing cry of *Si-i-kalel*. A profound and tremendous chorus responded, and a single tremendous stamp of feet. And the whole of Shanty Town, stamping, dancing, singing, came down the slope as one being. The earth palpably jumped. Clouds of dust rose through the dry grass and turned red in the flaming torchlight.

A few days later, a distinguished white sociologist and member of the Institute of Race Relations requested an interview with Mpanza. On Basner's advice, it was granted (though grudgingly), and she came — an able and imperious woman. Mpanza awaited her, sitting outside his shack, next to which a grey horse was tethered. A cloth covered the shoulders of his worn suit, a cap of spotted fur was on his head, and his bony fingers rested on the handle of a carved walking stick. A couple of his councillor-lieutenants stood nearby.

He greeted her civilly enough and they exchanged a few words before she put a practical but rather injudicious question to him. 'Mr. Mpanza,' she inquired, 'what will happen to all these people when it rains?' 'Madam,' he replied, rising to his feet, 'we will get wet', and promptly retired behind his hessian front door.

Within three months, the Johannesburg municipality persuaded the government to release building materials to put up four thousand breezeblock dwellings on Shanty Town's site and establish it as a location. What is more, Africans were employed on the job for the first time not just as labourers, but doing 'white work' (and thereby saving the authorities a good deal of money).

More squatters began to pour from every location, and more shanty towns sprang up in other places, led in some cases by steadier personalities than Mpanza, but by 1946, the end of the war had brought an end to administrative tolerance. The new settlements were surrounded by police armed with guns, and torn down. Their leaders were arrested for trespass and their people strewn to the winds along with the litter out of which they had constructed their homes.[8]

Meanwhile, Mpanza had become increasingly arbitrary, and probably more than a little mad, refusing to have anything to do with anyone (including his ADP deputy, Nchee) who gave him less than total allegiance. He was said, moreover, to have turned into a shameless racketeer, though there is no evidence of this. The Native Affairs Department, however, making use of the provisions of the Native Administration Act of 1927, banished him from the Witwatersrand, like the humane, conscientious Molepo of Pietersburg, many others before him, and many thousands more to come.[9]

22

THE SLEEP OF REASON PRODUCES MONSTERS (1945-1946)

For Basner the first three months of 1945 were primarily concerned with the inaguration of a new party and the launch of a journal which would speak for it. But before dealing with the political opinions which led him and others of his white friends to pursue these projects during the coming year, a little more may be said about his parliamentary foes, allies and activities.

Because of the war, Jan Smuts could govern the country under War Regulations, so the parliamentary legislative programme became very sparse and free time was available which could be filled by the native representatives with complaints about and reviews of government policy and the maladministration of the Native Affairs Department. In Basner's estimation, this explained, more than any other factor, why he spoke in the Senate more often and at greater length than he really intended to, causing Hansard to swell in size (to no political effect whatsoever).

Major Pieter van der Byl, the Minister of Native Affairs, was obliged

The Sleep of Reason Produces Monsters 173

to come to the Senate at least once during each session to descant on the policies of his department for the current year. This was an innovation introduced by General Hertzog when he was Prime Minister to make it appear as if the representation of seven million blacks by four whites meant something.

Van der Byl was the scion (no less pompous word, Basner felt, was applicable) of an old Cape Dutch family which had thrown in its lot completely with the British connection. They owned vast tracts of land on which they raised sheep, vines and coloured people, and the Major (an Oxbridge 'blue') was known to all — because of his height, elegance and extensive wardrobe — as 'The Clothes Horse'. He was a snob, a fop and a dolt in more eyes than Basner's[1], but had as much right to be in Smuts's cabinet as any other member, with the exception of Jan Hofmeyr, the Deputy Prime Minister, for it seemed to be deliberate policy on Smuts's part to fill his cabinet with duds. As long as he had Jan Hofmeyr, whom he rightly respected for his remarkable brains, to carry on everyday administration, he could be free to draft foreign policy plans for the British government or constitutions for international bodies such as the United Nations.

The one post Major Van der Byl had no claim to be fit for was that of Minister of Native Affairs. His part of the Cape had been denuded for generations of its original inhabitants. Seventeenth and eighteenth century slaves from Batavia and the dying Khoikhoi (Hottentot) herdsmen of the area (by 1824 as free as the sheep they shepherded) had been mingled together to create a work-force. Their women had in turn been obliged to breed the coloured people from white residents and sailors, and had created a society which speedily multiplied to meet increased labour requirements. Together with paltry wages and scraps of food, large tots of brandy were the daily apportionment which kept that part of the population quiet, and even sometimes, happy. If a Van der Byl saw any Africans from the 'tribal' areas of the north-eastern Cape, it was when shopping in Cape Town and if Major Van der Byl ever spoke to any, they would have been in a deputation introduced by one of his officials.

The Van der Byls were detested by most Afrikaners as renegades. Piet van der Byl was envied for his wealth, hated for his insolence and regarded as a brainless ignoramus by members of Smuts's own party as much as by his Nationalist opposition. Only Basner thought himself lucky to have him for 'his' minister, precisely because he was so easy to bait.

Despite his moral convictions and self-assurance, Basner had been surprised to find, during his first session in 1943, how painful the prospect of spending years in conflict with a whole House, including the three men with whom he should theoretically have collaborated, could be. Yet he could no more refrain from twitting Senator Brookes about his

Christian forbearance than from letting fly at his overt opponents for their racial bigotry and economic irrationality. He could not expect warm support from colleagues such as Malcomess and Campbell (Smuts-supporters in all but name) and Brookes, anymore than they could expect a little humanity for their electors from the government or its official opposition. If his own reason could comprehend his situation, it did not suffice to cheer him personally or encourage him tactically.

Unknown to him, however, crumbs of comfort had lain sprinkled near him quite early in his first session. Sitting silent but interested for the first time in a speech on African Affairs, were two Labour Party senators — Henderson from the Transvaal and Smith from Natal.

Henderson was secretary of the party, an ageing henchman rewarded for long years of service with his Senate seat. Sidney Smith, a far younger man, but similarly rewarded, was a well-to-do, rather notorious wheeler-dealer who had become mayor of Durban and was reputed to own a chain of liquor firms and stores financed by Indian merchants for whom he did many favours. He was also active in Moral Rearmament, a movement Basner detested nearly as much as he did the Broederbond.

The day after his speech, Sidney Smith visited him in his office, and Basner was rendered almost bashful by his intelligence and charm. Obviously of Irish extraction, tall, dark and handsome, it was no wonder he could weave rings round the bovine burgesses of Durban. By the time Smith had explained his reasons for coming and had finished telling his own story, Basner had learnt a lesson on how superficial, vulgar and misleading our judgements of public men can be if we depend on party labels, gossip and the media.

Henderson and Smith were not really interested in the Senate and only filled their seats to retain the prerogatives of Labour as a national party. Henderson, as an old trade unionist, still believed in the colour bar to protect white workers. Smith, according to what he told Basner that day, had never felt anything but dislike for racists, but also could never (unless he wanted to lose votes) challenge racism in Natal, where English-speakers of all classes were even more afraid of Indian competition than they and the Afrikaners were of African advancement.

Smith had been born in poverty and had clawed his way out — the expression was his — assisted by a series of miracles in which rich Indians had always been the ministering angels. As a Catholic, he could never have any truck with Communists, but lately, somewhat disillusioned with his church, had bolstered his socialist leanings with Moral Rearmament. It was not strange for Basner to hear that Henderson — a typical old-style British union man — had little time for the middle-class liberalism of Rheinallt Jones or Edgar Brookes, but he found it revealing that Smith, a genuinely religious man, did not so much dislike them for their liberalism as for their missionary-inspired approach to politics. Smith had gone on to pay Basner the compliment of saying that he had never, before listening to his attacks on the Native Trust, understood the relationship between the goldmining industry and South Africa's racial policies.

The point of Smith's visit was that both Henderson and he had come to the conclusion that Basner was a socialist, hence someone with whom they could work in a way they never could with the other Native Representatives. He was not sure how far Henderson would go as he was both tired and hidebound, but for his own part would be glad to help whenever necessary. It did not need long discussion for Basner and him to understand what this could mean for both of them. One person could do nothing, but two could transform the mechanics of the Senate. In a revising Chamber such as that, the reason was technical rather than political. It implied that each could find a seconder for any resolution he cared to move and would not have to wait for a bill or a minister's statement to offer him openings for assault. Without a seconder, Basner would be the dead duck he now believed 'Peg' Ballinger and her Senate associates intended to make him.

He became as cheerful as he had been depressed only a short while before. The fog of isolation and enforced idleness before him had been lifted from a quarter he had least expected. He could also enjoy another side of Smith's personality which was mischievous and fun-loving.

Their first conversation lasted all morning and through lunch and at the end of it they were firm friends, and continued to be so until Basner left the Senate five years later. Smith needed him because his own excellent and energetic mind had never before been used except for political shenanigans and Basner needed Smith because he had a store of human wisdom and experience more real — or at least easier to assimilate in a true sense — than most of the books on philosophy, economics, law and literature he had read.

Sidney had known and liked Indians ever since being helped by some in his early struggles to become educated and established in business. He knew little of the Zulus who lived and worked in Durban, and Basner was intrumental in widening his humanity to embrace that of yet another community. Smith in his turn taught Basner by personal example what the plight of an ambitious and intelligent white boy from a poor working-class family in South Africa could be, when battling with an environment in which racial competition and hostility were the privileged classes' most potent weapons.

Sidney was the tonic Basner needed to make the Senate seem more human. His mischievous streak, combined with his wheeler-dealer's instinct for capturing headlines, served both of them well. They were to collaborate in the future in concocting provocative themes for debate, and twice succeeded in creating something of public sensation — in 1945 and 1946. Typically, their success was due to the fact that their subject-matter appealed to large number of whites because it superficially appeared to have nothing to do with blacks and because it dealt aggressively with two powerful consortia and their capacity, respectively, to adulterate the South African press and South African liquor: the Chamber of Mines and the Cape wine and spirit producers.

Since his feelings about Margaret Ballinger, and, to a much lesser extent, Donald Molteno, were defined by political mistrust alone (in contrast to his personal distaste for Edgar Brookes), Basner was eventually able to have a relationship with them that allowed for easy conversation and co-operation on specific issues. But as he had discovered in the Senate, so in the House of Assembly; his only real friend was to be a Labour MP, Alec Wanless.

In 1943 the Socialist Party was formed, more in reaction to events than as an outcome of planned political tactics. As early as 1940, Basner and those younger whites with whom he had then become acquainted had begun to think of themselves as 'the Group'. They were all left-wingers no longer able to contemplate the Communist Party as a political home, who took to meeting regularly and informally to discuss how best they could act, as individuals or together, in the South African scene. Naturally, they considered that scene to be made up of a vast majority of people under the domination of a small class-cum-ethnic minority.

Basner had come to believe for a considerable time that not only white liberals but white socialists were habitually, and as if by right, paternalistic in their attitudes towards blacks. True, this was most obvious in the case of the Institute of Race Relations and its Joint Councils but it was not much less the case in the Communist Party and the trade union movement. His self-imposed task — as has previously been described — to spur the African people into assuming proper responsibility for their struggle against white dominance, may, to a contemporary cynic, suggest a paternalism of his own but it should be remembered that he had idiosyncratically planned to relinquish that task within a specific period of time. Furthermore, he and his African confederates were at that time all too conscious of the grievous shortage of blacks trained and equipped for the basic needs of political organisation, even typing and mimeographing. Telephones and cars were luxuries and pass and curfew laws added immeasurably to the simplest requirements of communication.

Although it was attacked by black nationalists and Stalinists in turn as 'white-dominated' and 'Trotskyist', the ADP soon turned out to be almost as broadly based ideologically, and certainly just as African, as the ANC itself. The political climate in which it had arisen had clearly bred it to become a militant black thorn in the purely black flesh of the ANC rather than a racially mixed and revolutionary alternative to it.

Hence, members of 'the Group' began to think it only right to direct more of their efforts towards influencing 'their own kind' — whites mentally and physically ghettoised inside South African society by the very privileges imposed upon them by their ancestry.

Early on, they had tried to infiltrate the Transvaal provincial branch of the Labour Party which was, by 1941, showing signs of division between racially exclusive and much more enlightened wings. By the end of 1944, war and the Allied democratic slogans adopted in order to win it, had produced what appeared to be a significant change in the attitudes of many ordinary whites — particularly soldiers who had fought or were fighting in North Africa. A wave of optimism among such whites as were already left-wing in their sympathies had come to affect Basner and outstanding trade unionists like Johanna Cornelius and Solly Sachs, almost as much as it did members of the Communist Party. Many, from time to time, supported or joined the Rev Michael Scott's Campaign for Right and Justice and the Springbok Legion of servicemen and ex-servicemen[2]. Most of them tended to share in a hope that some members of Smuts's administration and men like the doyen of the goldmining industry, Ernest Oppenheimer, were ready to consider at least some measures of obviously necessary reform.

It transpired, however, that nationwide, the old leadership of the Labour Party remained as firmly entrenched as ever. Because of this, a section of that party, which by that time included Solly Sachs, Johanna Cornelius and Jessie MacPherson (a former mayor of Johannesburg), was prepared to join members of 'the Group' and Basner in starting a new organisation, the Socialist Party.

He who had always so much wanted to be a journalist rather than a lawyer, certainly found more pleasure in becoming editor of the new party's journal — the *Socialist Review* — than from any of his other political commitments. Its first issue appeared as a monthly in June 1945, but unremarkably, and doubtless consonant with a sharp reactionary swing in white public opinion subsequent to the Allied victory in Europe, it only survived until the middle of 1946. By 1947, the Socialist Party — a minority within a minority — had also ceased to function[3].

It is of some interest to read what today seem to be the very limited aims implied in both the *Socialist Review* and a compilation of extracts from Basner's Senate speeches which he chose — in the same year — to distribute to his electorate. Compared with his address to that same electorate in 1942 and the opinions he was ever after to voice, these publications seem downright 'liberal'. That is to say, there is moral wrath enough, yet a moral wrath that seems to accept the South African power structure as something capable of amendment, could it only be persuaded to recognise the stupidity of its own brutality.

If extenuation is needed for a year or so's misinterpretation of reality, Basner may perhaps be allowed it as an individual, considering the quixotically courageous policy that was to be followed by thousands of Africans and Indians together with some dozens of whites (and wholeheartedly adopted by the Communist Party) for years to come.

This policy, based on Gandhist theories of passive resistance, was, as he soon recognised, no more than a delusion about the power of moral force to induce inexorable wielders of physical power to be so kind as to relinquish it.

On a different level, the view of a remarkably large number of radical blacks would seem to have agreed with those expressed in a pamphlet issued by Basner during this period, on the occasion of a black trade union conference in Johannesburg in 1945. Interesting for its confusion of lines of thought, it was a fierce attack on the Workers International League, a small group of Trotskyists on the Reef, for what he, as a Marxist, described as 'far-left adventurism' (an opinion from which, incidentally, he did not later depart). The attack, however, coincided with . . . a warning of what will happen unless African trade unions are organised and responsibly led by militants ready to do battle against the intolerable conditions of the urban workers, and unless the European (ie white) trade union movement comes to their assistance to gain recognition, rights of collective bargaining, a better standard of living and *proper education to acquire consciousness of socialism.*[4]

Since a very considerable number of senators were rural landowners, antagonism towards Basner in Parliament was probably greater because of his repeated attacks on farmers for their behaviour towards their labourers. Pay and working conditions on white farms were so notoriously bad that there was a perennial shortage of African labour despite the grim legal machinery employed to force men onto the land as well as into the mines. It had long been commonplace for magistrates in urban areas to sentence blacks found to have infringed the pass laws to work on farms in lieu of going to prison. Less well known was the practice among farmers — especially in the Eastern Transvaal — of using mercenary recruiters to tempt men from impoverished neighbouring territories into their employ. Both systems were open to appalling abuse. Many Transvaal farms were simply slave plantations, where beating was the norm and murder not abnormal[5].

Basner never forgot the complaint of an elderly, and, as it happened, lovable Afrikaner Senator, who, after a heated debate, approached him and said, 'It hurts me, young fellow, how you talk about us. Where I came from, I've never heard of the terrible things you say. We always treat our people right. It's true we're always short of labour and sometimes have to pay to get hold of it. I well remember my old father having to cross the border into Portuguese East (Mozambique) years ago, just to buy some little Shangaans, which he got for five shillings each. But I'll tell you, those little kaffirs grew up on our place and lived there all their lives . . . and my father would call them to the house at the end of every week to get their rations and they'd touch their hats and say "Thank you, my Baas" each time and you could see how happy they were'.

Perhaps the worst conditions were on the high 'platteland' east of Johannesburg where potato and maize growing, developed on a large scale but in no way mechanised, needed a great deal of manpower. The area surrounding the *dorp* of Bethal was typical in this respect.

There can be no question but that the behaviour of farmers in the Transvaal platteland was known to officialdom well before 1943. However, Basner at that time merely seems to have been aware that the Bethal area was more notorious than most, and it must be assumed that he made no specific investigations there until nearly two years later.

Prior to 1945, an Anglican missionary called Yates had approached the synod of his church, which eventually led to approaches to the Native Affairs Department, the SA Jewish Board of Deputies and to Basner in his Parliamentary capacity. It is probable that Basner would already have heard, if only through the press, of two particularly horrible murders by beating committed by African farm foremen in 1943 and 1944. But it is unlikely that he knew of the role played by their employers, Stein and Kadish, who were Jews. The pair of them were not only outstandingly brutish in a conventionally brutal environment, but outstanding in their rapacity as professional recruiters of labour from over the Portuguese colonial border.

It would seem that the first indication that these men were if anything guiltier of murder than their employees came to the Board of Deputies from a co-religionist, a Mrs Schwartz, employed by the Bethal court.

The available records of the Board of Deputies may not cover the subject in its entirety, and only imply that it was at some stage contacted by Basner. He, for his part, may have hoped to avoid a shocking scandal involving Jews almost as much as did the Board. The cases had been brought to court and the accused black foremen given typically mild sentences.

The truly guilty parties went scot free in a neighbourhood in which it was felt to be politically essential for everyone concerned to keep as quiet as possible. Afrikaner farmers, liberal-minded churchmen, conservative Jews and Smuts's government itself, all had different reasons for avoiding nationwide publicity. The correspondence between the Board and Mrs Schwartz and her husband, together with letters between the Deputies themselves, clearly disclose their feelings and fears. These were doubtless understandable at a time in South Africa when anti-Semitism was a major issue. Furthermore, the government was, with good reason, very much afraid for its future electoral chances in a part of the country where Afrikaner nationalism was on the ascendant.

Certainly, pressure was exerted on the Board by Basner and by the Board on the Jewish farmers concerned. It is possible that in Basner's case, his pressure was strengthened by threats of fully detailed public disclosures. All one may assume, though, is that in return for assurances, he then continued, as in the past, only to make general attacks on the treatment of farm labourers in the Bethal area during the Parliamentary session which began in the following year, 1945.

It is painful to note that despite the awareness of so many people of what had been happening, it took a least two years more for it to be properly publicised by the Rev Michael Scott. This was done through the Johannesburg newspaper, the *Rand Daily Mail*, in 1947.[6] Not surprisingly, Scott's campaign was held by many white supporters of General Smuts to be partially responsible for his defeat by Afrikaner nationalism in 1948.

The Parliamentary sessions of 1945 and 1946 were, with one exception, filled for Basner with impotent verbal battles about conditions on farms and in reserves, about mining, black trade unions and laws affecting Africans and Coloured people in the Cape. These were only relieved by the lively debates which Smith and he set going about the English-language press and the liquor industry. (These debates tended to delight Afrikaner Senators from the Transvaal and Free State who had no love either for mining magnates and their newspapers or for Cape vineyard magnates such as Van der Byl).

The exception was a serious one. In May 1946, Smuts introduced a bill, soon popularly to be known as the 'Indian Pegging Act', to minimise what little freedom of settlement Asians still had in Natal and the Transvaal. It was then that the Indian community — for the first time since Gandhi's Satyagraha movement early in the century — bravely embarked on a fruitless passive resistance campaign.

Basner engaged himself in mounting a filibuster against the bill in the Senate, as an attempt to pillory its iniquity if nothing more; and managed to interrupt the House's proceedings for a number of days. His hours spent in chatter which inevitably became more and more peripheral to his subject led, as he intended, to his suspension from the Senate — an occurrence scarcely requiring note today, but at that time unprecedented in an Upper House in the British Commonwealth.

The Pegging Act did more for Basner than keep him in mind of the futility of his verbal bombardments in a heedless parliamentary chamber or that of the Indian moral ones which burst into dusty air outside it. In retrospect, he was to speak of the four months of mid-1946 as a crucial period for him, one in which he was forced to reassess both the contemporary political climate and his own political behaviour. Indulgence in wishful thinking had led him, he felt, into near forgetfulness of his purpose in becoming a 'Native Representative'.

In August of that year he not only became hyper-conscious of the fact that the end of World War II spelt the end of liberal posturings in South Africa, but was consumed by what, for him, was an unusually personal form of fury — against Field Marshal Smuts. Not Smuts the mere expression of a political system, but Smuts the epitome, as a man, of the Platonic philosophy of the elite in a slave state.

Smuts, Basner felt, was the victim of power. In reality a head of state, although he was called Prime Minister, he was a national hero, a world-esteemed statesman and he was like any other person in a supreme position — completely insulated from reality or that aspect of reality which the ministers, officials, advisers, toadies, flatterers and hangers-on around him did not want to know.

By 1946 African mine workers were still waiting for the full implementation of the recommendations made by Mr Justice Lansdown three years earlier in his Mine Wages Commission report. The government had awarded a one-penny increase per shift in April 1944 but took no further action. Deteriorating conditions in the countryside, a decline in the quality of food served in the compounds and accelerating inflation combined to arouse amongst workers unprecedented support for their trade union. Basner, who was still closely in touch with its leaders, notably John Marks and James Majoro, conveyed urgent warnings to the then Minister of Labour, Colin Steyn and to Ernest Oppenheimer of the Anglo American mining corporation about the consequences of governmental and industrial obduracy. Though both these intelligent men expressed concern and apparent understanding, this was to turn out to be completely abstract — they were quite ignorant of African feelings.

In August 1946, the mineworkers demanded an increase in pay to ten shillings per shift — about twelve pounds ten shillings a month as against the existing wage of little more then three pounds. There was no recognition of the black miners' union, hence, no negotiation. No reply was received to letters sent by the union to the Chamber of Mines on 6 May, 24 June and 7 August. On 12 August 50 000 men went on strike.

Four days later, Smuts left South Africa for a peace conference in Paris, to be followed by a meeting of the United Nations at Lake Success, New York. By then, at least nine men had been killed and thousands injured by police who had literally scourged, clubbed and gunned them back to work underground.

The discovery of inordinately rich new gold reserves in the Orange Free State four months before these incidents may or may not have been as fearsome an omen to Basner as it appeared to him some time later. Another omen, however, was clear — Churchill's Fulton speech, which amounted to a formal declaration of the Cold War. The two events, though unrelated, combined to mark the end of the false dawn of reason in wartime South Africa.

Fury at Smuts's treatment of the miners made Basner determined to beard the man — not at home, but internationally, in his role of philosopher statesman cum humanitarian. At all costs, he decided, he must get to New York and put the truth about the South African government under Smuts before the United Nations.

23

A SMALL GLIMMER OF INTERNATIONAL LIGHT
(1946)

The difficulties facing Basner's proposed foray to New York seemed formidable. Yet such was his longing for revenge against Smuts, as the very personification of political arrogance and iniquity, that he welcomed each difficulty more as a diversion than a challenge. He felt clear-headed enough, however, about how to present segregation/apartheid as a major item for the agenda of the World Assembly.

There was need for both secrecy and haste. If his plans were disclosed too soon, the government, through its influence in Britain and the United States, might find ways to impede his journey. And the Communist Party and the African National Congress leadership might forestall him and blight his intentions: the former (he guessed) enlisting the support of the Soviet bloc in such a way as to ensure a solid Western counter-bloc and the latter merely calling for help from the NAACP and white liberals, who would interpret South African policies solely as a matter of colour prejudice and race relations, omitting all mention of goldmining and international finance . . .

He already knew which was the obvious country to ask to sponsor and word his own indictment of South Africa and Smuts: newly independent India. But he did not wish to approach the logical body to make such a move, the South African Indian Congress, which was already arranging to send representatives to brief the Indian UN delegation in a formal protest against the discrimination incorporated in the Asiatic Land Tenure Act. The Congress had only recently split, with its largest section — labourers on the sugar plantations of Natal, town workpeople and students — following Dr G M Naicker in Natal and Dr Yusuf Dadoo in the Transvaal, both of them leading members of the Communist Party. Basner had supported Dadoo in his efforts to oust the smaller section — mean-minded and reactionary merchants and petty shopkeepers who had controlled the funds and organisational structure of the Indian Congress in both provinces since the departure of Gandhi in 1915 — but he was no admirer of Dadoo, politically or personally, and his sentiments, he well knew, were thoroughly reciprocated.

Smuts himself was going to attend the Assembly, not only to rebut Indian accusations, but — and mainly — to apply for the incorporation of the mandated territory of South West Africa (now Namibia) into the Union of South Africa. So why should India not take on a double brief and formally question his and his government's right to rule over any black people at all?

As is often the case, large-seeming difficulties were quite easily overcome, and it was unexpected lesser ones that gave trouble.

As an ex-Communist, Basner was ineligible, not being an official delegate to the United Nations, for a visa to enter the United States. He had vague hopes of persuading the Indian government to arrange something once he could reach London and establish contact with its representatives there but to his surprise, he discovered a remnant of Roosevelt's New Deal among the personnel of the US embassy in Cape Town which was not only sympathetic towards his intended visit, but positively keen on it. A member of the Mining Attaché's staff had heard of his plans from a mutual friend who was a mining engineer, and Basner found himself not only furnished with a visa, but with a helpful letter of introduction to the State Department in Washington. Obviously the CIA was not functioning properly yet, or its precursors overestimated the muscle and mind of the World Assembly.

Years of neglect of his legal practice had seriously reduced his income, so much so that he had to seek financial help to pay for his fare and stay in New York. Yet that problem again was quickly settled — by a whip-round and a personal contribution from the same engineer friend. Shortly before the time of his departure, though, something more than shortage of funds came to trouble him. He learnt that one of his partners and some members of his staff were becoming lax at work and possibly more than unreliable over money. In a lawyer's office like his, with a large clientele of illiterate and vulnerable people, this was a particularly serious matter; but to take things in hand meant so much exertion as well as unpleasantness that he could be seriously hindered from getting away. He decided to leave the situation be until his return (with almost disastrous results, in the form of further and more crippling debts to cover the misdeeds of others and his own reprehensible lack of awareness of their extent).

If, in later years, he was to concede that his drive to reach Lake Success had been far more emotive than rational, he was also to hold that what he had schemed and pressed for made such good political sense that it outweighed any returns that caution would have brought.

Basner reached London but found himself turned away daily from the British Airways booking office. He began to wonder whether the obstacles he was meeting in getting a plane to New York were genuinely due to transport shortages, or were the result of official South African intervention.

Nearly a fortnight passed. He grew desperate, fearing that he would arrive — if ever — too late to do anything effective. Eventually, however, on a tip from an English Labour MP, who pointed out that French Deputies had much more influence with their national airways than British ones with theirs, he took a train to France and, four days later, was airborne. He had come to Paris with a letter from the English MP to some friends in the Chamber of Deputies, who handed him over to a woman in the colonial department of the trade union confederation. She was a former member of the Maquis and the widow of a Maquis leader killed by the Germans, and had no difficulty in arranging at once that he would have a seat on the next Air France flight to the States.

It was nearing the start of October when he arrived in New York. There, the contrast with weary, shabby post-war London was dramatic: brilliant streets crowded with well-fed, well-dressed, noisy, confident people. To Basner, it seemed incredible that they could have fought in the same war and also strange that he could look upon their vitality, air of success and general pushiness with affection (remembering his hatred for it all when he had quit Los Angeles some twenty years before). On the surface, the city was Johannesburg writ vast, yet lacking Johannesburg's ever-latent anxiety. He knew well enough that the same racist background was there — in Harlem, within a mile or two, in Georgia, hundreds of miles away. But a background is not a foundation. A background can change, a foundation hollow of all justice and humanity can only cave in.

It was a measure of his impulsive haste that he should have the addresses of only two contacts in New York. One of them was Leo Kerz, the German theatre director, for whom, when he was a fugitive in

Johannesburg in the thirties from Hitler's drive against 'non-Aryan' culture Basner had translated Bertolt Brecht's *Threepenny Opera* songs, but who was now determinedly non-political and unlikely to be of much help. The other was Max Yergan, who years before had been a YMCA missionary in South Africa and a friend of Charlotte Maxeke. Now he was the director of a radically-inclined organisation called the Council on African Affairs.

Basner immediately contacted Yergan, who seemed to know about him and suggested that they meet at his office the following day. The next morning, Basner stepped into the Council's front hall to encounter Dr Xuma of the African National Congress and HA Naidoo and S Rustomjee of the Natal and Transvaal Indian Congresses. They were clearly not surprised to see him, but he was, to say the least, taken aback at the sight of them.[1] Polite greetings were scarcely over when they were called into a committee room, where he was introduced to more people and briefed. He recognised at once the acting chairman of the Council on African Affairs — a huge man with the most distinguished head he had seen since his last glimpse of Fiodor Chaliapin. He was the world's other great bass, Paul Robeson. Next to him was a very tall, thin, ascetic-looking, paler man, Dr Alpheus Hunton, the Council's treasurer. Opposite them at the table sat Max Yergan and his stenographer, a robust Jewish blonde. On either side were Xuma, Naidoo and Rustomjee, with whom Basner took his place, still bewildered that his presence seemed taken for granted. The only person missing, he was told, was the Chairman of the Council, Dr WE Burghardt du Bois, famous as a writer, lecturer and founder of the NAACP, who was obliged to be away for the next few months.

Basner assumed that when the African National Congress conservatives and the Communist Party had heard of his departure for the United States, they must have grasped the political significance of his move. Having determined to claim an initiative equal to his, they had met with no difficulties over money, visas or transport. Xuma, through his church and social welfare affiliations and marriage to an American woman, had always had good connections in the USA, and the Indians had been efficiently assisted by the Indian High Commission in London.[2]

He discovered that his fellow South Africans, together with the Council's committee, had already asked the Indian delegation at the UN to put the racial policies of the South African government on the agenda of the Assembly. That delegation was an exceptionally strong and able one, led by Vijaya Lakshmi Pandit, Nehru's sister, and Krishna Menon, an intimate friend of the Nehru family. India as a country, and its representatives as individuals, would be taken very seriously by the United Nations, and, because of the size and disabilities of the Asian population in South Africa, was on strong grounds in pressing home a charge against its rulers.

It was unfortunate but necessary, Basner felt, that he should voice immediate objections to what he was now told had been planned. He agreed wholeheartedly to the use of the good offices of the Indian delegation, but not to the manner in which they would be used. A line of approach had been adopted that took no account of political reality. The indictment against South Africa had been — as he had anticipated — formulated in racial terms and based on generalisations about government policy. But the framers of the constitution of the United Nations (who included Smuts) had been careful enough to make sure that there would be no intervention in the internal affairs of any member state. For all the fine talk in the Charter of safeguarding human rights, there was also a clear provision safeguarding the rights of governments, and, more important still, the right of veto in the Security Council for the five major powers. With such provisions, why should it be necessary to close labour camps in Siberia, abolish chain-gangs in South Carolina, do away with slavery in Ethiopia, clip the wings of Orangemen in Ulster, hold back *colons* in Algeria, or compel South Africa to abolish the colour bar, passes, the Asiatic Land Tenure Act and similar legislation?

If the African and Indian Congress representatives based their case solely on the iniquity of race prejudice and discrimination, it would be easy for the Department of Native Affairs to rush a group of tame black chiefs over to Lake Success to complain about how Indian traders exploited the African population. Their evidence would then be followed by noble speeches from Smuts expatiating on the beauties and duties of Christian Trusteeship and the utopia waiting for all in South Africa as long as everything hastened slowly; and all reality would be lost in the harmony of black and white keys played on that elderly piano constructed in Dr Aggrey's head at Achimota on the Gold Coast.

Basner went on to say that he had come to the UN as he had come to the Senate, not expecting any practical results, but to use it as a forum from which to tell the world the truth about South Africa and why the apartheid state had been set up and was being maintained there. The fact that the goldmining industry might bear moral responsibility for the unique legal structure of that state, had not as far as he could see, entered the Council's deliberations at all and had to be brought to the forefront. The truth about Smuts himself, as the only South African in whom the world was interested, had to be told, and told effectively.

He suggested holding a number of public meetings before the session began. There would be enough black churches and white liberal organisations ready to open their doors to them. A platform made up of the President of the African National Congress, leading South African Indians and a white South African senator would attract attention. They could then call press conferences, and, with a bit of luck, the newspapers would be sufficiently interested to give them an impressive start.

When the discussion ended, Basner knew that he had two staunch

A Small Glimmer of International Light

allies in Robeson and Hunton and a wavering one in Yergan. Only the South Africans were put out. They wanted debate at Lake Success arising out of formal motions against the Asiatic Land Tenure Act and the absorption of South West Africa into the Union, but no public activities which could be interpreted at home or abroad as hostile propaganda against Smuts personally. To meet their objections, it was decided to put the matter to India's delegation, on whom, in any case, the feasibility of any plans they made depended.

Robeson asked Basner to lunch with him that day. This was the first of many such meetings. In fact they met on nearly every weekday — sometimes the two of them alone, most frequently with the South African Congresses' delegates and various members of the Council and its staff.[3]

Robeson was one of the brightest human stars in the American firmament. For kingly dignity, for a compassionate heart, for a lively intelligence, for the nobility men have always esteemed as a combination of great strength and great gentleness, there could not be anyone more complete than he. But because he was a black man, they had to travel long distances from midtown New York to find a hotel where he could sit down at a table with whites.

Once they became better acquainted, the people from the Council and the South Africans began to enjoy each other's company far better than might have been expected. Their gay and animated lunches and evening excursions into Harlem and Greenwich Village would have aroused envy in the dullest-witted offshoots of the master race that segregated them. Not dependent on liquor or fat wallets, their natural talent for living was augmented by their joint efforts and stimulated by the prospect of the contest ahead of them.

When they had met the delegation from the then Dominion of India and explained their mission in detail, its members had agreed, with only slight reservations, to Basner's evaluation of the role of the World Assembly and his strategic approach. Mrs Pandit, together with her brother, who was India's Foreign Minister at that time, had noted and considered the fatal contradictions in the UN Charter and its crippling effect on any action to invoke and assert human rights in a member country which claimed that this would constitute interference in its internal affairs. What Basner did not realise until a good deal later was how much the Nehru family's preoccupation with the coming struggle over Kashmir made Mrs Pandit appreciate that constitutional difficulty.

Mrs Pandit's deputy, Krishna Menon, had been a life-long participant in his country's drive towards independence, and was known to have Communist leanings. When Basner, in due course, learnt that the Council for African Affairs was an American Communist 'front' organisation, his chief regret was that most of its membership did not consist of the same kind of Communists as Menon. Though he was as different from Paul Robeson in looks and personality as he could possibly be, Menon was his equal in compassion and integrity.

He was as abrasive as a piece of cobbler's sandpaper, and his hawk-like, dour profile became a hatchet when he was listening to fools. Robeson's equanimity and courtesy could not be disturbed by human malice or foolishness (of which he had experienced more than his fair share). The Indian's intelligence was sophisticated and politically needle-sharp; the black giant, equally intelligent, but over-trusting, could be lured up blind alleys by any plausible tongue. The two became close during the weeks of work spent in preparing the case against South Africa. What happened to their natures later, when illness wrecked Robeson's life and Indian Congress Party reactionaries wrecked Menon's career after years of grossly misusing his loyalty[4], Basner was not to know.

The campaign was successful from the moment it started. Despite some public awareness that the Council on African Affairs was Communist-backed, Mrs Pandit, Naidoo, Xuma, Robeson and Basner made up a novel and colourful team upon which, as Basner had foreseen, the New York papers could not help but report.[5] They held a series of well-attended meetings at which Basner concentrated on the goldmining industry and Smuts's role in breaking the miners' strike. Some of the press coverage was relayed to South Africa, where it aroused a great deal of interest and indignation, although more in the English-language than in the Afrikaans press. The Nationalists were quite prepared to put up with adverse overseas comment on their country as long as they could announce that Smuts had been hammered or humiliated.

On one memorable, if troubling occasion all the unofficial delegates to the UN were invited to a large hall at Lake Success to meet Eleanor Roosevelt and Fiorello La Guardia. For Basner, Mrs Roosevelt's plain face, with its protruding front teeth and upper lip, was to remain a memory of gracious beauty. As for the 'Little Flower', now a very sick, shrivelled old man, no bigger than one of Disney's seven dwarfs, he was still an orator with a transcendent voice and words that went straight from his heart to every heart in the audience. No wonder he had been mayor of New York for twelve unchallenged years, as if that hard-headed city had been enchanted by a small angel in place of a politician.

The message the pair of them brought was menacing. They thought it was plain that Truman's new administration had decided to abandon Franklin Roosevelt's approach to world affairs. For Africans, Asians and Latin Americans, the main issue was that the State Department intended to stop contributing to UN agencies and give relief through US ones only, which meant that aid and development funds for the 'Third World' would in effect become instruments of US policy. As loyal American citizens, Mrs Roosevelt and La Guardia were calling on their hearers to protest while there was still time, so that their country could be saved from its own chauvinistic folly.

A Small Glimmer of International Light 189

Basner was sure they both knew nothing could be done. Theirs was only a desperate and pathetic attempt to warn the world that Churchill's Fulton speech (made in March that year), was taking effect, and that the Cold War was beginning.

A British lawyer, Sir Hartley Shawcross, flew in direct from the Nuremberg Trials to help Smuts and his accompanying officials who were in deep trouble. Not only had the preliminary war of words against them proved telling, but the Indian delegation, with Mrs Pandit at its head, promised to be very formidable. Moreover, the US State Department was still only feeling its way internationally, and had its own racial problems to consider, together with the possibility that its hegemony over Latin America might be shaken over an unpopular issue like colour discrimination in South Africa. Only the British could be relied on to put up an effective fight on Smuts's behalf.

Shawcross was Attorney General in Clement Attlee's Labour government. The glow of his success as chief prosecutor at the Nuremberg Trials was on him. His skills, combined with fierce moral indignation, had persuaded the judges there that the crimes against humanity of Hitler's chief accomplices deserved nothing less than death — implying that nothing less would reinstate democracy and ensure a future of freedom for the family of man on earth.

But now Smuts, heir of Demosthenes and Burke, a member of the cabinet of the Mother of Parliaments in the First World War, Field Marshal of armies against fascism in the second, co-architect of the free and democratic British Commonwealth, was arraigned, together with his country, on a related — even if lesser — charge to that against the Nazis, together with his country.

By this time, all the members of the South African team had worked hard and enthusiastically to collect material for Mrs Pandit, showing how segregation and the colour bar operated through the Mines and Works Act, the Land Acts, the Urban Areas Act, the Asiatic Land Tenure Act and so much other legislation, to deprive South Africa's black majority of all human rights as envisaged in the United Nations Charter. And she — a Nehru, daughter of India's most famous barrister, who had studied at the knees of Mahatma Gandhi — presented the Assembly with an unanswerable case. Her brief had mainly been compiled by Basner, whose knowledge of the legal legerdemain of white supremacy was the fruit of twenty years' almost unique experience. So well did she propound it, that for a while Smuts's position seemed untenable. A leading South African newspaper carried a cartoon of him sitting down at the UN to have a diminutive figure of Basner pull his chair from under him. On the Security Council, the United States had proved as unwilling to come to his support as had the USSR and Chiang Kai-shek's China.

But Smuts was not unseated. It was the United Nations itself that went to the floor. It would not pick itself up to save the Congo from the Union

Minière any more than the League of Nations saved Abyssinia from Mussolini, and on no occasion has it restored a legitimately elected regime toppled by a military coup or crushed by a fascist junta.

The same professional passion with which Sir Hartley Shawcross prevailed at Nuremberg enabled him to prevail at Lake Success. The UN merely approved a resolution criticising South Africa's treatment of Indians and requested her to mend her ways and report back at the next session. Although Smuts's application for the incorporation of South West Africa into his Union was not accepted, the League of Nations Mandate for the administration of that country by his government was not annulled.

Despite Basner's initial and categorical assumption that the UN would do nothing to change South African policy or practice, it was still as impossible for him as it was for his fellow delegates and their allies to feel anything but depression at the minimal outcome of their efforts. Perhaps they were depressed because they had done so much better than they had expected. Truths about South Africa had been forced upon a world which hitherto had seen it only as a democracy regrettably plagued, like others, by all-too-human prejudice and conflicts over culture and race.

Basner's return home had its comic as well as its serious side.

He had to fly from New York straight to Cape Town at the beginning of January, as both Houses of Parliament were in session and he did not dare be late in case this was taken for funk. He had scarcely expected a hero's welcome, but the chilly blasts of antagonism which blew at him through the corridors made air-conditioning against the humid Cape summer superfluous, to say the least. When he entered the Senate chamber and made his bow to its President, every eye lowered over the order papers. There was no sound from his three Native Representative colleagues as he took his seat among them. Clearly, he had been sent to Coventry — either by arrangement or on spontaneous impulse. He sat out the whole afternoon although normally he would not have wasted ten minutes after registering attendance, as the business on hand was dull and unimportant.

At tea time, he went to his usual table, a large one reserved for the seven Native Representatives in both Houses, three Labour members and a handful of Jewish MPs belonging to Smuts's United Party. The latter were on the UP's liberal wing and usually proved supportive when matters not fundamentally affecting the basic principles of apartheid were at issue. They were, that is to say, only opposed to the cruelties and humiliations of petty racial segregation(as, essentially, were the Labour Party and all but three of the Native Representatives — Peg Ballinger, Donald Molteno and Basner himself).

There was no one at the teatable, which was usually fully occupied at that hour. He already knew from the morning papers that the three Labour men, who included his close friends Alec Wanless MP and

A Small Glimmer of International Light   191

Sidney Smith, were in Durban for the annual conference of their party. The absence of the other Native Representatives and the Jewish MPs meant that the chill in the air extended to the lower House too. Basner was no longer a nuisance and a rebel, but an outcast.

The press knew what was going on but could not print a word about it. How do you report that a whole parliament has sent one of its members to Coventry? There was nothing to prove concerted action, and any speculation could be interpreted as contempt. Basner had more friends in the press gallery than in either House, but their frustrations did nothing to allay his own.

He finished his tea slowly and left the building. He had already experienced — on becoming the first person in the British Commonwealth to be ordered out of the Chamber of an Upper House — the sinking feeling occasioned when walking through ranks of disapproving faces without meeting a friendly eye. At such times it does not help to imagine oneself a noble and righteous victim of injustice, but on that day he had known his condition to be temporary — he could have apologised and been reinstated at once. Even without an apology, his supension could only have lasted three days. This time, it was a casting-out with no cover of ceremony, with no possibility on his part of apology, and he had not the faintest idea how long it would continue.

He thought of flight — back to Johannesburg, to the Africans in his office and the locations. He would find lots of friendly eyes there. But it would not do. If he left now, he could never come back. He might as well resign immediately — before the end of the year and his self-imposed term of office.

Next morning saw him back in the Chamber, to meet with exactly the same silence and avoidance. But by now he was damned if he would resign for the sake of this collection of old fools who in reality represented no one, whilst he represented three and a half million people. During the night, courage and brains had returned, and he had decided that if the Senate would not talk to him, it could certainly be obliged to listen. He retired upstairs to his office, to think.

A special arrangement in the South African Senate arose from a ruling that the Native Representatives should not be allowed to debate the budget. As compensation, they could, by tabling a special motion, call upon any Minister to discuss the policy of his department. Basner decided to call on no less a person than the Prime Minister, Jan Smuts, to report on foreign affairs and his relationship with the United Nations. It was a bold, even impudent, plan, but there was nothing anyone could do to interfere with it.

On the day of the debate, he was in the House before the other Senators, and now had his turn to keep his eyes down over the order papers whilst they took their seats. Sidney Smith arrived, to sit firmly beside him.

After the usual formal prayers, and before a full Chamber, the Prime Minister entered with some other Ministers and a retinue of civil servants. But Smuts did not go immediately to his place. Instead, he walked up the aisle to Basner's desk and leant upon it, shook hands, and said in a loud, clear voice, 'Good morning. I haven't seen you since New York, so haven't had a chance to congratulate you. You worked hard for your constituents and understand how much the world has changed. We must all change with it'. There was a moment's silence in which neither Basner nor, he supposed, anyone else, was likely to have noticed a clap of thunder. Then came a buzz of voices. Smuts went to his place and the President banged his gavel for silence.

That sly old politician, 'Slim Jannie', had stolen the show. With one chivalrous gesture, he had regained the stature of a great statesman rising above the petty sentiments and quarrels which bedevil ordinary men. In the style of a true democrat, he was acknowledging that Basner had a right to oppose him at the world forum which he had helped build on behalf of the black people of his own country. If he had merely said that he bore no malice, he would have been a superior officer forgiving the misconduct of a rebellious underling; but by stressing that they both understood a changing world, he lifted the issue of racial discrimination right out of its local context and on to the larger stage to which he always felt he belonged.

Smuts left the Senate Chamber with his retinue of civil servants, Ministers and Senators. Basner marched out after them . . . and into a comic finale to his grand opera at Lake Success.

The dining room, which was also the tea room, was full, and the table crowded. All seven Native Representatives were there, as were all the Labour members and the Jewish MPs. Basner was greeted with friendly and congratulatory noises about his trip to New York, about Smuts's greatness, and about the invaluable service they had both rendered to the Native people and to South Africa. His unnatural silence was ascribed to his being overcome by grateful emotion.

When he rose to go, several people accompanied him to the door, one putting an arm through his. It was an honour to walk and talk with someone who had been singled out for praise by the Prime Minister.

The United Nations debate with Smuts was to prove the only one of real importance for Basner during the five months of the session, which ended in June 1947. It encapsulated the war between Basner's obsessive, despairing desire for the UN to become a genuine instrument of world government and Smuts's determination that it should never be empowered to interfere with the internal affairs of a member nation.

Basner, whose sense of irony was acute, may have indulged it in relation to two other parliamentary events in which he found himself involved, had he bothered to write about them. The first of these was a typically obtuse government proposal to convert an African reserve in

A Small Glimmer of International Light 193

the Northern Transvaal into a game reserve and the second concerned the entertainment by the Senate of King George VI and Queen Elizabeth and their two young daughters. Their hosts were all so advanced in years that Basner, at forty-two, was reluctantly accepted as being the only one youthful enough to sit with Princess Elizabeth and Princess Margaret at table.

A further element of irony arose from what seemed at first to be a frightening incident. On a brief visit to Durban, he was assaulted by a large white thug in the lift of the hotel in which he was staying, and was lucky to escape with no more than a broken pair of glasses and some bruises. It was perhaps natural for him to take it for granted at the time that his attacker was a rabid Afrikaner Nationalist. He later found rueful amusement in discovering that, on the contrary, the man had been employed by well-to-do Natal Indians, enraged that they had been displaced by radicals such as HA Naidoo, and that Basner had joined these radicals in vilifying Field Marshal Smuts, to whom they persisted in giving their trust.

EPILOGUE

Basner resigned from the Senate in June 1947. He could have taken the option of a sixth year in Parliament at that time, because the government had decided to extend the tenure of both the Senate Native Representatives and the Native Representative Council until 1948, when a general election among whites was due, but by this time he was more than content to delegate his role to his once-despised rival, William Ballinger. Needless to say, he now shared completely the opinion of Paul Mosaka, who, in a famous phrase, had likened the NRC in its communications with government to a 'toy telephone'.

It was not easy to return to ordinary life, which meant a return to practising law and coping with personal matters. Both his finances and his marriage were in disarray.

Inevitably, his legal work was as political in content as ever. If he found a certain grim humour in the years between 1947 and 1952, it came from being one of the few people to forecast the defeat of Smuts's United Party by the Afrikaner Nationalists under Malan. But there was nothing humorous about the series of painful trials which dominated his practice during the period.

Epilogue

In the British Protectorate of Basutoland (now Lesotho), a combination of political demoralisation and cultural shock, largely derived from governmental attempts to change and intervene in chieftainly administration, manifested itself in an epidemic of so-called 'ritual' murders — desperate distortions of old magical means of defence and power. In Witzieshoek came a culmination of all the despairs engendered by the Land and Trust Act of 1936 — and the most painful and lengthiest trial of all, preceded by at least a year of useless negotiations with the Native Affairs Department, and of evidence before a commission of enquiry. It was to become a six-month ordeal for more than a hundred people impelled into outright resistance.

In 1950, Basner was divorced. After his subsequent marriage to me, we tried to settle in Swaziland, optimistically hoping to live there in semi-retirement. Events in Witzieshoek, however, wrenched him back to the realities of his profession and his natural clients. Later, another attempt to escape from the essentially political character of his work led us to move to Durban, where, again vainly, we dreamt of a clientele made up of thrifty burglars and solvent civil litigants.

By 1957, all attempts at professional impersonality had proved both humanly and financially unsuccessful and we returned to Johannesburg. Once again, he was tied to the sort of cases for which he was most sought after — the ones he most hated for their futility: courtroom battles over the non-existent rights of Africans in urban and rural areas, with fees paid or unpaid by the poor.

A visit to Basutoland as legal adviser to the then Paramount Chief — now King Moshoeshoe — early in April 1960, gave Basner something of a break from his usual routine. The notorious massacre at Sharpeville had taken place a little more than a fortnight before, and he was not greatly surprised when the King told him that he had heard on the radio of mass arrests of blacks and of unprecedented numbers of white opponents of apartheid in South Africa. Would it not be sensible, he asked, for Basner to invite his wife and three children to stay in Basutoland until the storm blew over?

Basner was amused. He had now been out of active politics for twelve years and could not be at risk. He started driving home while, unbeknown to him, dozens of other people were heading fearfully in the opposite direction. For once in his life, he was completely wrong in his estimation of police behaviour. At three o'clock on the morning after the night of his return came the classic bang-on-the-door, and he was whisked off, together with prominent white Communists and liberals, as well as a number of elderly remnants of dissent from the 1930s, first to detention in the Johannesburg Fort and then to Pretoria Central prison.

Four months or so later, they were all released, having been detained along with tens of thousands of blacks, though under infinitely more tolerable conditions.

Another irony was that the unexpected imprisonment, followed by restriction on his movements, was now to free him from the inhibitions that usually keep people from acting either spontaneously or rationally. Matters like concern for one's children and their education, or one's income and income tax, suddenly became of no serious account. He had felt impotent for so long, living in the midst of an increasingly intolerable society and feeling incapable of contributing intelligently to its overthrow.

He had, it is true, tried to redirect his political energies into writing, and had produced a lengthy — and, at that time, remarkably original and solid — history of South African racist legislation, to which he gave the provocative title *Apartheid is an English Word*. Not surprisingly, it had failed to find a publisher. Now, virtually confined to Johannesburg by the authorities, even his deep-felt involvement with the rural areas was cut off. On leaving the Senate, he had carried out his intention to distance himself from ANC politics and those of such whites as were then attempting to influence them. But only in September 1960 was he at last able to realise that he had not faced up to the implications of his conviction that his self-imposed role in South Africa was no longer useful to others. A new means of feeling of use had to be found — outside the mental and physical restrictions of home.

Within five months, a way of escape presented itself. In an elderly Land Rover, we managed a trundling getaway across the two thousand miles between Johannesburg and Dar es Salaam.

At that time Tanzania was nearing full independence with Julius Nyerere already its Prime Minister. Our year there failed to offer any prospects of real political or professional usefulness, although it was interestingly filled for Basner in making a collection of short biographies of the Tanzanian leaders of that time (including Nyerere), with whom he quickly established friendly contact; and for me, in being the barely-competent headmistress of a primary school. We were reacquainted with representatives of the ANC in exile, and embarked with them on joint efforts to help adjust young — and rather demoralised — black refugees from South Africa to living in a settlement provided for them by the new Tanzanian government.

There seemed little hope for a constructive way of life in the long term for either of us, so much so that we even contemplated withdrawal into the Serengeti Plains to run a safari camp or to an isolated mission station as English teachers.

At the end of 1961, however, he received an offer of work from the opposite side of the continent, in Ghana. We flew to Accra in January 1962, where, under the direction of Joseph Gillman, my previous chief at the Johannesburg Medical School, an institute for medical research was being established.

The living thus provided was more than adequate to maintain us during the first couple of months, which, for Basner, were both highly stimulating and highly frustrating. Before he left Dar es Salaam, the Ghanaian Embassy had given him hope that he would find a post as a lecturer in law or South African history at a university. These hopes soon collapsed because of the conservatism of the Ghanaian academic establishment, which was plainly entrenching itself to counter the radicalism of Kwame Nkrumah.

Having always believed that he had been sidetracked into law after leaving school, Basner's ambitions were still directed towards journalism. His sympathy for Nkrumah was already great and the newspaper in Accra that most plainly reflected Nkrumah's aims and feelings was the *Ghanaian Times* — edited by two men who were to become his friends — TD Baffoe and Kofi Badu. Its politics were enthusiastically left-wing, its print and sub-editing were eccentric, its news coverage erratic, and its distribution chaotic.

After making several appointments to see Baffoe (which were broken), Basner began to suspect that he was as much a victim of obstruction as he had been when looking for academic work. Happily, however, this proved to be a delusion, engendered by the muddle that typified the paper's management. He was warmly welcomed as someone whose good reputation had preceded him, and asked to write articles about Tanzania, followed by a series on South Africa. He soon became a regular columnist, putting out three pieces a week under the heading *Watching the World from Accra*.

The next four years were to be the happiest, and to his mind, the most positive, of his life. Within weeks, it became apparent that the President was reading his comments on foreign affairs with great interest and approval and within months, they became properly acquainted. This acquaintance speedily developed into true friendship and close collaboration, with Basner eventually becoming the President's chief speechwriter on international affairs — especially those concerning Nkrumah's great dream of a real union of African states. He also became intimately involved in drafting a proposed constitution for what was to become the Organisation of African Unity (OAU). Nothing resembling this constitution was ever adopted, and the OAU was set up in the loose and impotent form it has today.

Basner accompanied Nkrumah as a member of the Ghanaian delegation to two major conferences, in Addis Ababa and Cairo, about the formation of the OAU and also travelled on missions to Indonesia, Cuba, East Germany and Czechoslovakia.

Ghana at that time was an exciting centre of political ferment and intrigue. It was so precisely because it was by far the most lively country in black Africa. Cold war rivalries impelled governments all over the world to establish embassies in Accra and to staff them with some of their most able envoys. Many of these not only supplied a rich mix of international gossip, but of mental stimulus as well. Yet it was Ghanaian society itself, so innately vital and so particularly vitalised by Nkrumah, which attracted an influx of far more people than mere diplomats. Outstanding black and white refugees, academics, writers and artists, technicians, enquirers, and seekers and self-seekers, came in droves from every quarter.

Living in Ghana gave Basner some insight into the politics and psychology of exile of his own countrymen and women. His most distressing days in Accra were spent in fruitless efforts to obtain official recognition for the ANC. These efforts were obstructed largely by the machinations of a semi-lunatic, Barden, head of Ghana's Bureau of African Affairs. Barden had ensured that only the PAC was represented in Accra — by at best irresponsible and at worst venal people speaking for an ill-organised party of romantic nationalists. It was particularly deplorable to him to meet (for the last time) one of his oldest friends, JB Marks, and be unable to help him get permission to establish an ANC office in Accra.

Early on 24 February 1966, the army-police coup which toppled Nkrumah's regime coincidentally toppled Basner into Accra's Usher Fort prison together with virtually everyone holding a position in the ruling party. A month later, he was released and deported.

It was a relief to leave a place once loved that had, literally overnight, become quite another and, as yet, there was no leisure in which to look back in sorrow. It was necessary to cope with the problem of where to go. Our two elder children were at school and with my family in Britain, but we were debarred from going there. With no passports except Ghanaian travel documents which were due to expire within weeks, we were fortunate to be able to fly to Rome, through the good offices of the Italian ambassador in Accra.

In Rome, repeated visits to the British embassy proved as useless as were earnest efforts made on our behalf by senior members of the then ruling Labour Party in London. It was clear that the Foreign Office had decided that Basner was an unsavoury Red supporter of a pernicious black dictator, as well as a notoriously vociferous critic of British policy *vis à vis* Ian Smith's recent takeover of power in what was then Rhodesia. Since, however, we plainly could not return to South Africa, officialdom, it seems, was eventually prevailed upon to make a delicate suggestion: could we not emigrate to Israel, where, after a decent interval, we would be supplied with passports? We should then, we were led to understand, have no difficulty in being given visas to stay with our family in London (and could also be deported, but without fuss, in the event of our being deemed to be misbehaving.)

So, at the end of 1967, we found ourselves in Britain, on what was hoped to be a fairly temporary visit. Early the following year, however, Basner suffered the first of several heart attacks which impelled us to remain — and be allowed to become 'permanent residents' in Herefordshire — until his death in 1977. Those nine years were filled for him by writing: reminiscences of Tanzania and Ghana, revision and updating of his earlier history of apartheid, and finally, the beginnings of an autobiography, which has provided most of the substance of this book.

NOTES

FOREWORD

1 Paul Rich, *White Power and the Liberal Conscience*, Manchester University Press, Manchester, 1984, p 93.
2 Edward Roux, *Time Longer than Rope*, Victor Gollancz, London, 1948, p 309.
3 C M Tatz, *Shadow and Substance in South Africa*, University of Natal Press, Pietermaritzburg, 1962, p 93.
4 He worked most closely with Margaret Ballinger who wrote for *Umteteli*, 1 June 1946, an amused account of his marathon four-hour speech on the Indian segregation bill: 'In the course of these four hours, the elderly gentlemen of the senate heard a great deal about what the African thinks and feels. They groaned as the hours lengthened out but at the end of the time they were still listening. Possibly by that time they were more interested in Senator Basner's powers of endurance than receptive of his propaganda but something of what he said would remain in their minds.'
5 Miryana Roth, The Natives' Representative Council, 1937-1951, Doctoral Thesis, Department of History, University of the Witwatersrand, 1987, p 231.
6 *The Times*, 3 May 1977.
7 He was a pioneering advocate of the ANC's and the CPSA's participation in advisory boards, lamenting the 'missed opportunities in not using the Advisory Board elections for political purposes' (*Umsebenzi*, 10 July 1937), and recognising their importance in a local political system held together by patronage: '... being a member of the Advisory Board was a very important thing, no less so than because it was a sort of bribery; you could also depend on it that a lot of people would bring you money, because suppose you wanted to open a little shop in the location, you had to get a trading licence, suppose you wanted your daughter to come and stay with you, you had to get a lodger's permit, supposing you wanted to make beer, you had to get permission to make beer; well you went to the Advisory Board member who went to the Superintendent and got you a permit to make ten gallons of kaffir beer, you know, so there was always plenty of room for both prestige and for money and indeed it was a very important thing ... So these board meetings were fought with terrific ferocity, you know every year for election' (Transcript of interview with Brian Willan, 1975, held in the Institute for Commonwealth Studies, University of London).

8 Roux, *Time Longer than Rope*, p 304.
9 See Barrington Moore, *Social Origins of Dictatorship and Democracy*, Penguin Harmondsworth, 1969, p 487.
10 Though with qualifications. Though he 'accepted most of the fundamental theses of Marxist philosophy of politics... that political progress or political recession can only move on class tension... I've always had reservations about the dictatorship of the proletariat, not the way Marx formulated it, but the way Lenin evolved it' (Transcript of interview with Brian Willan, 1975).
11 Paul Rich, *White Power and the Liberal Conscience*.
12 Basner argued reciprocally that the league only served to 'confuse the black workers and frighten off the white workers', in the process serving 'the capitalist system because they enable the capitalist to divide and exploit both sections of the working class' (H M Basner, *Wreckers at Work: A Warning to Black and White Workers*, Johannesburg, 1945). Encouraged by his friendship with Solly Sachs, Basner continued to believe at this point that white workers could be mobilised in a progressive direction, given education and the right approach. In the first issue of his new journal, *Socialist Review*, Basner attacked the Communist Party for its unrealistic advocacy 'of immediate equality of Africans and Europeans on social and economic grounds'; at this stage, he continued, the workers' movement should be organised on racially parallel lines (cited in *Inkululeko*, 14 July 1945).
13 *Guardian*, 13 February 1947.
14 *Inkululeko*, 3 December 1945.
15 HM Basner, The Duties of a Native Representative, *The Table – The South African Socialist Review*, October 1945, p 25.
16 Basil Davidson, *Report on Southern Africa*, Jonathan Cape, London, 1952, p 133.
17 Paul Rich, *White Power and the Liberal Conscience*, p 82.
18 See Baruch Hirson's autobiography, to be published by Witwatersrand University Press. Other works in the genre include: Bernard Sachs, *Multitude of Dreams*, Kayor Publishing House, Johannesburg, 1949 and Eddie and Win Roux, *Rebel Pity*, Rex Collings, London, 1970.
19 Edgar Brookes, *White Rule in South Africa*, University of Natal Press, Pietermaritzberg, 1974, p 200.
20 Press clipping of article by Julius Lewin supporting Rheinallt Jones's candidature, September 1937. Rheinallt Jones Papers, University of the Witwatersrand.
21 Paul Rich, *White Power and the Liberal Conscience*, p 51.
22 John David Rheinallt Jones, *Official Report and Manifesto*, Esson and Co, Johannesburg, August 1942, pp 4-6.

23 J D Rheinallt Jones, 'Africans Awake! There is danger!', roneo'd leaflet, Johannesburg, September 1942, A B Xuma papers, 420900, University of the Witwatersrand.
24 *Inkululeko*, 14 April 1945.
25 Baruch Hirson, *Yours for the Union: Class and Community Struggles in South Africa*, Witwatersrand University Press, 1989, p 179.
26 *Inkululeko*, 24 November 1944. ADP leaders in Orlando since September had been trying to persuade residents to boycott trains against a fare increase. Police broke up a 'large gathering' called by the ADP and arrested Paul Mosaka. In the subsequent Orlando Advisory Board elections, the ADP candidates defeated their Communist rivals who had opposed the ADP's efforts to mobilise around train fares (Self Mampuru, the African Democratic Party and the Orlando Advisory Board Elections, *The Table – The South African Socialist Review*, December 1945, pp 19-22).
27 Papers relating to Hyman Basner versus the Incorporated Law Society of the Transvaal, Rand Supreme Court, 1952, Hyman Basner Papers, University of the Witwatersrand Library, A 2026.
28 Basner's literary and intellectual interests were wide ranging. He was an avid reader of English poetry, an early translator of the work of Bertolt Brecht and, amongst his other enthusiasms were the work of Leonardo da Vinci and the philosopher Kierkegaard. His aspirations as a writer found expression in his journalism during the 1940s and later in Ghana in the 1980s. He also wrote a substantial history of South Africa entitled *Apartheid is an English Word* which was never published. Its arguments anticipate much of the work of South Africa's revisionist school of historiography in the 1970s. A copy is held in the University of the Witwatersrand Library's collection of historical manuscripts under the title *The Black Price of Gold in South Africa*.
29 Hyman Basner, untitled and unpublished manuscript on Ghana, 1962-1966, written in the late 1960s. Original in possession of Miriam Basner; copy in University of the Witwatersrand Library. All subsequent unacknowledged quotations are from this text.
30 See, for examples, David Apter, *Ghana in Transition*, Princeton University Press, 1972 and Roger Genaud, *Nationalism and Economic Development in Ghana*, Praeger, New York, 1969.
31 Subsequent academic analysis suggests that Basner's view was mistaken. Victor T Le Vine, *Political Corruption: The Ghana Case*, Hoover Institution, Stanford, 1975, pp 28-30 and 135-136.
32 In an interview conducted in 1974, Joe Matthews recalled encountering Basner after the first OAU conference outside the assembly chamber after Nkrumah's speech, and a buoyant Basner asking him: 'How did you like my speech?' (Karis and Carter Microfilms, 2: XB6: 96). For a negative assessment of Nkrumah's

speech at the Cairo meeting to which Basner in his autobiography suggests he made a more important contribution see David Rooney, *Kwame Nkrumah: The Political Kingdom in the Third World*, Tauris, London, 1988, p 231.
33 Relevant excerpts from his journalism are quoted in Zdenek Cervenka, *The Unfinished Quest for Unity*, Julian Friedmann, London, 1977, p 11; Immanuel Wallerstein, *Africa: The Politics of Unity*, Random House, New York, 1967, pp 224-225; Basil Davidson, *Let Freedom Come*, Atlantic Monthly Press, Boston, 1978, p 288.
34 *West Africa*, April 2 1966, p 387.
35 Geoffrey Bing, *Reap the Whirlwind*, MacGibbon and Kee, London, 1968, p 373.

CHAPTER 1

1 Five reels of tape-recorded autobiographical reminiscences of Hyman Basner's political activities in South Africa and Ghana were acquired by London University's South African Materials Project. They can be consulted at the School of Oriental and African Studies. A transcript of an interview with Basner by Brian Willan and Baruch Hirson is kept in the neighbouring library of the Institute of Commonwealth Studies, together with various autobiographical manuscripts.
2 Post-war Soviet usage favours the Latvian name Daugavpils. When Basner was born the town was called Dvinsk and Latvia was a province of Imperial Russia. Latvia existed as an independent state between 1918 and 1940 before invasions by both the Soviet Union and Germany and incorporation in 1944 into the Soviet Union as Latvia SSR.
3 Chassidism: 'pietist movement which arose in the eighteenth century among the Jews of South-eastern Poland in opposition to the dry intellectualism of official rabbinic doctrine.' By the twentieth century, protagonists of enlightened Judaism viewed it as superstition and obscurantism but were themselves opposed by advocates of a powerful Chassidic revival. See G Saron and L Hotz, *The Jews in South Africa*, Oxford University Press, Cape Town, 1955, pp 283-291.
4 Russian provincial administration accorded to individuals who performed local government functions within Jewish communities the title of 'rabbi'. This brought no religious standing to such officials within their own communities.
5 The Pale of Settlement was fifteen Russian provinces in which after 1791 Jews were confined to certain localities and occupations. This followed the annexation of territories containing large Jewish

populations. The Pale contained 94 per cent of Russian Jewry. Most of Latvia lay outside the Pale and consequently Latvian Jews were relatively unrestricted, in Basner's father's case additionally so, for Jews who had completed military service acquired certain privileges. Dvinsk itself was on the frontier of the Pale.

6 Late nineteenth-century Russification policies and the establishment of heavy industry contributed to the rise of militant socialist and nationalist movements in Latvia. Jews played a conspicuous role in the former and were especially subject to the attentions of a political policing system instituted in the Baltic provinces in 1888. See Alfred Bilmanis, *A History of Latvia*, Princeton, New Jersey, 1951, pp 249-269.

CHAPTER 2

1 Afrikaners began entering the mining industry's workforce in significant numbers in 1907 when the Chamber of Mines began an energetic campaign to recruit unemployed Afrikaners during a strike. Two to three thousand Afrikaners gained employment between May and June 1907 but most were once again jobless by Christmas (Charles van Onselen, *Studies in the Social and Economic History of the Witwatersrand, Volume Two: New Nineveh*, Ravan, Johannesburg, 1982, pp 142-144). By the time Basner arrived in Johannesburg a quarter of the white miners were South African born (David Yudelman, *The Emergence of Modern South Africa*, Greenwood, Westport, 1983, p 75)

2 In certain cities, Pretoria for example, municipal regulations prohibited blacks from walking on the pavement.

3 Indunas were appointed by mining management to keep order in the compounds, one for each tribal group. Their title indicated that they were supposed to correspond to village headmen.

4 For other memoirs of Jeppe Boys' High School during this period: Eddie and Win Roux, *Rebel Pity*, Penguin Harmondsworth, 1972, pp 21-24; Bernard Sachs, *Multitude of Dreams*, Kayor Publishing House, Johannesburg, 1949, pp102-112; Bernard Sachs, *Herman Bosman as I knew him*, Golden Era, Johannesburg 1974, pp 26-34. Sachs has vivid recollections of his experiences of anti-Semitism at the school.

5 In 1921 the Helpmekaar school was established in Johannesburg as the first Afrikaans-medium secondary school. Sachs (*op cit*, p 95) existing before that date. These included Vrededorp's Die Trap der Jeugd attended by children of all ages.

6 In 1927 Johannesburg's African population (excluding mining

employees) numbered 96 000 of whom less than 15 000 lived in municipally controlled hostels or locations (Maud, *op cit*, p 140). See also: Eddie Koch, Slumyard Culture in Johannesburg, in Belinda Bozzoli (ed), *Town and Countryside in the Transvaal*, Ravan, Johannesburg, 1983, pp 151-175, and The Witches of Suburbia, in Charles van Onselen, *op cit*.
7 In 1920, 29 000 African children attended school in the Transvaal (Ellen Hellman (ed) *Handbook on Race Relations in South Africa*, Oxford University Press, Cape Town, 1949, p 318). A government school for Africans did exist in Johannesburg, at Klipspruit location. It was exceptional — all other African schools in the province were church or mission ventures (Charles Loram, *The Education of the South African Native*, Longman, London, 1917, p 63).
8 The Keystone Cops were a series of slapstick comedies from the studio of the same name, directed by Mack Sennett between 1914 and 1920 and featuring Ford Sterling, Mark Swain and Fatty Arbuckle.
9 Mack Sennett, owner, producer and director of the Keystone Company, specialised in a 'primitive humour of undress and obesity' in which pretty young women in daring costumes were an essential ingredient.
10 Gloria Swanson was an early Sennett bathing beauty before being rewarded with more ambitious roles.
11 Pola Negri was a Polish-born starlet famous for her roles in films made in Berlin by Ernst Lubitsch. In the United States her prominence was chiefly due to an affair she had with Charlie Chaplin in 1923.
12 Roscoe 'Fatty' Arbuckle, a 136kg comedian teamed up with Charlie Chaplin and Buster Keaton to star in a series of outstanding comedies. His career effectively ended when bit player Virginia Rappe died in his bedroom during a riotous party he threw in a San Francisco hotel. He was tried for manslaughter and acquitted after two hung juries had reviewed evidence so lurid it could not be repeated aloud in the court room (Axel Madsen, *Gloria and Joe*, William Morrow, New York, 1988, pp 80-82).
13 Wallace Reid was a matinée idol who frequently starred with Gloria Swanson. He died in 1926 after a year's confinement in a private asylum as a drug addict. His death, together with the Arbuckle affair were two of a series of scandals which shocked America just before Basner's arrival, heralding a decade of puritanical reaction to the more relaxed social climate of the 1920s.
14 Yudelman, *op cit* pp 178-180; Rob Davies, The 1922 Strike and the Political Economy of South Africa, in Belinda Bozzoli (ed), *Labour, Townships and Protest*, Ravan Press, Johannesburg, 1979, p 312.

15 Norman Herd, 1922: *The Revolt on the Rand,* Blue Crane Books, Johannesburg, 1966, pp 118-122.
16 Africans were attacked outside compounds in Brixton, Vrededorp, Ferreirasdorp and Sophiatown, as well as at New Primrose Mine. See: Herd, *op cit,* and Edward Roux, *Time Longer Than Rope,* Victor Gollancz, London, 1948, p 158.
17 The strike was one of a series in San Pedro, led by the syndicalist Industrial Workers of the World between 1922 and 1924. It is described in Peggy Dennis, *The Autobiography of an American Communist,* Lawrence Hill and Co, Westport, 1977, pp 37-39.
18 Upton Sinclair, 1878-1968, leading American left-wing novelist and pamphleteer. In the mid-1930s, Sinclair, as a Democratic nominee with the support of large sections of the unemployed narrowly missed winning the California governorship. His books include *The Jungle, World's End,* and *Dragon's Teeth.*
19 Sinclair subsequently wrote a short play about the episode entitled *The Singing Jailbirds* (published privately, Pasadena, 1924).
20 Georgi Plekhanov, founder of the Russian Social Democrats and before Lenin (whom he opposed) the foremost Russian Marxist. The book was probably his *Anarchism and Socialism,* translated into English in 1895. Plekhanov's *Fundamental Problems of Marxism* was available in English only from 1929.
21 Henry Mencken, 1880-1956, editor, literary critic, and essayist in *The American Mercury,* a journal he founded in 1925. Mencken was an iconoclastic opponent of American social conventions and political values with a particular dislike for clergymen, farmers and patriots. His popularity was largely attributable to such sardonic one-liners as his characterisation of romantic love being the delusion that one woman differs from another.

CHAPTER 3

1 The Labour Party was formed in 1909 and began contesting Johannesburg's municipal elections in 1911 when it won eleven out of thirty seats. It controlled the Council between 1919 and 1921 during which period it implemented a ten-shilling minimum wage for white employees, adopted a union closed shop policy (again for its white workers only) and established its own iron foundry and coal field. Such policies did not win universal approval; by 1925 Labour members were relegated to minority status on the council and the party's representation declined thereafter. In 1918 a Labour-influenced city administration achieved the historical distinction of making Johannesburg the first city government ever to support a

strike by its own workforce (John Maud, *City Government*, Oxford University Press, Oxford, 1938).
2 Hebrew and Religion school for Jewish children.
3 African Methodist Episcopal Church. Established by the former Methodist preacher, Reverend James Dwane in 1896 with the help of the Black American parent church. With 10 000 members by 1898, it was a major channel for black South African recruitment to American negro colleges.
4 The AME educational centre included amongst its teaching staff in 1928 a future General Secretary of the Communist Party, Albert Nzula. The Evaton school was named after Wilberforce University, originally a black secondary school established in Ohio by the AME in 1856.
5 Curfew laws for the two northern provinces were systematically unified under the 1923 Native (Urban Areas) Act.
6 Gana Makabeni and W Thibedi of the Native Clothing Workers' Union (E S Sachs, *Rebel's Daughters*, MacGibbon and Kee, London, 1957, pp 95-96).
7 The number of unskilled white workers on the railways rose from 6 363 to 12 042 between 1926 and 1930 while the number of African unskilled workers halved. Other government departments took on an extra 14 000 whites in response to rising 'poor-white' unemployment. In 1926 government policy set aside street cleaning, road repairs, school janitorship and doorkeeping and messenger duties in government offices as tasks which should be reserved for white employees (Rob H Davies, *Capital, State, and White Labour in South Africa*, 1900-1960, Brighton, Harvester, 1978, p 225).

CHAPTER 4

1 Of the Cape liberal politicians, only William Schreiner was to keep faith with African supporters by opposing the Act of Union (which maintained the political exclusion of Africans in the northern provinces and deprived Cape Africans of the right to hold elected office).
2 *Ilanga* survives today, though no longer as a vehicle for African National Congress sentiment. In 1987 it was purchased by a company owned by Chief Buthelezi's Inkatha movement.
3 A poll-tax was first introduced in Natal in 1905, sparking off the Bambata rebellion. Dube's newspaper gave outspoken support to King Dinizulu during his trial in 1906 for complicity in the rebellion. The poll-tax was not implemented after the revolt until 1925 when the Native Tax and Development Act applied a uniform imposition

throughout the four provinces. Resistance to the tax was strongest in Natal, provoking the Minister of Justice, Oswald Pirow personally to conduct an armed raid on defaulters in Durban in 1929.
4 A bilingual (Zulu-Xhosa/Sotho-Tswana) rendition of the word for people, an expression of the intertribal unity represented by the ANC's formation.
5 For a full description see Philip Bonner, The Transvaal Native Congress, 1917-1920: The Radicalisation of the Black Petty Bourgeoisie on the Rand, in Shula Marks and Richard Rathbone (eds) *Industrialisation and Social Change in South Africa*, Longman, London, 1982.
6 Clements Kadalie founded the ICU in 1919. *White Man – I see you* was what he said the initials meant. The ICU was a militant protest movement by black workers against low wages, the Pass Laws and the 1923 Urban Areas Act. For formation and development of the ICU see Edward Roux, *Time Longer Than Rope*, Victor Gollancz, London, 1948, pp 161-203; Clements Kadalie, *My Life and the ICU*, Frank Cass, London 1970; Philip Bonner, The Decline and Fall of the ICU — A Case of Self Destruction, in Eddie Webster (ed), *Essays in South African Labour History*, Johannesburg, Ravan Press, 1978, pp 114-120; P L Wickens, *The Industrial and Commercial Workers' Union of Africa*, Oxford University Press, Cape Town, 1987; Helen Bradford, *A Taste of Freedom: The ICU in Rural South Africa, 1924-1930*, New Haven, Yale University Press, 1987. By the time Basner returned to Johannesburg, the ICU was largely a rural movement, having acquired one hundred new branches in country districts between 1926 and 1928. For a description of Kadalie's opposition in 1930 to the CPSA anti-pass campaign in the Orange Free State see Eddie and Win Roux, *Rebel Pity*, Rex Collings, London, 1970, p 91.
7 Bonner, The 1920 Black Miners' Strike, in Belinda Bozzoli (ed), *Labour, Townships, and Protest*, Ravan Press, Johannesburg, 1978, suggests that if all the participants over the seven days of the strike are counted, the total reaches 71 000 workers in twenty-one mines, making it the largest black strike until the 1980s.
8 The ICU made an unprecedented effort to recruit women in 1920, holding a women's meeting in Cape Town (Cherryl Walker, *Women and Resistance in South Africa*, Onyx Press, London, 1982, p 59). ICU leader Selby Msimang had, earlier in his career, helped in the legal defence of the Free State resisters, and Basner believed that Msimang and OFC secretary Keable Mote were important in sustaining women's support for the ICU.
9 Peter Wickens (*The ICU of Africa*, Oxford University Press, Cape Town, 1978, p 204) suggests that 150 000 people actually joined the ICU though its normal support could well have been even more extensive. In Miriam Basner's own experience, the ICU's continuing

influence was evident in at least a dozen small towns and villages in the southern Free State and the western Transvaal in 1941-1942.
10 A former labour tenant sadly told University of the Witwatersrand researchers in the 1980s that the ICU 'all ended up in speeches' (Helen Bradford, *A Taste of Freedom*, Yale University Press, New Haven, 1987). Much of the disappointment was attributable to the ICU's failure to keep its promises to provide land through purchase schemes.
11 On the connection between the effective prohibition of consumption by Africans of liquor, and the labour requirements of the mining industry see Charles van Onselen, *Studies in the Social and Economic History of the Witwatersrand, 1886-1914: New Babylon*, Ravan Press, Johannesburg, 1982, p 92.

CHAPTER 5

1 The *Contemporary Review* was a liberal monthly journal founded in 1866 by Bunting aided by Sir Jesse Boot. A D Godley (Under-Secretary at the Indian Office) wrote a piece of doggerel about them entitled *Two Liberal Knights*.

> Freshmen on the Cherwell punting, twanging on the festive lute
> Magnify Sir Percy Bunting and extol Sir Jesse Boot.
> Engines in the act of shunting suddenly forget to hoot
> When they spy Sir Percy Bunting, or behold Sir Jesse Boot.

Percy Bunting was knighted in 1908 for philanthropy and services to the Liberal Party.

2 The League of African Rights was formed in 1928 through a CPSA initiative as a consequence of its adoption of the Native Republic policy which party officials at the time believed required them to collaborate with African Nationalist leadership. The LAR's President was Joshua Gumede, President-General of the ANC and it included on its executive Bunting, Albert Nzula and Doyle Modeighotla from the ICU. The League looked as if it was set to replace the crumbling ICU in African political affections. Large meetings popularised a petition of rights and launched a million-signature campaign under a striped red, black and green flag. On the eve of a conference called for Dingaan's Day 1929, a telegram from the Executive Committee of the Comintern called for the League's dissolution, charging that it served to bolster reactionary and reformist African leadership.

3 Established under the Native (Urban Areas) Act of 1923, the Advisory Boards were constituted as mediums of consultation. Their elected and nominated members had no policy making powers; they

met under the chairmanship of the location superintendent who would funnel their suggestions and opinions to the municipality's (white) Native Affairs Committee. According to Sir John Maud (*City Government*, 1938, p 209) 'More intelligent natives regard Advisory Boards without enthusiasm.'

4 The first case in which the argument was used to challenge a prosecution under the Urban Areas Act was in Rex vs Hodos and Jabbe, Transvaal Provincial Division, no 101, 1927. Unfortunately the *South African Law Report* does not mention the name of the attorneys; the advocate was Leslie Blackwell. The Supreme Court subsequently declared null and void the Act's requirement that Africans should live in segregated locations, because of the absence of sufficient housing.

5 African Communists may have contested board elections in 1929, when the Party actively sought the African vote in parliamentary elections. The first systematic efforts by the Party to win seats on the boards began after 1936 after a policy shift favouring the development of broader political alliances, in conformity with Comintern's popular front advocacy. See *Umsebenzi*, 20 September 1936. On Comintern's prescription of a United Anti Imperialist Front for the CPSA see the autobiography of the CPGB official who represented Comintern in South Africa in 1935: George Hardy, *Those Stormy Years: Memoirs of the Fight for Freedom in Five Countries*, Lawrence and Wishart, London, 1956, pp 228-236.

6 The Greyshirts were started in 1933 by Louis Weichart. Openly anti-Semitic, their meetings protesting against Jewish immigration attracted substantial crowds in the course of 1936.

7 By 1929 it had become very difficult to sort out which of the eight ICU factions constituted the breakaway group. After his resignation Kadalie formed an Independent ICU in Bloemfontein at the end of March 1929. Ballinger's group continued to claim it was the original ICU and to receive British support. The ICU of Africa (Ballinger) collapsed as quickly as its rivals and was defunct by 1934. Kadalie was prohibited from addressing meetings on the Rand in 1930 and his ICU became increasingly localised in East London, where its leader made his home from 1931.

8 The reorganisation of the CPSA on Bolshevik lines took place after its December 1930 conference under the direction of its new English secretary, Douglas Wolton. Prostrate obeisance to Comintern directives was accompanied by the withering of internal democracy and an intensification of polemic directed towards 'reformist' nationalist organisations. By late 1932 these developments had reduced membership to 300. See Sheridan Johns, *Marxism Leninism in a Multiracial Environment: The Origins and Early History of the CPSA*, PhD dissertation, Harvard University, 1965.

9 Bunting contested the Tembuland constituency in the 1929 'Black Peril' general election. His campaign lasted from March to June and included two arrests and convictions for incitement under the 1928 Native Administration Act. He was accompanied by Gana Makabeni; their joint efforts were rewarded with 289 votes, just over a tenth of the total. Makabeni was to remain loyal to Bunting, attempting to defend his friend against expulsion from the party two years later.

10 Soviet theorists, taking their cue from the 1929 recession, forecast bright revolutionary prospects in South Africa as elsewhere in the capitalist world, and hence ordered the CPSA to lead and dominate political alliances rather than merely foster them. Hence the Party should have used the League of African Rights as a compliant 'transmission belt' rather than treating it as a partner (Johns, *ibid*, pp 535-543).

CHAPTER 6

1 Here Basner was ahead of his time; locating the origins of modern segregationist legislation in the policies of the Milner administration was fairly unconventional among South African historians until the late 1970s. See Shula Marks and Stanley Trapido, Lord Milner and the South African State, *History Workshop*, Issue No 8, Autumn 1979.

2 The 1926 amended Act limited certificates of competency in engineering, surveying, blasting and other selected occupations to 'Europeans, Cape Coloureds, and Mauritius, Creole and St Helena persons'. But, as David Yudelman argues (*The Emergence of Modern South Africa*, Greenwood Press, Westport, Conn, 1983, p 33): 'in fact, the color-bar regulations had existed before and were not siginificantly expanded by the regulations attached to the (1911) Act.'

3 Seme began his presidency by provoking a split in the ANC in the Western Cape because of his antipathy to Communists. He alienated remaining loyalists with his efforts to introduce an authoritarian constitution which would have given the President the right to appoint his executive and invested control over finances in the Congress 'Upper House'. By 1933 only sixty-nine delegates attended the ANC's annual conference in Bloemfontein. Thirty-seven of them came from Bloemfontein itself (Peter Walshe, *The Rise of African Nationalism in South Africa*, Ad Donker, Cape Town, 1987, pp 254-255).

4 By 1932, Party spokesmen were routinely characterising the ICU

212   Am I an African?

and the ANC as 'counter-revolutionary' (Brian Bunting, *Moses Kotane: South African Revolutionary*, Inkululeko Publications, London, 1975, p 61). According to Kotane, though nineteen of the twenty-three members of the 1930 CPSA executive were black, 'most of the Africans were dummies, they never spoke at meetings' (Bunting, *ibid*, p 58).

5 Basner's earlier work on Urban Areas Act prosecutions may have directly contributed to the growth of the slumyards. After the Supreme Court ruling on the Act the populations of the yards leaped from a total in 1925 of 8 000 to 40 000 at the close of 1927 (Eddie Koch, 'Slumyard Culture in Johannesburg', in Belinda Bozzoli (ed) *Town and Countryside in the Transvaal*, Ravan Press, Johannesburg, 1983, p 154).

CHAPTER 8

1 For commentaries on the relationship between goldmining, racialism and international capitalism by Marxist contemporaries of Basner see: A T Nzula, I I Potekhin and A Z Zusmanovich, *Forced Labour in Colonial Africa*, Zed Press, London, 1977 (first edition, Moscow, 1933); Max Yergan, *Gold and Poverty in South Africa*, New York, 1938. Currently the standard analyses are: R V Kubicek, *Economic Imperialism in Theory and Practice: The Case of South African Gold Mining Finance, 1886-1914*, Duke University Press, Durham, North Carolina, 1979; David Yudelman, *The Emergence of Modern South Africa*, Greenwood Press, Westport, Conn, 1983; F A Johnstone, *Class, Race, and Gold: A study of Class Relations and Racial Discrimination in South Africa;* Routledge, London, 1976; Marion Lacey, *Working for Boroko: The Origins of a Coercive Labour System in South Africa*, Ravan Press, Johannesburg, 1981.

2 The Jewish Workers' Club existed between 1929 and 1950 with a peak membership of 300, mainly Yiddish-speaking Baltic immigrants. Politically it was close to the CPSA, being anti-Zionist and supportive of Birobidjan, the Jewish autonomous region of the USSR. See: Taffy Adler, 'History of the Jewish Workers' Club', African Studies Institute, *Papers Presented at the University of the Witwatersrand*, Johannesburg 1977, pp 1-66.

3 For more on the strike see Bettie du Toit, *Ukubamba Amadolo: Workers' Struggles in the South African Textile Industry*, Onyx Press, London, 1978; Basil Davidson, *Report on South Africa*, Jonathan Cape, London, 1952, pp 176-188.

4 Interview with Bettie du Toit.

5 Comintern's emissary to the CPSA in 1936, George Hardy, was later to praise the Party's 'constructive decision to unite all democratically minded people irrespective of color, nationality or creed.' This was in accordance with the 1935 Comintern decision in favour of the formation of popular fronts. For Hardy the Party's previous 'ultra leftism' was attributable entirely to 'Trotskyites'. All the quarrels between advocates of a bourgeois native republic and the partisans of a workers' and peasants' government could now, happily be superseded by the main task of convincing white workers 'that it was in their interest to put an end to segregation and help in the organisation of black workers' (George Hardy, *Those Stormy Years*, Lawrence and Wishart, London, 1956). Presumably they could do this more easily if they didn't have to sit next to them at meetings. Party publications pandered to racial prejudice without quite endorsing it: for example a pamphlet discussing the issue of racially mixed marriages asserted that 'neither race *wants* to mix with the other. Where racial intercourse (sic) does take place, it is largely due to the poverty and backwardness of the native women which leaves them without self respect' (*Communism and the Native Question*, CPSA, Johannesburg District, nd c 1936). On Friends of the Soviet Union: Kurt M Campbell, *Soviet Policy Towards South Africa*, Macmillan, London, 1986.

CHAPTER 9

1 Contemporary conditions in the Cape reserves were most richly documented in a survey commissioned by the Chamber of Mines: Francis Fox and Douglas Back, 'Preliminary Survey of the Agricultural and Nutritional Problems of the Ciskei and the Transkei', ts 1937, held at the University of the Witwatersrand. The report characterised the reserves' populations as living in a state of semi-starvation.
2 In 1922, African and Coloured voters comprised more than one-fifth of the electorate in twenty-one constituencies. In two of these, Tembuland and Woodstock, they were in the majority. By 1929, there were 15 780 African voters in the Cape. Black voters had been enfranchised in the Cape since 1854 though they were barred from holding office by the terms of the 1910 Act of Union. Their vote was halved in importance when white women were granted the franchise in 1930. Figures from Noel Garson, 'The Cape Franchise in Action; the Queenstown by-election in 1921', paper presented to the 1984 History Workshop, University of the Witwatersrand.

3 The 1936 Native Trust and Land Act authorised the state to purchase another 7,25 million morgen for African settlement, established a South African Native Trust to administer the development of the reserves, and outlined a timetable for the elimination of the remaining black squatters on white farms. Baruch Hirson argues that the immediate effect of the Act was to increase overcrowding and intensify state interference; the additional land hardly compensated for the influx of evicted squatters and the presence of white officials employed by the Trust to regulate the way in which land was used (*Yours for the Union*, WUP, Johannesburg, 1990, pp 122-129).
4 'Parliamentary idiocy' was the phrase used by Marx in his essay 'The Eighteenth Brumaire of Louis Bonaparte' (K Marx and F Engels, *Selected Works*, Lawrence and Wishart, London, 1970, p 148). He refers to 'that peculiar malady which since 1848 has raged all over the continent, *parliamentary cretinism*, which holds those infected by it fast in an imaginary world and robs them of all sense, all memory, all understanding of the rude external world'. Lenin in his 1920 polemic, *Left Wing Communism and Infantile Disorder*, suggested that Communist parties should exploit every opportunity supplied by parliamentary institutions and trade unions, if necessary using 'every kind of trick, illegal means, concealment of truth or prevarication'. Lenin shared Marx's contempt for parliamentary representative systems, a somewhat different position from Basner, who seems to have believed in their essential merit but saw them as corrupted under capitalism. At a more pragmatic level, in 1936 Basner wrote in the *South African Worker* (19 September 1936) 'We must also have a positive attitude during elections ... the party which comes closest to meeting our immediate demands is the Labour Party. Because the natives have no franchise is no reason why they should not interest themselves in elections'.
5 Roux is less charitable. In *Time Longer than Rope* he wrote: 'There was one outstanding traitor: the Reverend John Dube publicly declared himself in favour of the Bill. But who cared for Dube? He was known to be a government man.'
6 Naudé was appointed acting State President (the republican equivalent of Governor-General) in May 1967.

CHAPTER 10

1 Dr J E K Aggrey toured South Africa in 1921 as a member of a Commission on African Education set up by the New York-based Phelps-Stokes Fund. Aggrey was a graduate of Livingstone College

in North Carolina. After his three-month visit to South Africa he accepted an appointment as Principal of Achimota College in the Gold Coast where he was to teach the young Kwame Nkrumah. During his tour of South Africa, Aggrey addressed 120 meetings of African students, religious leaders and political notables. See E W Smith, *Aggrey in Africa: A Study in Black and White*, SCM Press, London, 1929; W M McCartney, *Dr Aggrey: Ambassador to Africa*, London, 1949; Baruch Hirson, 'Tuskegee, the Joint Councils, and the All African Convention', Institute of Commonwealth Studies, *The Societies of Southern Africa*, Collected papers, Volume 10, University of London, 1981, pp 66-69.

2 Initial funding for the SAIRR came from the Phelps-Stokes Fund, The Rhodes Trust, and the Carnegie Corporation, but by 1934 the greater part of its finances came from South African sources. SAIRR Director, JD Rheinallt Jones, resigned his position at the head of the Institute in 1947 to become welfare adviser to the Anglo American Corporation in the Free State goldfields. See Ellen Hellman, '50 years of the SAIRR' in Ellen Hellman and Henry Lever, *Conflict and Progress*, Macmillan, Johannesburg, 1979; Paul Rich, 'The SAIRR and the Debate on Race Relations', *African Studies*, XL 1 1981, pp 13-22.

3 On Rheinallt Jones's social and political philosophy see Paul Rich, *White Power and the Liberal Conscience*, Manchester University Press, Manchester, 1984. For a sympathetic portrayal: Edgar Brookes, *John David Rheinallt Jones*, SAIRR, Johannesburg, 1953.

4 For more of Thema's views on this issue see JH Simons and RE Simons, *Class and Colour in South Africa*, Penguin Harmondsworth, 1969, p 496.

5 The electoral arrangements established under the 1936 Act included the placing of Cape African voters on a separate roll to elect three members of the House of Assembly and a process of indirect voting to select four senators to represent Africans throughout the country. In the senatorial elections, chiefs, local councils, committees in white farming areas and advisory boards would constitute voting units with weighting according to the number of registered tax payers. Candidates would first be nominated at meetings at which electors would vote through a show of hands and then, in a second stage, the voting colleges (the Chiefs, boards, committees and councils) would choose between the two candidates receiving the most nominations. For a fuller description see Marjana Roth, 'Domination by Consent: Elections under the Representation of Natives Act' in Tom Lodge (ed), *Resistance and Ideology in Settler Societies*, Ravan Press, Johannesburg, 1986, p 145 and pp 148-149.

6 American universities and philanthropic organisations supplied the main channels for ideas and expertise flowing to South Africa in the

1910s and 1920s on the management of race relations. Columbia University and the Phelps-Stokes Fund were especially important in this respect. Between 1914 and 1948, for example, about seventy South Africans attended Columbia University's Teachers College. Both Paul Rich (*White Power and the Liberal Conscience*, Manchester University Press, Manchester, 1984) and Saul Dubow (in Shula Marks and Stanley Trapido (eds), *The Politics of Race, Class and Nationalism in Twentieth Century South Africa*, Longman, London, 1987) have noted how the 'discourse of positivist American race relations' began to affect South African social thought in the 1920s.

CHAPTER 11

1 See Edward Roux, *Time Longer Than Rope*, Victor Gollancz, London, 1948, pp 227-229.
2 Eddie Roux attempted to achieve the residential qualification which would have enabled him to stand for the Party in the Western Cape, just failing to do so. See Eddie and Win Roux, *Rebel Pity*, Rex Collings, London, 1970, p 148.
3 See Baruch Hirson for early efforts by Communists to organise mineworkers in the 1930s (*Yours for the Union*, WUP, Johannesburg, 1990, p 169). There are reports of an African Mineworkers Union in *Umsebenzi*, 8 June 1935, 14 December 1935 and 4 April 1936. W Thibedi is cited in these reports as its secretary. Thibedi was a veteran member of the CPSA but was expelled from the Party in 1931.
4 There were five candidates in the first stage of the election. The two others were so obscure as to be irrelevant, obtaining between them only a few thousand votes.
5 After the nomination stage the electoral colleges would vote on the first two candidates. If there was a tie, the unit chairman would exercise a casting vote. As chairmen, therefore, in addition to their informal influence, the chiefs could have a decisive effect on the ways in which the colleges voted.
6 In an apparently contradictory reference, *Umteteli Wa Bantu* 17 April 1937 stated that Mote was attached to the Rheinallt Jones camp and spoke on Jones's behalf in the election, but it is possible that Mote might have publicly identified himself with one candidate and discreetly helped the other (the author is grateful to Baruch Hirson who supplied the *Umteteli* reference).
7 L T Mvabasa was an important figure in the ANC from its inception, participating in delegations to the government in 1914 and to Britain in 1919. He founded a newspaper in 1912, *Umlomo wa Bantu* which

merged with *Abantu* the following year. He attended ISL and IWA meetings in 1917 and 1918 and was a member of a secret ISL/Transvaal Native Congress committee which planned strategy before and during the 1918 Johannesburg municipal workers' strike. Later he became identified with the more conservative wing of Congress leadership, joining Seme's cabinet in 1930 but remaining on the ANC executive after the latter's departure. See Philip Bonner, The Transvaal Native Congress, 1917-1920, in Shula Marks and Richard Rathbone (eds), *Industrialisation and Social Change in South Africa*, Longman, London, 1983, pp 291-295.

CHAPTER 12

1 Basner's memory may have misled him on this point. Contemporary newspaper reports suggest that Thomas Mapikela actually supported Basner in Bloemfontein whereas Keable Mote opposed him, gaining for Rheinallt Jones the local advisory board's endorsement. Reports may not have been accurate; both Mote and Mapikela may have switched sides during the campaign or even worked for both candidates simultaneously, so the text has been allowed to stand. See Paul Rich, Managing Black Leadership, in Bonner, Hofmeyr, James, Lodge (eds) *Holding Their Ground*, 1989, Johannesburg, WUP.
2 For the Witzieshoek rebellion see Sean Moroney, The 1950 Witzieshoek Rebellion, *Africa Perspective* 3, February 1976, pp 1-15.

CHAPTER 13

1 Charles van Onselen's forthcoming study of a South African sharecropper, *A Chameleon Amongst the Boers: The Life of Kas Maine*, 1894-95, will point to the role played by small-town Jewish lawyers, traders and shopkeepers in shifting support of black sharecroppers voting in the District Councils from Rheinallt Jones to Basner in the 1937 and 1942 Native Senate elections. Mirjana Roth attributes Basner's 1937 defeat mainly to his refusal to appeal to the chiefs in the rural voting units (Formation of the Native Representative Council, Master's Dissertation, University of South Africa, 1979, p 173). Roux attributes Basner's comparative success in this election to his having developed an extensive legal practice amongst rural African communities. According to Roux, Pietersburg was one of the voting units (20 639 votes) where a majority of

two on the District Council awarded the votes to Jones *(Time Longer Than Rope,* Victor Gollancz, London, 1948, p 303).

2 S P Matseke was President of the Transvaal African National Congress between 1933 and his death in 1941. He was a member of the ANC's National Executive Committee from 1928 and one of the guiding influences behind the formation of the African Mineworkers Union in 1941.

3 In fairness, not all the Party's leaders in the late 1930s were foreign-born newcomers. Much of the day-to-day work of keeping the Party going between 1936 and 1939 was undertaken by Issy Wolfson and Willie Kalk, both South African-born trade unionists. At that stage, though, both of these men were mainly active in the Trades and Labour Council, fighting a rearguard action to defend the Party's remaining influence within white labour. According to the Simons *(Class and Colour in South Africa,* Penguin Harmondsworth, 1969, p 485), their understanding of popular front policies led them on occasions to side with white labour conservatives against other socialists and communists.

4 The Party's efforts to win over white workers included the advocacy, during the 1938 election, of a racially discriminatory minimum wage — five shillings for Africans, ten shillings for whites *(South African Worker,* 12 February 1938). In this context Mofutsanyana's proposal was not unreasonable. With the move to Cape Town at the end of 1938 the leadership shifted to Cape-based people with the election of a Politburo, headed by Jack Simons, Ray Alexander, Bill Andrews, Z Gool, Sam Kahn and Moses Kotane.

5 André Marty led the Black Sea mutiny in the French Fleet in 1919 during the Russian Revolution. He joined the French Communist Party in 1923. As Chief Political Commissar of the International Brigade he was partly responsible for a series of internal purges conducted with psychopathic cruelty. As a base commander at Albacente he gained an additional reputation for arrogant incompetence. He was expelled from the Party shortly before his death in 1955. For a literary portrait of Marty see the depiction of 'Comrade André Massart', 'as crazy as a bed bug, he has a mania for shooting people', in Ernest Hemingway's *For Whom the Bell Tolls,* Penguin Harmondsworth, 1967, pp 391-400.

   Marty headed the Comintern Commission which in 1935 resolved a dispute between the CPSA's 'Ultra-leftists', Lazar Bach and Paul and Maurice Richter, and the more pragmatic Moses Kotane. Kotane's views were in the end found to conform to Comintern's recently adopted United Front policy. He returned to South Africa but Bach and the Richters, all of whom were of Latvian origin, remained in the Soviety Union. In 1937 they were expelled from the South African Party and according to some reports sentenced to death (Brian Bunting, *Moses Kotane: South African Revolutionary*, Inkululeko Publications, London, 1975, p 291) after accusations of complicity with Soviet Trotskyites. The three were rehabilitated by an SACP Congress in 1989.

CHAPTER 14

1 In 1939, the Northern Transvaal reserves were the first regions to be proclaimed ás Betterment Areas. For more detail on the effects of proclamation see Baruch Hirson, *Yours for the Union*, WUP, Johannesburg, 1990, pp 128-129.
2 Popular histories of Shaka's kingdom available to Basner in the 1930s suggested that such punishments were routine. Modern historians believe that there is little evidence to support such contentions.
3 The Native Administration Act was used to banish 153 people between 1948 and 1980; before then it was employed more sparingly. The law also gave the Minister of Native Affairs the authority to relocate whole tribes, to prevent people from leaving their place of residence, and to detain without trial people disturbing the peace. All these powers were exempt from any challenge in court. Powers of banishment were also conferred on the Minister of Justice through the 1930 amendment to the Riotous Assemblies Act. Both measures were important instruments in curbing ANC/CPSA popular campaigning between 1928 and 1930. For an extensive discussion of the Native Administration Act see Marion Lacey, *Working for Boroko*, Ravan Press, Johannesburg, 1981, pp 84-119.
4 Basner's speeches to the Senate in the course of 1943 supply the main source material for modern historical analysis of 'betterment' in the Transvaal (Hirson *op cit*). In Parliament, Basner described the removal of families to stony two-morgen plots and their subjection to harsh regulations concerning ploughing, grazing, and foraging firewood. It was also Basner who first drew attention to the employment of former 'poor-whites' as agricultural officers. For a survey of organised political responses to the government's agrarian policies: Colin Bundy, Land and Liberation: Popular Rural Protest and the National Liberation Movements in South Africa, 1920-1960, *Review of African Political Economy*, No 29, 1984.
5 See Basner's speeches in the *Senate Hansard*, March and April, 1943, Debate on Administration of Trust Farms.
6 Basner and Self Mampuru prepared a paper about the effects of the Trust Administration which they sent to the Natives Representative Council in December 1942. Typically it was only made use of in December 1943, when the next session of the Council could make it

the subject of a debate sparked off by the news of 'disturbances' in Pietersburg. See Natives Representative Council, *Minutes of Proceedings*, 3 December 1943, pp 79-84.
7 CPSA assistance to Maliba included the publication of a pamphlet, A M Maliba, *The Conditions of the Venda People*, Inkululeko Publications, Johannesburg District Committee of the CPSA, 1939. Such support notwithstanding, the Party's attitude to rural organisation was tartly summed up by George Findlay, a Pretoria-based Communist advocate who defended Maliba in Louis Trichardt in 1941. He noted in his diary (Findlay Papers, University of the Witwatersrand) that 'the platteland Africans are a secondary area — mere propaganda is needed there, not peasant revolts' (quoted in Richard Haines, 'Resistance and Acquiescence in the Zoutpansberg, 1936-1945', University of the Witwatersrand History Workshop, 1981, p 6).

Maliba died in a Louis Trichardt police cell in September 1967 while detained under the Terrorism Act. The police claimed he had hanged himself. His detention and death may have been linked to the efforts of ANC guerilas to cross the Rhodesian Wankie game reserve and establish a presence in the Northern Transvaal.

CHAPTER 15

1 Referring to the SAIRR, A B Xuma wrote to D M Buchanan: 'I honestly feel that the Institute . . . stands in the way of African organisation and democratically thinking Europeans especially as it is taken in official quarters as a body that represents African opinion. The position is most embarrassing to some of us who are personal friends of its officials, but who do not have the same outlook in Race Relations' (Gail Gerhart, *Black Power in South Africa*, University of California Press, Berkeley, 1978, p 37). See also correspondence between Hoernle and Xuma and from Buchanan to Hoernle and Jones, December 1942, A B Xuma Papers, University of the Witwatersrand, ABX H21228.
2 Molepo was President of the Transvaal African Teachers' Association until his removal from his teaching post in 1944. He was deported under the Native Administration Act between 1944 and 1946. Basner used him as his translator and interpreter in the Northern Transvaal.

CHAPTER 16

1 For Xuma's efforts to create a local branch structure for the ANC and revive Congress finances see Peter Walshe, *The Rise of African Nationalism in South Africa*, Ad Donker, Cape Town, 1987, Chapter XIV.
2 The Non-European United Front was established at a meeting in April 1938 in Cape Town attended by delegates from forty-five organisations including the ANC, the CPSA and the Trades and Labour Council. The CPSA's Cissie Gool was elected President. The main force behind the formation of the NEUF was the National Liberation League, itself assembled in 1935 by young coloured intellectuals, many of them Marxists, but divided between Trotskyites and CPSA supporters. The NEUF's most spectacular achievements were the massive torchlit rallies it staged in Cape Town in 1939 to oppose draft legislation which would have codified coloured residential segregation. A Transvaal NEUF under the aegis of Dr Yusuf Dadoo was comparably active at the same time. See Gavin Lewis, *Between the Wire and the Wall: A History of South African Coloured Politics*, St Martin's Press, New York, 1987, pp 174-198.
3 Basner's election manifesto is reproduced in full in this book.
4 Bishop Edward Lekhanyane was the older of two brothers of the Lekhanyane lineage who led the Zion Christian Church in the 1940s. Centred on a farming settlement at Moriah (a biblical name for Jerusalem), Lekhanyane and his fellow bishops administered 'a fund of spiritual, material and symbolic power' (Jean Comoroff, *Body of Power, Spirit of Resistance*, Chicago University Press, Chicago, 1985, pp 237-250). For the hierarchy at least, membership of the Church conferred considerable material wealth; the Moriah headquarters was by the 1940s equipped with a fleet of forty-five American limousines and Easter collections were taken in a ten-gallon oil drum. The Church was established in 1912 by Edward's father, Engenas, originally a Scottish Presbyterian who became influenced by the American Apostolic leader Joseph Downie, whose Chicago-based church first won converts amongst newly-urbanised Afrikaners. The Church's support is strongest amongst the elderly and the middle-aged, the poorly educated and the unskilled, and poorer city dwellers in general who have retained strong social and ideological connections with the countryside.
5 See B G M Sundkler, *Bantu Prophets in South Africa*, Oxford University Press, London, Second Edition, 1961.
6 The best collective biography of this generation of political leadership remains Gail Gerhart's *Black Power in South Africa*, California University Press, Berkeley, 1978.

7 Significantly, Basner's victory is not mentioned in the Simons's treatment of the 1940s in their *Class and Colour in South Africa*. *Inkululeko* (20 September 1942) did acknowledge the wide support for Basner evident at meetings. The Senate and NRC elections were, for the CPSA, rather overshadowed in importance by its own 'Defend South Africa' initiative. The three CPSA NRC candidates, Mofutsanyane, Maliba, and OFS teachers' leader, S M Lekgetho, garnered between them 200 000 votes but did not succeed in winning a seat. By 1944, rural issues were beginning to attract attention in some quarters of the Party; *Communists in Conference* (Cape Town, 1944), the booklet summarising the proceedings of the 1943/44 CPSA National Conference records a motion from Rusty Bernstein on behalf of the Johannesburg District Committee arguing for 'the need to distribute land among the peasants'.

CHAPTER 17

1 The Argus Printing and Publishing Company, which owned ten newspapers, including *The Star* and the *Cape Argus*, was owned jointly by several mining groups of which the most prominent was Johannesburg Consolidated Investments. The *Rand Daily Mail's* shareholders were at that time more representative of the manufacturing industry. For a comprehensive analysis of newspaper ownership in the 1950s see Gwendolen Carter, *The Politics of Inequality*, Thames and Hudson, London, 1958, pp 37-48.
2 See *Senate Debates*, 21 January 1943. This also includes a description of the effects of the 1913 Land Act and the 1936 Land and Trust Act.
3 See *Senate Debates*, 26 March and 12 April, 1943: Administration of Trust Farms.
4 This is a reference to Oswald Pirow, who after serving in Hertzog's 1929 cabinet as Minister of Justice became an adherent of republican fascism, visiting the Berlin Olympiad in 1936 and forming the New Order Study Group within DF Malan's HNP in 1940. He was expelled from the HNP at the end of 1941 but remained within the House of Assembly as the leader of a national socialist minority until losing his seat in 1943. As a Queen's Counsel he opened the prosecution of ANC leaders in the 1956-61 Treason Trial.
5 Provision existed within the 1936 legislation for senators to be appointed by the government for their presumed expertise in 'Native Affairs'. Senator Welsh was a beneficiary of this measure.
6 This was a reference to the powers conceded by the Native Administration Act to the Minister of Native Affairs, and hence, indirectly, to civil servants within the Ministry.

CHAPTER 18

1 The Broederbond was founded in 1919 'to arouse Afrikaner national self consciousness and further every concern of the Afrikaner nation'. Described as subversive by General Smuts in 1945, its influence was mainly exercised through a pervasive network of cultural and functional organisations, established, manipulated and controlled by its secret membership. For detail see: Dan O'Meara, The Afrikaner Broederbond, 1929-1948: Class Vanguard of Afrikaner Nationalism, *Journal of Southern African Studies 3, 1977;* Ivor Wilkins and Hans Strydom, *The Super-Afrikaners: Inside the Afrikaner Broederbond,* Johannesburg, Jonathan Ball, 1980; JHP Serfontein, *Brotherhood of Power,* London, Rex Collings, 1979.
2 On the Ossewa Brandwag see: N M Stultz, *Afrikaner Politics in South Africa, 1934-1948,* University of California Press, Berkeley, 1974; Brian Bunting, *Rise of the South African Reich,* Penguin Harmondsworth, 1964, Chapter 6.
3 Both the police's Special Branch and Military Intelligence concerned themselves with internal security matters during the Second World War. For a narrative of Special Branch operations directed against the Ossewa Brandwag including the forestalling of assassination attempts (though with no mention of Basner) see: George Visser, *OB: Traitors and Patriots,* Macmillan, Johannesburg, 1976.
4 A wartime report by Military Intelligence is reproduced as an appendix in W H Vatcher, *White Laager: the Rise of Afrikaner Nationalism,* Pall Mall, London, 1965. In 1944, Smuts, acting on advice from the Director of Military Intelligence, launched a purge of Broederbond members from the civil service; 1 094 officials left government employment, including the Chief Clerk of the Treasury, the Under-Secretary of Commerce, and the Head of the Division of Diplomatic and Consular Affairs (Ivor Wilkins and Hans Strydom, *The Super Afrikaners,* Jonathan Ball, Johannesburg, 1978, pp 81-82).
5 During the war both compound conditions and labour discipline were to become more unpleasant and oppressive as a consequence of food shortages and 'scientific' management. See: W G James, Grounds for a Strike: South African Goldmining in the 1940s, *History Workshop,* University of the Witwatersrand, 9-14 February 1987.
6 The best narrative describing the spread of trade union ideas on the mines and the form they took in organisers' speeches to meetings assembled outside compounds is in T Dunbar Moodie's The Moral Economy of the Black Miners' strike of 1946, *Journal of Southern African Studies,* Vol. 13, No 1, October 1986.
7 Gaur Radebe had a background of trade union experience from the pre-war years; in 1937 he was secretary of the African Stone, Cement

and Building Workers' Union. In 1941 he was the ANC's 'Secretary for Mines' and in this capacity chaired the AMWU's founding committee. The following year he was expelled from the CPSA for running the Gaur Radebe Moneylending Agency (*Inkululeko*, 17 June 1942) 'which our party does not consider to be in the interests of the people'. By 1945, though, he must have been reinstated, because the Simons in *Class and Colour* describe him as leading the Alexandra branch of the Party.

James Majoro was a friend of Edwin Mofutsanyana; the two men came from the same area, Witzieshoek, and worked together on the same mine in the 1920s, and both joined the ANC in 1923. Majoro was the leader of the five-hundred-strong Mine Clerks' Association; his involvement in the AMWU was to lead to the loss of his post at Nourse Mines in 1942.

8 Moodie (op cit) suggests that 'home boy' networks supplied much of the organisational underpinning in mineworker protest and that the 'moral economy' of protest was partly shaped by the rural culture mineworkers brought with them to the compounds.
9 See the *Report of the Witwatersrand Mine Natives' Wages Commission*, 1943, Government Printer, Cape Town, April 1944. The Commission recommended a 3d per shift cost of living allowance, a boot allowance and an annual wage increase of £10-£11. The Government determined that employers should concede a 4d-5d per shift pay increase (about £6 a year) as well as extra payments for overtime.
10 As Ray Alexander put it at the CPSA's 1943/44 conference (*Communists in Conference*, Cape Town, 1944, p 5): 'Our party's policy is directed towards a peaceful settlement of disputes and avoiding any strikes that will hinder the war effort.'
11 30.19 per cent from the Cape, 4.75 per cent from Natal and Zululand and 7.72 per cent from the Transvaal and the Orange Free State (Transvaal Chamber of Mines Gold Producers' evidence for the Native Laws Commission citied in its *Report*, 1946-48, UG 28, 1948).
12 Dan O'Meara has noted that the average annual shortfall between wages and family subsistence levels rose from 2d in 1939 to £9.4.10 in 1943 ('The 1946 African Mineworkers' Strike and the Political Economy of South Africa,' Journal of Commonwealth and Comparative Politics, Vol. 13, No 2, 1975).
13 Francis Wilson, *Labour on the South African Gold Mines, 1911-1969*, Cambridge University Press, Cambridge, 1972.
14 Colonel A E Trigger was a former head of the CID who had, in 1925, sought to have Eddie Roux convicted on a sedition charge for distributing leaflets criticising an official visit to South Africa by the Prince of Wales. Trigger claimed £1 000 for defamation arising from

Basner's evidence to the wages commission. He was initially awarded £50, though the judge expressed his reservations about 'the method adopted by the plaintiff to safeguard the interest of the mining industry (which) was to insinuate a spy into the councils of the native union . . . a method which leaves an unpleasant taste'. Basner took the case to the Appellate Division and won; the award was rescinded (Eddie Roux, *op cit*, pp 343-344).

CHAPTER 19

1 For more information about the wartime bus boycotts see: Baruch Hirson, Azikwhelwa — We Shall not Ride, Chapter 11, in *Yours for the Union*, WUP Johannesburg, 1990; Alf Stadler, A Long Way to Walk: Bus Boycotts in Alexandra, 1940-45, in Philip Bonner, *Working Papers in Southern African Studies*, Volume 2, Ravan Press, Johannesburg, 1981; Edward Roux, The Alexandra Bus Strike, *Trek*, 21 September 1945; P H Guenault, Alexandra Bus Boycott, *The South African Treasurer*, February 1945.
2 Vernon Berrangé was a member of the Communist Party. He successfully defended Moses Kotane against a subversion charge in 1942. Later he was a defence advocate in the 1956-61 ANC Treason Trial. In exile in Swaziland from 1960, he died in 1983.
3 Self Mampuru's association with William Ballinger dated back to the mid-1930s. In 1938 he served as patron of the African Domestic Servants' League, an initiative of the Friends. In 1943 he played a leading role as a workers' representative in the negotiations which succeeded a wave of strikes on the Witwatersrand. That year he was chosen to preside over the Transvaal African National Congress, but then left the ANC to help establish the ADP. In 1947 he was a vigorous opponent of the ANC's boycott of the Natives' Representative Council leading that year a newly formed South African Democratic Socialist Party. He was elected to the NRC in 1948.

CHAPTER 20

1 For discussion of the ANC's role in the 1943 boycott see Alf Stadler, A Long way to Walk, in Philip Bonner (ed), *Working Papers in Southern African Studies*, Volume 2, Ravan Press, Johannesburg. In this essay Stadler documents Xuma's personal interest in acquiring a stake in the bus company as well as detailing Basner's role in

organising lifts, helping to form the Emergency Transport Committee and in proposing state subsidies.
2 The ADP's nucleus was the Emergency Transport Committee, the body established to co-ordinate assistance to the 1943 boycotters. Its members included leading Alexandra personalities as well as Basner, Lillian and Vincent Swart, and two Communists, J B Marks and Vernon Berrangé. The ETC was re-established in 1944 as the Worker's Transport Action Committee with its members within the ADP camp. A disagreement over whether to defy bans on public meetings, with Basner opposing civil disobedience, created the split which eventually destroyed the ADP (Baruch Hirson, Prices, Homes and Transport, unpublished paper, p 30).
3 For early career and intellectual development of Anton Lembede see Gail Gerhart, *Black Power in South Africa,* University of California Press, Berkeley, 1978, pp 45-84. Gerhart records that Lembede also worked in Seme's office as an articled clerk after gaining his LLB in 1943 (p 45). MacDonald Maseko was expelled from the ANC in 1954 for leading an anti-Indian faction called the *Bafabegiya* ('those who die dancing'). At that time he chaired the ANC's Orlando branch and was a member of the National Executive. Later he organised farm workers for the SA Congress of Trade Unions (SACTU) and in 1959 he joined the Pan-Africanist Congress. He later lived in Swaziland.

CHAPTER 21

1 See especially the *Report of the Inter-departmental Committee on the Social, Health and Economic Condition of Urban Natives,* 1942-43, Chapter XVII, p 10 and p 15.
2 Organised expressions of such sentiments included the servicemen's Springbok Legion, Ruth First's Federation of Progressive Students and the Campaign for Rights and Justice which was led by the Rev Michael Scott.
3 See Hilary Sapire, 'The Stay-away of the Brakpan Location, 1944', in Belinda Bozzoli, *Class Community and Conflict,* Ravan Press, Johannesburg, 1987, pp 358-400. For a disparaging description of the Anti-Pass Campaign and the Communist Party's role in it see IB Tabata, *The Awakening of the People,* Spokesman Press, Nottingham, 1974. To avoid confrontation, the Witwatersrand march took place along the deserted streets of a Sunday morning Johannesburg.
4 See Basner's motion on Removal of Natives, *Senate Debates,* May 8, 1944. See also Xuma's complaint in his ANC President's Address, December 1944, reported in Peter Walshe, *Rise of African Nationalism in South Africa,* Ad Donker, Cape Town, 1988, p 388.

5 A short biography of Mpanza as The Father of Soweto, is included in *Learn and Teach*, No 1, 1982. Mpanza was later to become a dominant figure in Soweto municipal politics in the 1960s. The best analysis of the squatters is A W Stadler, Birds in the Cornfield: Squatters in Johannesburg, 1944-47, *Journal of Southern African Studies*, Vol 6, No 1, October 1979.
6 *'Sikalel' izwe la kiti'* ('We are crying for our land') was frequently sung to open early SANNC meetings before *'Nkosi Sikelel'i-Afrika'* was adopted as its anthem in 1925 (Walshe, *op cit*, p 35). One of its lines, 'Zulu, Sotho, Xhosa, hlanganani', called for unity between all tribal or linguistic groups.
7 Antipathy between Mpanza and Mofutsanyana may have originated in the Advisory Board contests in which they were rival candidates. The Party in 1944, according to Hilda Watts in *Freedom*, 1946, 'actively discouraged squatters'. As she put it: 'It was generally agreed that the Party could not have been so irresponsible as to send thousands of people to set up hessian shanties at the beginning of winter, with all the resultant dangers, particularly for children.' For more on Communists and squatters see Kevin French, *James Mpanza and the Sofazonke Party in the Development of Local Politics in Soweto*, Dissertation, Development Studies, University of Witwatersrand, 1983, p 77 and pp 118-128.
8 On other squatter movements, some led by Communists: Philip Bonner, We are digging, we are seizing great chunks of the muncipality's land: Popular struggles in Benoni, African Studies Institute paper, University of the Witwatersrand, October 1985. *Learn and Teach*, No 3, 1982, pp 19-22, has a profile of Schreiner Baduza, the Communist Party member who led a squatter movement in Alexandra.
9 Mpanza successfully contested his deportation though, and returned to be declared King of Orlando amid feasting and rejoicing. Basner's role in his appeal against deportation is unclear from the press reportage but Basner had successfully defended Mpanza in an earlier court hearing when he was charged with incitement. This was after a riot in 1944 when Mpanza's followers attempted to prevent the Council from establishing a soup distribution centre in the camp. In his later career as a municipal politician, Mpanza's concerns included the establishment of a civic guard, efforts to obtain African freehold home ownership, the preservation of pass exemption privileges, and horse-racing.

CHAPTER 22

1 Van der Byl cheerfully admitted to the name of 'clothes horse' himself in his autobiography, *Top Hat to Velskoen*, Howard Timmins, Cape Town, 1973, pp 214-215. He is not to be confused with his son, also named Pieter van der Byl, the Rhodesian UDI administration's Foreign Minister, disliked with almost equal intensity by his black Zimbabwean compatriots and his fellow Afrikaners in the South African government (David Martin and Phyllis Johnson, *The Struggle for Zimbabwe*, Faber, London, 1981, p 108).

2 The Springbok Legion was established in September 1941 as a non-racial servicemen's organisation in opposition to the reactionary British Empire Service League. Its membership peaked at 40 000 according to the Simons (*Class and Colour in South Africa*, Penguin, Harmondsworth, 1969, p 540). The League's six-point programme undertook to secure a fair deal for soldiers, ex-servicemen and their dependants, to preserve racial unity and to defend democracy. Its journal, *Fighting Talk*, was published in English and Afrikaans. For a brief description of Basner's socialist student coterie see Boris Wilson, *A Time of Innocence*, Murray Coombes, Johannesburg 1991 p 87.

3 The Socialist Party was formed in 1943 and disbanded in 1947. It was started at the same time as the African Democratic Party with fifty foundation members, all white, and mainly drawn from the Independent Labour Party which was formed by Solly Sachs and other GWU organisers earlier in 1943 with the purpose of contesting industrial seats in the general election. ILP members also included poeple active in the Progressive Labour Group, referred to in the text as the 'Group'. The Chairman and Vice Chairman of the Socialist Party were the GWU leaders Johanna Cornelius and Anna Scheepers. The party began publishing a monthly journal, *Socialist Review*, in June 1945. Shortly before disbanding the Socialists merged with the ADP. For more detail: Lesley Wits, The Rise and Fall of the ILP in Belinda Bozzoli, *Class, Community and Conflict*, Ravan, Johannesburg, 1987, p 285.

4 The leaflet, *Wreckers at Work*, attacked the WIL's leadership of the African Milling Workers' strike in which, according to Basner, after a few arrests 'the members of the ultra-revolutionary group took such fright that they advised the Union to surrender and were prevented, with difficulty, from begging the officials of the Labour Department for a settlement on any terms'. It also praised the loyalty of African workers in the last five years in 'not striking and in not upsetting the economy of the country'. Basner's pamphlet was published at a time when the WIL's Progressive Trade Union Group was trying to wrest

CNETU leadership from Communist trade unionists. On the PTUG's efforts to pack a CNETU conference see: *Inkululeko*, 11 August 1945; Eddie Roux, *Time Longer than Rope*, Victor Gollancz, London, 1948, p 334. *Inkululeko's* columnist, 'Umlweli' (Michael Harmel) praised the pamphlet as a 'brilliant and biting exposé of the Trotskyites'. Basner delivered the opening speech at the 1945 CNETU conference. In his address he was critical of the WIL's antipathy to white workers and advocated black and white worker unity (*Inkululeko*, 14 April, 1945). For an account which is sympathetic to the WIL see David Harries, 'Daniel Koza', *Africa Perspective*, No 19, 1981. Communist Party approval of Basner did not last very long after this occasion; see *Inkululeko*, 14 July 1945, for a sharply critical evaluation of the first issue of *Socialist Review*.
5 For reports on torture and killing of farmworkers by employers see Patrick Duncan, *South Africa's Rule of Violence*, Methuen, London, 1964, pp 92-105.
6 Bethal farm conditions were widely publicised in a series of articles in the *Guardian* and the *Rand Daily Mail* in June 1947 after the investigations by Michael Scott, Ruth First, and Gert Sibande. See *Inkululeko*, 2 July 1947 on the impact of Michael Scott's disclosures. Later revelations of continuing mistreatment of Bethal prison labour: Mr Drum (Henry Nxumalo), 'Bethal Today', *Drum*, March 1952, Anthony Sampson, *Drum*, Collins, London, 1956, pp 37-54; Peter Abrahams, *Return to Goli*, Faber, London, 1953, pp 121-139. The first reports of abuses in Bethal were in *Inkululeko* in 1943. Basner's personal papers help document his sustained efforts to draw attention to the plight of Bethal farm workers in the course of 1944.

CHAPTER 23

1 Dr Xuma had already met Smuts at a reception. At least two versions of their encounter exist: Peter Walshe, *Rise of African Nationalism in South Africa*, Ad Donker, Cape Town, 1987, p 330 and Mary Benson. *Struggle for a Birthright*, Penguin Harmondsworth, p 112.
2 Xuma's papers do indicate that ANC leaders began to consider petitioning the UN in September 1945 over the proposed incorporation of South West Africa and the threat of South African subjection of the High Commission Territories. See Walshe, *op cit*, pp 329 and 371.
3 Robeson's first connection with South African politics dated from the mid-1930s when he was invited by the ICU to visit the country. The invitation was resisted by Mrs Robeson who was trying to curb

her husband's political commitments. Unfortunately Paul Robeson's contacts with Basner are not mentioned by his most recent biographer, though Duberman (*op cit*) does mention the singer's friendship with Dadoo which led him to share a platform with the TIC leader in London in 1948 (p 350).

4 Krishna Menon was the leader of the London-based Indian League during the 1940s. He had an intellectual affinity with Nehru though he was considerably more left-wing. From 1947 to 1952 he represented India in London as High Commissioner. He led the Indian delegation at the United Nations between 1953 and 1956. In 1956 he became a Minister without Portfolio in the Indian cabinet. During the 1950s his career was overshadowed by allegations of financial irregularities during his tenure at the Indian High Commission as well as accusations of Communist affiliations. In fact notwithstanding antipathy between him and Clement Attlee his closest external political connections were with the British Labour Party.

5 Basner's activities in the United States were extensively reported in the *New York Times*. Its edition of 22 October 1946 profiled AB Xuma, emphasising his university training at Minnesota and Northwestern and the CAA's call for the Assembly to resist the incorporation of South West Africa into the Union. On 9 November 1946 the *Times* reported 'Three African Leaders Assail General Smuts', citing speeches by Xuma, Basner and HA Naidoo, leader of the Natal Indian Congress at a reception organised by Max Yergan and the CAA and attended by representatives of Negro organisations including the NAACP and the National Urban League as well as representatives of the Indian Government. Basner described himself as a 'political middleman to represent Africans in their dealings with the White leaders as required by the sort of government we have'. He went on to criticise General Smuts 'for being prepared to argue that South Africa is a democratic country'. On 15 November a report summarised the speech of Sir Maharaj Singh, the Indian representative at the Assembly which cited the injury of 1 245 Africans during the mineworkers' strike. Sir Maharaj referred to Basner as his source. Basner was quoted after the Assembly session as saying that 'Africans of the subcontinent (were) totally opposed to the incorporation of any of the territory into the Union until Field Marshal Smuts and his government abandon the principle of white supremacy'. Another item, on November 18, described a CAA meeting at the Abyssinia Baptist Church in Harlem in which Basner appeared on the speakers' platform with Mrs Vijaya Pandit, Krishna Menon, A B Xuma, H A Naidoo and Max Yergan. *New York Times* coverage extended to Basner's reception back home; an article on 28 November noted a United Party resolution which deplored 'the

attitudes of political parties and political leaders who are damaging South Africa's good name among the democracies of the world'. The newspaper suggested that the resolution was aimed both at Basner and at Margaret Ballinger, then currently touring India. Pieter Van der Byl argued that 'even if they were true' Mr Basner's strictures should not have been voiced.

WHO'S WHO

RICHARD GRANVILLE BALOYI, Alexandra businessman, estate agent and bus company owner, was ANC Treasurer General from 1937 to 1939 and a member of the NRC from 1937 to 1942. He broke with the mainstream ANC leadership after supporting a National Party senatorial candidate in 1948. He died in 1962.

DAVID BOPAPE who was born in 1915 in Thabamopo near Sekhukhuneland, was drawn into politics through his participation in the Transvaal African Teachers' Association's salary campaign of 1940-1941. He joined the ANC then and in 1943 helped to establish the ANC Youth League. Elected as Chairman of the ANC branch in Brakpan, he refused an ultimatum to give up political activities to retain his teaching post. His subsequent dismissal in August 1944 resulted in a well-supported local school boycott and a one-day general strike. In 1944 he also served as secretary of the Anti-Pass campaign. In 1945 he was elected as the ANC's Provincial Secretary, in which capacity he proposed a motion at the annual conference that 'Africa was for the Africans'. The motion was deemed to be 'not in accordance with Congress spirit'. His ideological position shifted quite quickly thereafter. In 1946 he may have joined the Communist Party (he was 'listed' as a CPSA member in 1952). Banned from political activity just before the ANC's Defiance Campaign, he opened an estate agency in partnership with J B Marks. He is described by Mary Benson (*Struggle for a Birthright*, Penguin Harmondsworth, 1966, p 88) as a 'good psychologist with crowd appeal' and 'an exceptionally hard worker, he even organised the street hawkers'.

SIDNEY PERCIVAL BUNTING (1873-1936) won the Chancellor's prize for Classical Languages on graduating from Oxford in 1897. He arrived in South Africa in 1900 and after military service gained an LLB at South Africa College and subsequently practised as a lawyer in Johannesburg. He joined the Labour Party in 1910, defended workers after the 1913 miners' strike, was elected that year to the Transvaal Provincial Council, and helped to form the War on War League in 1914. He resigned from the Labour Party one year later, founding with other Labour dissidents the International Socialist League, within which he became the principal advocate of 'native rights'. He visited Moscow in 1922, attending the Fourth Congress of the CPSU as a CPSA delegate. In 1926 he was elected secretary of the CPSA. In 1928 he opposed the Communist International's prescription of a Native Republic programme for the CPSA. Expelled from the Party in 1931, he worked as an apartment building caretaker and died of a stroke five years later.

An obituary in the CPSA newspaper, *Umsebenzi* (6 June 1936) noted his 'persistent disagreements (with the Party) on fundamental principles' but conceded that 'his honesty and devotion were unquestioned' and acknowledged his historical significance for recognising 'the growing importance of the native masses'. See also Edward Roux, *S P Bunting: A Political Biography*, African Bookman, Cape Town, 1944.

HESTER CORNELIUS was born in 1908, the daughter of a Lichtenburg building worker and former Boer commando. Brought up an ardent Afrikaner nationalist she arrived in Johannesburg in 1930 to work in a clothing factory. Recruited into E S Sachs's Garment Workers' Union in 1932 she joined the Union's executive in 1934, the first of a series of positions she would hold in progressive unions through the next three decades (E S Sachs, *Rebel's Daughters*, MacGibbon and Kee, 1957, pp 40-43).

JOHANNA CORNELIUS, Hester's sister, was only eighteen when she was imprisoned after a strike in 1935. She was a member of the Labour Party in the 1950s and secretary of the Johannesburg branch of the Textile Workers' Industrial Union in 1972 (Bettie du Toit, *Ukubamba Amadolo: Workers' Struggle in the South African Textile Industry*, Onyx Press, London, 1978; Basil Davidson, *Report on South Africa*, Jonathan Cape, London, 1952, pp 176-188).

YUSUF DADOO was born in Krugersdorp in 1909. He received his university education in India and Edinburgh where he qualified as a doctor in 1936. While in Britain he joined the International Labour Party. In 1939 he established the 'nationalist bloc' of the Transvaal Indian Congress and called for a campaign of passive resistance against the 'Pegging Bill' which would have halted Indian land purchases. In June 1939 a meeting held by Dadoo was broken up by hirelings of SM Nana, a Congress conservative, and one person died. This action swung Transvaal Indian support in favour of Dadoo's radical faction, though the campaign was blocked by the Gandhi family. By 1943 the radicals were in full control of the TIC. Dadoo, as Treasurer of the Non-European Unity Front, opposed the 'Imperialist War' and was arrested and convicted under emergency regulations in September 1940. He was by then a member of the Communist Party. Dadoo later became President of the South African Indian Congress and was Chairman of the SACP at the time of his death in exile in 1983.

JOHN DUBE (1871-1946), son of an American Board Mission pastor, educated in the United States at Oberlin College between 1887 and 1992, founded the Ohlange Institute in Natal in 1901, modelling his school on Booker T Washington's Tuskegee Institute in Alabama. That year he also helped to organise the Natal Native Congress, and two years later he established a newspaper, *Ilanga lase Natal*, making it an influential medium for his gospel of racial self help and commercial empowerment.

He was elected the SANNC's first President in 1912 but fell out with his colleagues in 1917, ostensibly because of a letter he wrote appearing to support territorial segregation but really because of his more general conservatism. See Shula Marks, *The Ambiguities of Dependence in South Africa*, Ravan Press, Johannesburg, 1986, pp 42-73.

DR W E BURGHARDT DU BOIS (1868 - 1965) was a leading figure in African American political and intellectual life from the turn of the century. As a radical advocate of civil rights integrationism his thinking ran counter to the economic self-sufficiency doctrines of Booker T Washington and the racial nationalism of Marcus Garvey. A socialist from 1911, he joined the US Communist Party after the Second World War. Internal conflicts led to his departure from the NAACP in 1934. By the 1940s, he had become an advocate of an African American economy based on producer and consumer co-operatives, a socialist counterpart to Garvey's programme. He died in Ghana, a committed pan-Africanist.

HARRY HAYNES was born in Ireland in 1877. After fighting in the South African War he became a gold miner and was elected to the executive of the Kleinfontein branch of the Mineworkers Union, leading its strike committee in 1913. He joined the ISL in 1915 and left the mines to recover from phthisis in Durban. In Durban he led the municipal 'soviet' during the 1920 strike. He resigned from the CPSA in 1923 because he felt its 'native policy' was 'being forced down the throats of white workers' (Brian Bunting, *Moses Kotane: South African Revolutionary*, Inkululeko Publications, London, 1975 p 27). He joined the Labour Party and by 1924 was editor of its newspaper *Forward*.

JOHN TENGO JABAVU (1859-1921), teacher and editor, founded *Imvo Zabantusundu* in 1884 and became a major force in African politics in the Cape, using his newspaper to marshal African voting support in favour of liberal Parliamentary candidates. To this end he founded and led the Cape Native Voters' Convention and followed liberal Parliamentarians John Merriman and Jacob Sauer in opposing the Jameson Raid and backing the Afrikaner Bond. He disliked what he understood to be a confrontationist path followed by the SANNC which by his death had completely eclipsed his claims to African leadership. His son, Davidson Jabavu, followed his course in opposing the ANC and continuing to orchestrate African voter support for sympathetically disposed white politicians.

DANIEL KOZA trained as a teacher near Pietersburg in the mid-1930s but left the Diocesan Training College in 1936 without qualifying. Subsequently he joined Max Gordon in organising the African Commercial and Distributive Workers Union just before the Second World War. His trade unionist activities continued into the war itself; he led an important strike in the Johannesburg coal yards in 1941.

Joining the ANC in the late 1930s, he became its Secretary for Labour in 1942. He participated in the Alexandra Emergency Transport Committee and helped found the ADP but later in 1943 also joined Hosea Jaffe's Trotskyist Fourth International of South Africa. By this stage he was sharply at odds with Basner.

Between 1944 and 1946 he worked with the Progressive Trade Union Group, a Trotskyist faction of the Transvaal Council of Non-European Trade Unions. Later he was involved with the All African Convention. He took a BA at the University of the Witwatersrand in 1948-1950 and enrolled as a law student at the University of London in 1951. He returned to South Africa in 1952 and died in 1960 aged forty-eight (David Harries, Baruch Hirson, Daniel Koza: Working Class Leader, *Africa Perspective* 19, 1981).

THOMAS MTOBI MAPIKELA (1869-1945), a carpenter and building contractor from Bloemfontein, was a member of the 1909 delegation to Britain to protest against the Act of Union. He was President of the Orange Free State Native Congresss, a founder member of the ANC and ANC Speaker for twenty-five years. He was a member of the 1914 ANC deputation to Britain to oppose the 1913 Land Act, Chairman of the Bloemfontein Advisory Board during the 1920s and Treasurer of the South African Location Advisory Boards Congress, a member of the ANC National Executive in the 1930s and a member of the Native Representative Council from 1937 to 1945.

JOHN 'BEAVER' MARKS (1903-1972) was, according to his obituary in *African Communist* (No 51, 1972) born in Ventersdorp, the son of an African railway worker who married a white woman. Educated at Kilnerton Teacher Training College, where he led a strike in 1919, Marks first worked as a teacher in his home town of Ventersdorp. He was recruited into the Party by S P Bunting in 1928. He lost his teaching post three years later as a consequence of his political activities. In 1932 he stood as a demonstration candidate in the white Germiston Parliamentary by-election. He underwent training at the Lenin School in Moscow in 1933. Excluded from the Party between 1937 and 1939 he joined Mofutsanyana in efforts to reconstruct the ANC. From 1942 he chaired the African Mineworkers' Union. In 1950 he was elected Transvaal President of the ANC. Later he served as Party Chairman, in this capacity presiding over the SACP's Fifth Congress in 1962. He left South Africa shortly thereafter to help administer the ANC's offices in Dar es Salaam. He died in the Soviet Union in 1972 after a short illness.

CHARLOTTE MAXEKE (1874-1939) was educated in Uitenhage and Port Elizabeth. She was the first President of the Bantu Women's League and in this capacity in 1913, the year of the League's formation, successfully lobbied the authorities on behalf of Free State protesters against passes for women. The League was incorporated into the SANNC in 1919. As a member of a choir, she toured Britain and the United States in the mid 1890s and enrolled for a BSc degree at Wilberforce University, Ohio, which she completed in 1900. She joined the AME Church at the same time. She married the Rev M Maxeke, another Wilberforce student. As the first black South African professional social worker, she was a conspicuous member of the Joint Council movement which, by the late 1920s, marked her as one of the more decorous and conservative African public figures. In 1936 she was elected President of the newly founded National Council of African Women.

EDWIN MOFUTSANYANA was born in Witzieshoek in 1899, the son of a well-to-do sharecropper. He attended school up to Standard Four then, in 1916, began working in a goldmine compound near Johannesburg. Between 1919 and 1922 he trained as a teacher at the Bensonvale Institute before resuming work as a mine clerk. He joined the ANC in 1923 and was recruited into the Party five years later. Between 1928 and 1931 he worked for the CPSA, building up a huge branch (1 600 members) in Potchefstroom where he married Josie Mpama, subsequently another important Party activist. In 1931 he travelled to the Soviet Union to study Marxism at the University of the East. General Secretary of the Party in 1935, he later edited its Johannesburg newspaper, *Inkululeko*. During the 1940s he was heavily involved in Orlando Advisory Board politics, winning his first election in 1940. He opposed the dissolution of the Party in 1960. For more detail on Mofutsanyana in Potchefstroom see Julia Wells, The Day the Town Stood Still in Belinda Bozzoli, *Town and Countryside in the Transvaal*, Ravan Press, Johannesburg, 1983, pp 281-300; The Old Man in the Mountain, *Learn and Teach*, 6, 1985, pp 1-8.

E P MORETSELE was born into a chiefly lineage in Sekhukhuneland in 1897, joined the ANC in 1917 and was a vigorous participant in Congress activities in the 1920s and 1930s. He preceded David Bopape as ANC Provincial Secretary. He owned a cafe in Pritchard Street until his dispossession under the Group Areas Act. He served as President of the Transvaal ANC from 1953 through the rest of the decade. He died in 1961, just before the end of the Treason Trial in which he had been a defendant. See Peter Delius, Sebatakgomo; Migrant Organisation, the ANC and the Sekhukhuneland Revolt, *Journal of Southern African Studies*, 15, 3, October 1989.

JAMES S MOROKA (1891-1986) was born in Thaba Nchu and educated at Lovedale and the University of Edinburgh where he studied medicine. He established a medical practice in Thaba Nchu. He entered politics with his opposition to the Hertzog Bills as a member of the All African Convention in 1936 and became its Treasurer. He was a member of the NRC from 1942 to 1950. Moroka was elected President General of the ANC in 1949 and served until 1952 when he lost the Presidency after engaging a separate defence from other ANC leaders when he was put on trial on charges under the Suppression of Communism Act.

L T MVABASA was an important figure in the ANC from its inception, participating in delegations to the government in 1914 and to Britain in 1919. He attended ISL and IWA meetings in 1917 and 1918 and was a member of a secret ISL/Transvaal Native Congress committee which planned strategy before and during the 1918 Johannesburg municipal workers' strike. Later he became identified with the more conservative wing of Congress leadership, joining Seme's cabinet in 1930 but remaining on the ANC executive after the latter's departure. See Philip Bonner, The Transvaal Native Congress 1917-1920 in Shula Marks and Richard Rathbone (eds), *Industrialisation and Social Change in South Africa*, Longman, London, 1983, pp 291-295.

HOWARD PIM, a Quaker and a friend of Lord Milner was an accountant (Howard Pim and Hardy) and a liberal segregationist who believed that Africans should remain rooted in a 'natural' rural culture which could be reconstructed in the reserves. In the 1920s he was secretary of the Bantu Men's Social Centre. He organised William Ballinger's salary when the Scottish trade unionist arrived in South Africa to help Kadalie administer the ICU. Shortly before his death in 1934 he wrote his Report on the Transkei (Lovedale, 1934). At that time he was President of the South African Institute of Race Relations.

EDWARD ROUX began his career as a botanist at Wits in 1926 when he was appointed a junior lecturer. He subsequently did research in plant physiology at Cambridge, obtaining a doctorate in 1929. He worked for the Party for six years but was removed from the editorial offices of the Party newspaper and took a job as a municipal bath attendant in Cape Town until he resumed his scientific career in 1936, the year in which he was expelled from the Party as a right deviationist. After his expulsion, he remained on good terms with African Communists including Moses Kotane who arrived in District Six to share a house with him and his wife Winifred just before the Second World War. He rejoined the University of the Witwatersrand in 1946 and was appointed to the Chair of the Botany Department in 1963, one year before the government forced him to resign because he was a former Communist. In the interim, he had joined the Liberal Party. He died of aplastic anaemia in February 1966. See Eddie and Win Roux, *Rebel Pity*, London, Rex Collings, 1970. As a botanist he published more than thirty scientific papers, a standard textbook on plant physiology and a series of popular books on ecology and conservation. *Time Longer than Rope: A History of the Black Man's Struggle for Freedom in South Africa*, Victor Gollancz, London, 1948 was written largely between 1935 and 1939 with updating chapters added in 1946 and just before the second edition (Wisconsin University Press, Madison, 1964). On Roux's attitude to Marxism, a contemporary, Bernard Sachs, noted that Roux was 'particularly hostile to the Marxian concept of progress through opposition which formed an essential part of dialectical materialism'. (*Multitude of Dreams*, Johannesburg, Kayor Publishing House, 1949, p141).

E S 'SOLLY' SACHS gave up his studies at the University of the Witwatersrand to become general secretary of the Witwatersrand Tailors' (later Garment Workers') Union in 1928. After his expulsion from the CPSA in September 1931, he continued to serve as secretary of the Garment Workers' Union. He attempted in 1943 to try to transform his labour following into a political base, founding the short-lived Independent Labour Party to contest working class Johannesburg constituencies in the 1943 general election (Martin Nicol, Rise and Fall of the ILP in Belinda Bozzoli (ed), *Class, Community and Conflict*, Ravan Press, Johannesburg, 1987). Later the GWU affiliated to the Labour Party which Sachs represented as a municipal candidate in 1951. In 1952 the government banned him from attending all gatherings, effectively barring him from any employment. After the defeat of his effort to challenge the ban in the Supreme Court, Sachs left South Africa in 1953 to take up a fellowship at the University of Manchester.

PIXLEY KA I SEME (1881-1951) was, like Dube, a protege of American missionaries who sent him to a Massachusetts prep school from which he graduated in 1902 to attend Columbia University in New York between 1902 and 1906. His education was rounded off with legal training at Oxford, after which he returned to his homeland in 1910 to play a key role in establishing the ANC and drafting its constitution. His Presidency was notorious for his domineering manner. 'I must command all under me,' he once said, sacking four executive colleagues who disagreed with him. His political reputation, tarnished by such admonitions as his exaltation of the Minister of Native Affairs - 'We all love him and respect his person and his position', was partly restored in the 1940s. During the war he provided material help and moral encouragement to the ANC Youth League, whose founder Anton Lembede served in his office as an articled clerk in 1942. His funeral in 1951 was attended by thousands of ANC mourners. See Craig Charney, Pixley Seme: Father of the ANC, *Columbia College Today*, Spring, 1987, pp14-17.

T D MWELI SKOTA was born in 1890 in Kimberley. Between 1913 and 1919 he worked as an interpreter before moving to the Rand in 1920 to become a clerk at Crown Mines. From 1923 he resided in Pimville in what is today Soweto, by which time he worked full time for *Abantu-*

Batho, the ANC's newspaper. He was to serve as Chairman of Pimville's Advisory Board from at least 1943 into the 1960s and, until his death in June 1976, held office in the Urban Bantu Council, the body which succeeded the Advisory Board. He was a founder member of the ANC, edited *Abantu* from 1918, established another newspaper, *The African Shield*, in 1922, was elected ANC Secretary General in 1925 (in which office he was responsible for the organisation's adoption of a new name, anthem and flag that year), joined Seme's 'Cabinet' in 1930 and in 1935 and 1936 was put onto the executive of the All African Convention. His most notable achievement was the compilation of the *African Yearly Register: An Illustrated Biographical Dictionary of Black Folks in South Africa*, Johannesburg 1938 (Second edition, 1966). See J T Campbell, *T D Mweli Skota and the Making and Unmaking of a Black Elite*, History Workshop, 9-14.

LILIAN TSHABALALA participated in the African Democratic Party but resigned in 1945.

MAX YERGAN visited South Africa in 1921 on behalf of the Negro YMCA. He remained in the country for fifteen years, concerning himself with improving black educational facilities, before returning to New York in 1935. In South Africa he founded the Bantu Christian Association and acted as its secretary, organising student conferences every year. In 1938 he published in New York a pioneering study of South Africa's political economy, *Gold and Poverty in South Africa*. In 1937 he founded the Council of African Affairs, assuming the position of Executive Director. The Council functioned as a lobbying organisation and information centre, its two dozen members meeting twice a year. It was anti-colonial and generally pro-Soviet. At the time of its formation Yergan was close to the Communist Party, if not actually a member. He served as Robeson's 'political liaison' in 1942. The Council's most auspicious moment was the convening of a 'Conference on Africa' in New York attended by 112 people including Kwame Nkrumah whose political career began at that meeting. In 1947 the CAA was listed by the US Attorney General as a Communist front. Intimidated, Yergan denounced Communism in early 1948, splitting the CAA Board. Yergan then moved sharply to the right and in the 1960s became an outspoken supporter of apartheid, Katangan secession and Rhodesia's UDI. The Council disbanded in 1955 by which time it was a shadow of its former self. Yergan died in 1974 shortly after apologising for his political turnabout twenty-five years before. See Immannuel Geiss, *The Pan-African Movement*, Methuen, London, 1974; Martin Duberman, *Paul Robeson*, Alfred Knopf, New York, 1989.

To the African Electorate
of the Transvaal and O.F.S.
by
H. M. BASNER.

At the last election in 1937, I contested the seat of senator for the Transvaal and O.F.S. with Mr. J. D. Rheinallt Jones. I then addressed you on many public platforms, in urban locations and rural areas.

I said :—

"The abolition of the native franchise in the Cape will lead to the greater exploitation of the African, because it removes from Parliament a number of members who had to consider the native vote. The seats in the Senate are not effective to counterbalance this loss. Only a very strong national organisation can do that."

"The election is very important to you because of the opportunity it affords you for political organisation and education. The office of senator is important not so much as a voting instrument but as a medium to express the grievances and aspirations of the African Race. As the Native Representation Act has denied you the right to be represented by Africans in the Union Parliament your elected senator must be the voice of your political leaders, in that body. He can only be such a voice if he represents an African organised political movement, which includes Chiefs and people. **Your senator will only be respected and carry weight with the Government if and when he speaks in the name of a strongly organised African National Congress.**"

You did not listen to me or to the African National Unity Committee which supported me.

YOU DID NOT ORGANISE—YOU MERELY VOTED.

You elected Mr. Rheinallt Jones. You voted for him because he was known to you as Advisor on Race Relations to the "Institute of Race Relations," as a social worker, as a trustee of the "Bantu Welfare Trust ; you voted for him because the "BANTU WORLD", the "UMTETELI WA BANTU", the social workers, the joint councils, the negrophilists, the missionaries, the school superintendents, and the location superintendants told you to do so. You voted for him because a large sum (£50,000/0/0 of the Bantu Welfare Trust) was dangled before your eyes for education and improvement. You voted for him because his supporters travelled around the country with large maps and large promises. The maps were for the Chiefs to shew them how much land they would receive from the Native Trust. The promises were for the teachers—larger salaries for them and larger grants for Native Education.

In the other provinces, men of similar claims to "social service" were elected to the Senate.

The consequences were disastrous to your national and political organisation and to yourselves.

WHAT HAPPENED TO AFRICANS IN THE FIVE YEARS, 1937-1942 ?

The All-African Convention which started in a blaze of glory went out in smoke.

The African National Congress stagnated and very nearly died. It is today a head without a body.

The chiefs are unorganised and do not meet together in council.

No organisation of any importance or influence can speak as the voice of the African race.

No African organization has the authority or prestige to place before you candidates for the Senate, or the Native Representative Council.

NATIVE EDUCATION HAS NOT IMPROVED.—The teachers' salaries have not been raised.

Native education cannot and will not improve until the social and economic conditions of the Africans improve. It will not improve to any appreciable degree until the Government takes over native education and it is administered by the Education Department. It will not improve until compulsory primary education becomes the law of the land for all children of all races. Above all, it will not improve until the Government feeds the children and raises the pay of native teachers. **Hungry children cannot learn and hungry teachers cannot teach.** The abolition of school fees means nothing if there are no schools. The raise of 5/- per month for the teachers is an insult to a profession starving on £5 0s. 0d. per month. It is inexcusable on the part of the Government which tells other employers through a commission, presided over by Mr. Smit, Secretary of Native Affairs, that no native family on the Reef can live on less than £7 10s. 0d. per month.

Instead of boasting how much he has done for native education your Senator should have roused public opinion on this point.

THE AFRICAN PEOPLE GOT NO LAND. The Chiefs have no control whatsoever over Trust Land.

Up to August, 1941, the Native Trust bought 1,491,739 morgen of "released" land. This, for six and a half million people, dependant for their living on land. Who got this land? How is it administered? NO CHIEF, NO TRIBE, NO INDIVIDUAL AFRICAN GOT THIS LAND.

A Trust Farm is administered on exactly the same principles as is Municipal Location. It is administered by agricultural officers, servants of the Native Affairs Dept. The African is a tenant, perpetually paying rent. If he fails to pay his poll tax for two years, he can be ejected. There is no security of tenure. What will happen to his wife and family when the taxpayer dies? In a municipal location the wife and children of a deceased resident are ejected, no matter how long they have resided there, no matter if they have no tribal home. In town or country, the African owns no land (with negligible exceptions). Homeless and landless, the African supplies cheap labour for the mines and industries in which he has no part.

The maximum of land allowed to a tenant on a Trust Farm is 5 morgen.

No African can extract food, clothing, medicine and taxes from 5 morgen of land. There is no present and no future for the tenants of a Trust Farm.

This is what Mr. Rheinallt Jones did not foresee, and his supporters did not warn the Africans about, when they travelled the land with maps on the eve of the last election.

Trust farms must be administered by the Chiefs on a tribal basis if the Native Trust is to be accepted as some solution of the land hunger of the African race.

THE CONDITIONS OF THE AFRICANS IN THE TOWNS DID NOT IMPROVE.

The pass laws have not been abolished.
The beer raids have not ceased.
The location regulations are as harsh as ever.

Whatever increase of pay has taken place has nowhere nearly kept pace with the rising cost of living. The POVERTY, MISERY, ACTUAL STARVATION HAS NOT DIMINISHED SINCE 1937. It has increased and will continue to increase until the pass laws are abolished and native trade unions organised and recognised. African trade unions are not represented on the Industrial Councils. **Collective bargaining is closed to Africans, because they carry a pass, and no pass-bearing native is an employee under the Industrial Conciliation Act.**

On the eve of the elections, the Minister of Native Affairs has decided to try an experiment, to "relax" the pass laws in certain areas. The police will not be asked not to ask Africans for a pass unless they are suspected of another crime. The experiment is left to the discretion of the police. The Native Commissioner of Johannesburg immediately made it clear that Africans will still require a pass when they seek employment.

The Manager of the Johannesburg Municipal Affairs immediately made it clear that Africans will still require a pass when they seek a house in a municipal location.

The Minister of Native Affairs is undoubtedly anxious to ease the burden of the Native People. **But what will this experiment prove? It will prove nothing!**

THE PASS IS NOT JUST A PIECE OF PAPER. IT IS AN INSTRUMENT OF ECONOMIC EXPLOITATION.

By the pass laws the African is bound to his employer—he is bound to current wages.

An African must report to the Pass Office as soon as he enters an urban area. He must report as soon as he finds employment. He must report as soon as he leaves his employment. An African cannot seek employment without a "special" pass to look for work. He must have it renewed periodically if he does not find work. The "special" can be renewed or refused by the Pass Officer. The African can be ordered out of an area or "compulsorily endorsed" to another area. The Pass Officer can irrigate an area with native labour, as a barren field is irrigated with water. The African without trade unions is like water.

No African can trade or be an independant craftsman without an exemption or a daily labourer's pass. This can be granted or refused by the Pass Officer.

No Africans can live in an urban area. No African can obtain a house in a location without producing his pass.

In other words, no African can live, except as a lawbreaker, without a pass.

With a pass: He cannot choose his employment; he cannot wait for the wages which he thinks he is entitled to receive; he cannot refuse work except for a period which is limited by the Pass Officer. HE IS NOT A FREE AGENT IN THE LABOUR MARKET-What does it mean then, when the pass laws are "relaxed". It means that the indignity of being stopped by the police is relaxed. It means that the economic exploitation continues. A social burden is eased but the economic oppression continues. The president of the African National Congress, who gave the Minister the figures of arrest which horrified him, asked for the total abolition of the pass laws.

What did your Senator, Mr. Rheinallt Jones, ask for?
" The relaxation of the pass laws will lead to a considerable reduction in crime, in the opinion of Senator J. D. Rheinallt Jones. In an interview with the 'Daily Mail' yesterday, he stated that the police would now be able to bring the real criminals to book. 'I urged this very step in the senate' said Senator Rheinallt Jones."

Rand Daily Mail, May 14th, 1942.

So this is what your Senator urged in the senate. Not the total abolition of the pass laws, but a relaxation of the pass laws. Not an end to economic exploitation but an end to a social grievance.

This is what happens when a social worker becomes a politician. He stresses the "social" aspect, the superficial aspect, and forgets about the main problem.

ONLY THE TOTAL ABOLITION OF THE PASS LAWS CAN HELP THE AFRICAN WORKER.

THE CONDITIONS OF AFRICANS ON THE FARMS HAS NOT IMPROVED.

There is no need for me to say anything under this heading. Nothing has been done for the African farm labourer. His condition has not grown worse because it could not (except under Hitler or our local fascists) grow any worse.

THE SITUATION FOR AFRICAN TRADERS HAS GROWN WORSE.

In the O.F.S. Africans were not allowed to trade in 1937. They are still not allowed to trade.

In the Transvaal, where hundreds of Africans made a living as butchers, tailors, shoe-makers, carpenters, grocers, etc., the position has deteriorated rapidly in the last few years. Most of these traders and craftsmen have been driven back to the condition of labourers. They have not been prevented from trading. Nothing as brutal as all that. The European landlords have been notified that they would be prosecuted under the Native Law Amendment Act, for letting their premises to natives. The municipalities have refused licences under the Town Planning Ordinance. African traders must go to a location. But a location has only a few trading sites. The Africans number millions. **This is the history of the last five years.** Why is it so?

I would be wrong if I blamed your parliamentary representatives or The Prime Minister or the Minister of Native Affairs for this. I believe the present Government is not unconscious of the misery of the Native people, not unsympathetic to your just demands (both ministers have openly expressed their sympathy), and not without some plans for your future relief.

But can any politician, even with the authority and respect which Field Marshal Smuts commands, go further than the voters will allow him to go? No politician in a democratic country can do that.

No parliamentarian representing a constituency of employers and farmers can legislate or even advocate for the substantial social, political and economic relief of the African, without endangering his own seat, his own political career. (You will remember that the Prime Minister in his Cape Town speech made it clear that he was speaking in a personal capacity, not in his capacity of Prime Minister).

In South Africa certain conditions must be fulfilled before the African can hope for relief. These are, briefly:—

Firstly, the Africans must organise trade unions, and a strong African National Congress must come into being. This will win respect for you as a social, industrial and political force.

Secondly, the European section must be educated to think in economic terms and not in racial terms about the "Native Problem"; to see that poor-blacks make poor-whites; to understand that **Industrialisation, Socialisation of the means of production, State-ownership of the land**, these and these only, will bring economic security, social justice, and political peace to this land for all its citizens; white, black and coloured.

You Africans are responsible for not having fulfilled the first condition.

The European racialist politicians are responsible for the low level of political and economic thought in South Africa.

BOTH THESE DEFECTS CAN ONLY BE REMEDIED BY ENERGETIC PROPAGANDA AND POLITICAL COURAGE.

Of all your elected representatives, in my opinion, only Mrs. Ballinger and Mr. Molteno brought the economic facts home to Parliament and to the people of South Africa.

Five years ago I urged you to form trade unions and to organise a powerful African National Congress. I urged the Chiefs to unite into a mighty council. I pledged to help in this work if I was elected. You did not elect me and you did not unite or organise.

This time I know that you will elect me and I repeat this pledge. But I also repeat my warning:

" Elect me only if you decide to organise. I do not want to be elected as a saviour. **A race can only free and save itself.**

A senator is a mouth-piece, not a saviour. Your salvation lies in hard organising and effective propaganda."

I think you know by now that I am one of the few Europeans who know the needs of your race and how to help you.

This election will, like the last one, be a contest between myself and Mr. Rheinallt Jones, or—if the Institute of Race Relations feels the claims of the ex-senator to be too weak for re-election—between myself and some other "Social worker" from the Institute.

Why does the Institute meddle in politics to this extent? It describes itself as follows:

" SOUTH AFRICAN INSTITUTE OF RACE RELATIONS, a NON-POLITICAL ORGANISATION (incorporated under the Companies Act)".

Its purpose is to work for the "Peaceful and orderly adjustment of conflicting racial interests and thereby promote the welfare of all sections of the population".

Its membership consists of "individuals, firms, municipalities, universities, and other public bodies. It is independant of the Government and of all political parties. It includes men and women of varied interests and opinions".

Independant of the Government? Its headquarters, strangely enough, are at the University of Witwatersrand, a semi-government institution.

Independant of all political parties? The firms, municipalities, public bodies, individuals, owe their allegiance to political parties, have political convictions, have party ties. I would be the last to quarrel with the Institute if it stuck to social work, and remained strictly non-political, I would not even quarrel with it if it took on a political complexion of some definite sort.

But when the Adviser of the Institute entered politics, the Institute entered the political field with him.

AND IN POLITICS YOU CANNOT REPRESENT "MEN AND WOMEN OF VARIED INTERESTS AND OPINIONS". YOU CANNOT REPRESENT FIRMS AND MUNICIPALITIES AND THE NATIVE PEOPLE.

Firms and municipalities want low wages, Africans want high wages.

Firms and municipalities need the pass laws, Africans need collective bargaining.

(You will remember that the Manager of the Johannesburg Muncipal Native Affairs appeared at several commissions and enquiries and opposed, on behalf of his municipality, higher wages for Atricans.)

Firms and municipalities want the location regulations. Africans detest the location regulations. They do not

want fences round their suburbs.

WHOM DOES MR. RHEINALLT JONES REPRESENT IN PARLIAMENT. THE FIRMS AND MUNICIPALITIES AND OTHER PUBLIC BODIES WHO DONATE FUNDS TO THE INSTITUTE, OR. THE POVERTY-STRICKEN, LANDLESS, PASS-BEARING AFRICANS WHO ELECTED HIM?

When the Institute, as presently constituted, interferes in politics it does a dis-service to the Native people; it does a great service to the firms and municipalities who exploit the Native people.

THE ECONOMIC ISSUE, IN SOUTH AFRICA, MUST NOT BE CONFUSED. CONFUSION IS A GREAT SERVICE TO THE EXPLOITERS.

EACH ONE OF THE OPPRESSIVE AND DISCRIMINATORY LAWS AGAINST THE NON-EUROPEAN AIMS AT THE ECONOMIC EXPLOITATION OF THE NON-EUROPEAN.

Economic exploitation can only be resisted by trade union and political organisation.

The joint councils have taken the best Africans out of politics into social welfare work, Social welfare relieves misery but does not remove the causes of your misery.

The negrophilists sap the political energy and political independance of your leaders.

The "BANTU WORLD" and "UMTETELI WA BANTU" are the organs of the liberal employers, negrophilists and social workers. They are not the organs of African trade unions and political organisations.

Let the social workers, the liberal employers, the negrophilists, the joint councils, the "Bantu World" and "Umteteli wa Bantu" and the Institute of Race Relations leave politics alone and they will serve the Africans better.

You Africans lost a quarter of a century when you forsook the African National Congress for the joint councils. IT IS MR. RHEINALLT JONES' PROUDEST BOAST THAT HE ORGANISED THE JOINT COUNCILS.

You Africans lost five years when you preferred his policy to mine, at the last election.

You will have to accept my policy eventually. Accept it now.

In this election, judge between the policy of any other candidate and my policy.

Judge between my record and the record of any other candidate. AND JUDGE WITHOUT FEAR OR FAVOUR

If your job does not allow you to vote freely, dont seek to become a member of a voting unit. If you do become a member, dont forget that NO ONE CAN THREATEN YOU OR COERCE YOU IN YOUR VOTING. This is a criminal offence under the Electoral Law, and the Government must and will protect you.

Cast your vote like free men. Cast your votes for any candidate chosen by the tax-payers who elect you to the voting unit. I am sufficiently confident in my policy and record to leave it at that.

Lastly, and above all, I ask you to remember that we are living in a difficult and important moment of the world's history. The forces of reaction (fascism) and the forces of democracy are locked in mortal combat.

THE AFRICAN RACE MUST TAKE A FULL SHARE OF THE RESPONSIBILITIES OF THIS MOMENT.

The Government must allow the African race to do so. **No race which values and wants and is worthy of freedom can say "This is not my war".** The defeat of fascism is even more important to you than to the European section, because Fascism aims at a greater and crueller exploitation of the workers and peasants of other races. Fascism's main characteristic is race oppression. If the Government is in earnest about this war it must arm the African soldiers.

If the Government is in earnest about this war it must give the Africans some democratic rights to fight for.

The Africans must share, and claim a reward for sharing, in the defeat of Hitler, Mussolini, and the Japanese aggressor.

I will stand behind the Government in its war policy, but I will not compromise or wait until after the war to express your demands for:—

LAND.

ABOLITION OF THE PASS LAWS.

RECOGNITION OF THE AFRICAN TRADE UNIONS.

A MINIMUM LIVING WAGE FOR AFRICAN FARM LABOURERS.

ABOLITION OF THE COLOUR-BAR IN INDUSTRY.

ABOLITION OF THE LOCATION SYSTEM.

ABOLITION OF THE POLL TAX.

TRADING RIGHTS.

COMPULSORY EDUCATION.

These are the particulars for the Nomination Form.

Surname	Christian Names	Address	Occupation
BASNER	HYMAN MEYER	8 Somerset House, 110 Fox Street, Johannesburg.	Attorney.

Index

Abantu-Batho (newspaper) 26, 69, 83
Accra 197-198
Advisory boards 114
African Commercial and Distributive Workers Union 160
African Democratic Party 158-9, 160-2, 169, 176
African Methodist Episcopal Church 18, 22
African Mineworkers Union 106, 139, 141-2, 145, 153
African National Congress 18, 23-5, 27, 34-5, 50, 64, 81, 93, 115, 117, 153-7, 160-2, 166, 169, 196, 198
Africans, treatment in court 17-20, 25, 49-50
Aggrey, Dr J K, 68
agricultural officers 100, 103
Alexandra Emergency Transport Committee 148
Alexandra Township, bus boycott 146-54, 158
Alexandra Women's Brigade 153
All African Convention, Bloemfontein 62-5, 67, 70-1, 83
Anti-Fascist League 56
Apartheid is an English Word 196
Asher's Building 42, 47
Asiatic Land Tenure Act 180, 183, 187
Attlee, Clement 189

Badu, Kofi 197
Baffoe, T D 197
Ballinger, Margaret 75, 79, 110, 127-30, 175-6
Ballinger, William 35, 75, 79-80, 88-9, 110, 153, 194
Balmoral Chambers 6-7, 20

Baloyi, R G 94, 115, 117, 122, 154, 157
Bantu Men's Social Centre 113
Bantu Restaurant 113
Bantu Women's League 23, 28
Bantu World 69, 73
Barden, A K 198
Basner, David 3
Basner, Israel 3
Basner, Abraham 2, 13, 14, 20
Basner, Baruch (Bendik) 2-3
Basner, Hannah 2, 14
Basner, Hyman Meir
  articled clerkship 16-19
  detention 195
  early life 1-8
  election campaign, 1936 77-9
    1942 114-116
  election as Senator 123-4
  final years 196-9
  formation of African Democratic Party 172
  friendship with Charlotte Maxeke 22-3
  law practice 39-46, 48-51, 150-4
  membership of Communist Party 33-7, 55-8, 96-8
  parliamentary career 126-36, 178-80
  resignation 194
  University of California 8-14
  visit to United Nations 182-90
Basner, Marusya (Cherniavsky) 3, 9
Basutoland, 'ritual' murders 195
Batty, A H 28
Belgravia Dairy 14-15
Berrangé, Vernon 150-1
Bethal, treatment of farm labourers 179
Bopape, David 115, 121, 166

Botha, General Louis 8, 23
Broederbond 138-9
Brookes, Dr Edgar 71, 76, 127, 173, 174, 176
Bunting, Rebecca 32, 54
Bunting, Sidney 30-3, 35-7, 47-8, 51-2, 54, 57, 139

Calata, Rev James 94
Caluza, R T 168
Campaign for Right and Justice 177
Cape Province, African franchise 61-2
Cement Fort 40-2
Chamber of Mines 69-70, 73-4, 77, 139, 142
Champion, George 28
Cherniavsky, Gregor 9, 11
Churchill, Winston 189
Coka, James 79
Communist Party 32-7, 39, 47-8, 51-6, 62, 65, 71, 76-8, 95-8, 106-7, 112, 114, 122, 140, 176
Congress Youth League 162
Cornelius, Johanna 56, 177
Council on African Affairs 185, 187-8
Cresswell, Colonel 15
Crouse, Hetta 56

Dadoo, Yusuf 183
dagga sellers 43
Dönges, Dr 138
Doornfontein 8
Du Bois, W E Burghardt 23, 185
Du Toit, Bettie 56-7
Dube, Rev John 25-7, 64, 71, 94, 123
Dvinsk 2-3

Ellis Park, battle of 10
Emergency Transport Committee 154
Ethiopian Church 18, 119-121

Eyles, Mr 151-2

Farm labourers, treatment of 178-9
Fish, A E P 155
Friends of Africa 153
Friends of the Soviet Union 54, 57
Fusion Coalition 59-60, 97

Gaiety Café 7, 20-1
Garment Workers Union 52, 57
Garvey, Marcus 68
Gemmill, William 93, 142-5
George VI, visit to South Africa 193
Ghana 196-9
Ghanaian Times 197
Gillman, Joseph 196
Godlo, R H 123
Gordon, Max 140, 160
Gow, Rev Dr Francis 22
Greyshirts 54, 56-7, 96, 138

Haynes, Harry 73
Hemming, G K 75
Henderson 174-5
Hertzog, Albert 60
Hertzog, J B M 15, 58, 59-66, 97
Hertzog Bills 58-66
Hirson, Baruch 106
Hofmeyr, Jan 173
Hollywood 11
Holtby, Winifred 79
Hunton, Dr Alpheus 185, 187

Ibarruri, Dolores 97
ICU 28-9, 35, 51, 65, 69, 82-3, 139, 159
Ikaka laba Sebenzi 48
Ilanga Lase Natal 25
Imvo Zabantsundu 26, 62
India, delegation to UN 185-7
Indian Pegging Act (see Asiatic Land Tenure Act)
Industrial Workers of Africa 83
International Socialist League 139

Jabavu, A M 62, 71, 94, 110
Jabavu, Tengo 24-6
Jeppe High School 8
Jewish Board of Deputies 179
Jewish Workers' Club 56
Johannesburg 8-9
Johannesburg elections 88-9
Johannesburg General Hospital, police raid 45-6
Johannesburg Theosophical Lodge 16
Joint Council of Europeans and Natives 67-8, 73, 176
Jones, Arthur Creech 79
Jones, J D Rheinallt 68-9, 71, 73, 76-7, 80-1, 86, 88-9, 91-3, 105, 109-11, 115, 118, 122-3, 174

Kadalie, Clements 27-9, 69-70, 80-3, 89, 93, 110, 139
Kerz, Leo 184
Kotane, Moses 58
Koza, Dan 160, 162, 166
Kroonstad 82, 88

La Guardia, Fiorello 188
La Grange, I J 69, 70
Labour Party 177
Lansdown, Mr Justice 141-5, 181
Larkin, J 56
League of African Rights 33, 48, 51
Lekganyane, Bishop Ignatius 115, 119-20, 121
Lembede, Anton 162
Lesolang, J J 115, 121, 159-60, 162, 166
Lesotho, visit to 195
Lewis, Ethelreda 69, 77
Lion, Bishop Solomon 115, 120-1
liquor laws, effects of 29-30
liquor sellers, defence of 43
Louis Botha Avenue 146, 148
Louis Trichardt 107
Los Angeles 9, 11
Los Angeles Law School 12

Lowenberg, Fred 16, 18, 32-3
Luthuli, Chief Albert 120
Lydenburg 103, 107

MacPherson, Jessie 177
Mahabane, Rev Z R 112
Mahlangu family 114
Majoro, James 141, 181
Malan, Dr D F 139
Malcomess 76
Maliba, Alpheus 106-8, 114, 122
Mampuru, Self 79, 153, 159, 161, 162
Mandela, Nelson 162
Mapikela, Thomas 71, 85-6, 93-4, 114
Marks, John 55, 58, 64, 78, 81-2, 86, 93-5, 106, 112, 122, 141, 181, 198
Marty, André 97-8
Maseko, Macdonald 162
Matseke, S P 95, 117, 141
Matthews, Prof Z K 123
Maxeke, Charlotte 18, 22-6, 28-30, 40, 45, 55, 112
Mayfair 20
Menon, Krishna 185, 187, 188
Messina 107
mine strikes 139-40
Mine Wages Commission 153, 181
mineworkers
  proposed rise in wages 145, 181
  strike, August 1946 181
  union, black 117, 140-1, 181
Mofutsanyana, Edwin 54-5, 58, 64, 71, 78-9, 81-2, 86, 88-9 93, 96, 106, 112, 117, 122
Mogale, Frank 82, 88
Molepo, M K 81, 89-90, 93, 114, 115, 121-2, 166
Molepo, Mary 89
Molteno, Donald 75, 127, 151, 176
Mopeli, Chief Charles 88
Moretsele, Elias 113, 115-7
Moroka, Dr J S 88, 113, 122, 123

Mosaka, Paul 113, 115, 122-3, 158-9, 160-2, 169, 170, 194
Moshoeshoe, King 195
Mote, Keable 82-3, 88
Mpama, Josie 55
Mpanza, James Sofazonke 168-70
Mvabasa, L T 83-4, 86, 93, 114, 139, 161

Naicker, Dr G M 183
Naidoo, H A 185, 188, 193
Natal Code of Native Law 102-3
Native Administration Act 102
Native Affairs Department 118-9
poll tax receipts 149
Native Land and Trust Act 60, 62-3, 64, 65, 90, 100-8, 130-6, 195
Native Land Act 24, 27, 60
Native Laws Amendment Act 100-2
Native Representation Act 60, 61, 62, 80, 112
Native Representative Council 61, 70, 113, 121, 122, 123, 194
Naudé, 'Dop' 65
Naudé, Tom 65-6
Nchee 169, 171
ngakas 44
Nkrumah, Kwame 197-8
Non-European United Front 117
Nyerere, Julius 196

Ohlange Institute 25
Oppenheimer, Ernest 177, 181
Orange Free State
Orange Free State electioneering 84-5
Orange Free State African Teachers' Association 71
Organisation of African Unity 197
Orlando 166-71
Ossewa Brandwag 138

Pan Africanist Congress 153

Pandit, Vijaya Lakshmi 185, 187, 189
Parnell, James Stewart 63
pass laws, campaign against 166
Paver, B G 69
Phillips, Rev Ray 74
Pietersburg 81, 89-90, 100, 106, 107, 119
Pim, Howard 23, 25, 68-9
Pimville 114
Pollitt, Harry 97-8
Prisoner's Friend 17-8

Radebe, Gaur 114, 141, 153, 154
Radebe, Samuel 40, 42, 55
Radin, Mr 31
Rand Revolt 10
Rangata, Abel 114
Reserves, African 100-8
Rhodes, Cecil 60
Robeson, Paul 185, 187, 188
Rome 198
Roosevelt, Eleanor 188
Roux, Edward 33, 34, 36, 52, 54, 107
Rustomjee, S 185

Sachs, E S 52, 57-8, 177
San Pedro dock strike 12-3
Seme, Dr Pixley Ka 26-7, 65, 93
Scott, Rev Michael 177, 180
Sekhukhuneland 103
Senate constituencies elections 80-4
Shanty Town 168-71
Shawcross, Sir Hartley 189-90
Sieff, Dr Bessie 32
Sinclair, Upton 12
Skota, Mweli 114
Smith, D L 93
Smith, Sidney 174-5, 191, 192
Smuts, General Jan 8, 10-1, 15, 25, 59, 60, 61, 97, 105, 107, 127, 138-9, 141-2, 160-1, 180-1, 183, 186, 188-92, 194

Sobhuza II, King 25-6
Sobukwe, Robert 162
Socialist Party 176-7
Socialist Review 177
Society of the Friends of Africa 79
Sofazonke Party 168
South African Indian Congress 183
South African Institute of Race Relations 67, 68-9, 70, 73, 76, 77, 106, 109, 115, 118, 176
South African Native National Congress 23
South West Africa, incorporation of 183, 190
Soweto 167
Springbok Legion 177
Steyn, Colin 138, 181

Taberer, H M 68-9
Tanzania 196
Thaba Nchu Reserve 88
Thema, R V Selope 69, 70-1, 81, 94, 114, 115, 122
Thema (Pietersburg) 81, 89-90, 93, 114, 117
Transvaal African Teachers' Association 71, 115, 121, 159
Trigger, Colonel 145
Truman, H S 188
Tshabalala, Lilian 153

Umsebenzi 69
Umteteli wa Bantu 69, 73
United Nations meeting Lake Success 181-90
University of California, Los Angeles 9, 12
University of the Witwatersrand 15
Urban Areas Act 101
  prosecutions under 34, 48-9

Van der Byl, Major Pieter 172-3
Vendaland 103

Wanless, Alec 176, 191
Wasserzug, Herman 16, 18, 33, 34, 35, 40
Welsh, W T 76
Wilberforce Institute 18, 22, 24
Witwatersrand Mine Native Wages Commission 139, 141-5
Witwatersrand Native Labour Association 142-3
Witzieshoek 86-8, 195
Workers International League 178
World War II 97-8, 163-6

Xiniwe, B B 123
Xuma, Dr A B 115, 117, 157-8, 161, 166, 185, 188

Yergan, Max 74, 185, 187

Zion Apostolic Faith Mission Church 120
Zion Christian Church 119-21
Zoutpansberg Balemi (Farmers) Association 107